A COMMUNITY IN TRANSITION

The Bishop of Portsmouth, John Henry King,
blesses cattle at a Jersey farm, circa 1948

The picture shows the farm of cattle breeder Michael Hickey and his family at
Cambrai, Trinity, who owned the 'Forget-me-not' cow family. Michael came from
Ireland and was a devout Catholic - hence the visit by the Bishop.

(Information thanks to Derrick Frigot)

A COMMUNITY IN TRANSITION

The Catholic Church in Jersey in Modern Times

By Alasdair Crosby

With contributions by the present and former Catholic Deans in Jersey,

Monsignor Nicholas France, MBE

and

Canon David Mahy

This book is dedicated to the memory of Fr Francis Isherwood, Assistant Priest at St Mary and St Peter's Church from 1970 – 1976. He was editor of the Jersey Catholic Record for many years and editor of a series of Jersey Church History booklets published by the Jersey Catholic Record.

Published in 2016 by
Crosby Media and Publishing Ltd
La Cohue Maisonette
St John
Jersey
JE3 4FN

Printed by
Dolman Scott
1 High Street,
Thatcham,
Berks,
RG19 3JG.

CONTENTS

CONTENTS

8

CONTENTS

9

Monsignor Nicholas France MBE
Catholic Dean in Jersey 1999 -

FOREWORD

THIS book tells a story. It is not dry history, but the story of a people to which we belong. It tells of the heritage and patrimony we now enjoy and which we must pass on to succeeding generations, adding to it along the way.

I always think that the Acts of the Apostles has an unfinished ending with St Paul in Rome, not even recounting his martyrdom and that of St Peter. In truth, the story has continued in the history of the Church throughout 19 centuries, which tells the history not just of the global church, but of local church communities in places such as our own.

Sometimes it is easier to understand local church history, as it is all about the place in which we live, the buildings in which we worship and the people who once were members of our congregations. But it is more than a human story.

In the same way that we see Scripture as relating how the hand of God has guided his people through the Holy Spirit, so with the story of the Catholic Church in Jersey, when we tell of priests and people, religious brothers and sisters, who have sought to respond to God's grace in the lives they have lived and the communities they have sought to build.

In Jersey, as in other places, there has not always been a balance between mission and maintenance in the way we have understood the purpose of being Church. We have sometimes been inward looking, partly due to prejudice against Catholics in the past, but also out of a loss of missionary impetus.

The challenge of Pope Francis, echoed by Bishop Philip Egan of Portsmouth, is for us to become a missionary Church: 'Evangelisation is the church's reason for being,' the Pope has said. 'The church must not become wrapped up in itself. It is called to come out from itself and go to people on the periphery of society where there is sin, pain, misery and injustice to bring them the good news of the gospel of Jesus Christ.' Both within our community and outside there are many on this periphery whom we need to serve, as our predecessors did in days when the Catholic community was so much poorer.

May this book provide us with knowledge of those who have gone before us and inspiration for the future in the story, in which we are still involved in word and action.

I thank Alasdair Crosby for composing and writing this book, using many different sources, in such a readable and interesting manner.

Nicholas France
Catholic Dean
2016

ACKNOWLEDGEMENTS

I would like to thank all those who have helped, supported and encouraged me during this project.

Mgr Nicholas France and Delia Hardiman, who worked most closely with me, are due special thanks. The team was enhanced by Canon David Mahy, Deacon Iain MacFirbhisigh, Tony Pezet and Terry and Angela Le Sueur, all of whose contributions and help have been most useful and much appreciated.

For helping me with research and providing me with information I would also like to thank Leo Harris, Fr Kevin Hoiles, Deanna Greene, Gio Pollano, Deacon Tony Ward, Deacon David Cahill, Mary Cahill and and Ron Satchell.

A big debt of gratitude goes to the *Jersey Evening Post* for generously allowing me to quote from past articles and for providing me with pictures. The JEP is very frequently quoted in the pages of this book and I would have been lost without the co-operation and help of my former colleagues there, Andy Sibcy, Peter Mourant and Jan Hadley.

Equally, the Jersey Archive and its senior archivist, Stuart Nicolle, have been more than kind at making available pictures for use as book illustrations.

I also owe a debt of gratitude to Diane Moore, the author of the book *Deo Gratias, a history of the French Catholic Church in Jersey*. Her book was an invaluable source of information, especially with regard to the earlier and pre-war history of the Catholic Church in Jersey. I recommend it unreservedly and I am grateful to her for her generosity in allowing me to make use of so much of her material.

May I also thank all those who, by helping to sponsor the book, have ensured that it saw the light of day:

Heilette & Grant Barbour	Jennifer Lort-Phillips	John Scally
Christopher Beirne	Diarmuid Lynes	Robin & Rita Seymour
Michael Cassidy	Angela & Martyn Magee	Sister Marie-Louise Serveau
Yvonne Culver	Aurelie Norman	Nigel Sweeny MBE
Peter & Kate Farrell	Anthony Pezet	Kath Tizzard
Carol Garton	Gio Pollano	Andrée & Neil Wakeling
Alan Hamel	Jurat Jerry & Pat Ramsden	Bernard White
Rosemarie & Stuart Hill	Mary Renouf	
Veronica Langlois	Dorothy Rowcliffe	
Jane Laurent	Robin Rumboll	

Alasdair Crosby

PRELIMINARY

THE CATHOLIC CHURCH IN JERSEY IN 2016

IN Jersey, as everywhere in the world, the Catholic Church has gone through major changes in recent decades. Much of this stems from the Second Vatican Council (1962-1965), which provided a catalyst for major change. But irrespective of the Council, the changes in society and the increased tempo of change in daily life, as well as the destruction of concepts that half a century ago were considered to be moral certainties, has had an equal effect on the Church, religious and lay people.

Another factor has been the decrease in the number of priestly vocations and consequently in the number of clergy in the parishes.

At the time of writing, there are around 2,500 church-attending Catholics in Jersey, perhaps a slight decline on previous estimates, but it is believed that there must be around ten times that number who do not attend church or who do so very rarely.

Over the past two centuries there have been hundreds of members of religious orders, such as French Oblates, De La Salle Brothers, Carmelite Sisters, Christian Brothers and Jesuits. Fifty years ago, there were still some 25 Catholic priests and religious in the Island (in contrast to five Priests in 2016). In the post-war years Priests would visit schools and parishioners in their homes. That is something that has now almost disappeared, but much of a priest's former duties and 'work routines' are now carried out by lay people. The greater involvement of the laity is the biggest contemporary change being seen in the Church in Jersey.

The change since the turn of the Millennium from seven different parishes to one 'Pastoral Area' is something that has, according to the former Bishop of Portsmouth, Crispian Hollis, put Jersey ahead of many parts of the Diocese and could well make the Island Catholic Church a template for it.

The following pages chronicle some of these changes and, it is hoped, show how the Church has coped with combining transient change with eternal verities.

I. AN INTRODUCTION

Chapter 1

NO ABIDING CITY

"We've no abiding city here" says the hymn. As true for Jersey as for anywhere else.

I T is the glorious late summer of 1949, and you have been back home in the Island for just over a year.

You could not have had a better summer to recover from your war service. Jersey has looked at its best and there is a real feeling of 'getting back to normal'. Tourism is taking off again and the hotels are full. As you walk along the Esplanade charabancs pass you laden with holiday makers on their way to the holiday camps in St Brelade or Plémont. They have just arrived on the mailboat at the start of a fortnight's holiday – their main break from work in the year – and the sound of them singing 'Roll out the Barrel' and 'Happy Days are Here Again' wafts over the road. They wave as they pass you. This is peace.

It has been a good summer. In June you were among the crowds that gave a rapturous welcome to Princess Elizabeth and her new husband, the Duke of Edinburgh, on their first visit to the Island. The Battle of Flowers earned a double page spread in the Daily Mirror and the warm summer has spawned such a glut of tomatoes that they are being given away - boys are having their own tomato battles on the beach.

The streets of town are crowded as well – at times it is hard to make your way along the pavements of Queen Street or Colomberie because of the press of the crowd. You think it would not be a bad idea to make them traffic-free, since you are so often elbowed off the pavement by other pedestrians and narrowly avoid, on one or two occasions, being hit by passing cars or bikes.

Things are not the same, of course, as they were pre-war, certainly not as in the spring of 1940 when you had to leave Jersey in such a hurry, being torn apart from friends and family members who elected to stay. The signs of war are still too visible: not the acres of bombed out buildings that you have seen in London, thank goodness, but the alien grey of concrete towers and fortifications and defensive sea walls left behind by the Occupiers. In the political world there have been changes of an almost similar magnitude: at elections the previous autumn you helped to elect these new-fangled Senators for the first time in place of the Jurats. The political landscape, as well as the physical landscape, looks very different.

And so does the landscape on the international scale: a Communist takeover in China, for example, seems worrying, and as a Catholic, you take due note of Pope Pius XII's recent *Decree against Communism* excommunicating all Catholics who collaborate in communist organisations – it is estimated that perhaps several million Catholics might be affected. And then there is that absurd anti-Catholic book that has just appeared in the USA: *American Freedom and Catholic Power* that everybody appears to be reading. Also there is the scramble by the Labour government to give away the Empire, seemingly as fast as possible, events that seem to jolt the foundations of your perception of your own British identity.

Fortunately, in Jersey things are quieter – despite the political changes and certainly quieter at least as far as Catholicism is concerned. One of your first visits on your return to the Island was to St Thomas', and here, at least, the transient has not taken over from the eternal. On your visit there you happen to meet again Père Maré, the Rector before and during the Occupation and still in residence in the Oblate community, still looking much the same as always, still wearing his wig. The interior has not been affected by the Occupation: it has not changed at all since you remember it as a child in the 1920s when you were an altar server. With the Feast of Corpus Christi due shortly, he says he hopes that you will be taking part in the procession – and, yes, why not! In June you were among the crowds taking part.

It is a high point in the Church's year and for the first time since before the war you are part of a vast throng of Catholics winding their way slowly from St Mary and St Peter's, via the grounds of the Sacré Coeur Orphanage for Benediction and to St Thomas' for the final Benediction. The procession is headed by Ferdinand Lecrivain, the imposing '*Suisse*', wearing his uniform and carrying his halberd and silver-topped staff, marching in a dignified manner in front of the procession.

You are amazed quite how many Catholic clergy there seem to be in the Island: French Oblate priests from St Thomas' (you never quite know how many of them are tucked away in the presbytery next door to the church), Anglo-Irish Oblates that have taken over at The Sacred Heart parish, teaching brothers from Bon Secours College, Religious Sisters, lay organisations and, of course, all the ancillary help of acolytes and canopy-bearers. It is a grand spectacle as well and one that brings all traffic to a halt as it snakes slowly past.

In a way, it seems another manifestation of a sense of 'Catholic self-confidence' that existed in the years of peace following the war: the completion of Sacred Heart Church, the new church at Samarès, begun in the midst of the Occupation, the Centenary of St Mary and St Peter's last year... new parishes formed, vocations steady. The Church Militant, on such occasions as a Corpus Christi procession, does seem like an army arrayed in its splendour.

Fortunately the Corpus Christ Procession of 1949 took place in bright and warm sunshine. There have been years before the war that you remember when it chose to rain steadily throughout; on one occasion the dye ran from the vestments and formed puddles underfoot and the paper of the hymn sheets and order of service booklets turned into soggy pulp.

But not, fortunately in this present fine summer of 1949.

As you settle back into civilian life you regularly attend High Mass on a Sunday. It is, of course, in the old Tridentine Rite, and it has always seemed to you to be a magnificent and transcendent spectacle and one which always takes you back to the Sunday Masses of your childhood. Little do you realise then that you will live to see this form of Mass swept away, in Jersey as in everywhere else.

Attending Mass with you are often some young people from Dublin or Glasgow who have come to the Island, initially for seasonal work and now looking as if they want to settle down – Jersey has always had that effect on people! As their employer, you feel somewhat in *loco parentis* and have been concerned that, living in rooms in town, their evening entertainment consists only of going to the pub – there is little else for them to do and going to the pub is the only alternative for them to staying in their rooms and looking at the walls. The same problems will occur and re-occur with subsequent generations of 'young workers' in the years ahead.

Fortunately, through the Church they can make friends and contacts through the Church sporting clubs and they spend at least a couple of evenings there a week playing snooker, darts and table tennis.

As for yourself, you will experience in the years ahead not only a transformation in Jersey: a dramatic rise in population; a dramatic alteration in its aspect – townscape and landscape - and a dramatic change in its economic activity from agriculture and tourism to finance-related industries, but also a dramatic change in the nature of Catholicism. The changes wrought by the Second Vatican Council will transform the familiar interior of the churches you knew, the form of the services and the 'Catholic principles' that you thought immutable.

As in the Anglican hymn, Jersey is 'no abiding city' and the history of the Catholic Church in the Island over the post-war decades into the 21st Century is mostly the history of a faith community in transition, just as it is the history of the Island community of which it is a part.

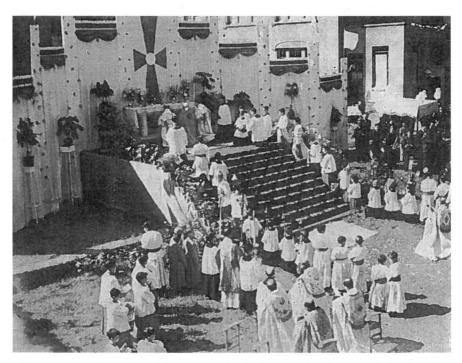

Benediction of the Blessed Sacrament in the Summerlands grounds during the Corpus Christs Procession, 1948, (photo, Jersey Evening Post)

Chapter 2

'OUR HELP IN AGES PAST'

AN apprehension of the numinous and the super-natural – it seems to be part of what it means to be truly human.

This can be inferred from archaeological excavation: both Neanderthal and Cro-Magnon buried their dead with some sort of ceremony; the departed were not just thrown out with the remains of dinner but carefully and – apparently - tenderly and reverently buried. Neanderthals used La Cotte in St Brelade for thousands of years as a hunting camp; Magdalenian Cro-Magnon man also came regularly to the land that would become Jersey – we know they camped at a hillside site near Les Varines, overlooking the low land that would one day be swamped by the sea and become the channel between Jersey and Normandy.

Many thousands of years later in Jersey there was manifestly a vibrant civilisation in Neolithic times – circa 4,000 BC. Jersey – certainly its coastal lands and the high grounds that over-looked them - comprised a sacred landscape: dolmens, menhirs, very possibly a ceremonial avenue leading towards La Hougue Bie.... a whole reverent, religious culture in place for thousands of years. It might be presumed - and it seems a reasonable presumption – that at least part of its function was to celebrate mysteries that, in ways we can only speculate, were otherwordly – perhaps, as

The window of the crypt of the mediaeval chapel on top of La Hougue Bie is aligned with the doorway of the Neolithic monument below - an example of the 'Christianisation' of pagan places of worship (Photo Warwick Rodwell)

23

in ancient Egypt - focusing on the hope of survival of the essence of human personality after physical death. Who knows? There are too many theories and not enough facts.

And some of the dolmens were built in a design that any modern visitor to a church would recognise: nave, transept and chancel, forming the shape of a cross.

St Saviour's Parish Church seems to have megalithic stones as part of its foundation and signs of prehistoric occupation have been found by St Peter's Church.

Further ages would elapse and Jersey would become an outlying part of the Gaulish and Celtic culture of France. Were there Druids in Jersey? Does the French name for the Parish Church of St John - St Jean des Chênes (St John of the Oaks) - suggest that it was built on the site of a sacred oak grove? It seems that in Jersey, as elsewhere, sites that were deemed to be sacred remained so for millennia and ultimately were never abandoned, but often just 'baptised' and Christianised.

—ooo000ooo—

HOW did Christianity come to Jersey? There are legends of Apostles in both France and England at a very early period in the 1st Century and whether or not there is any fact in these legends, it seems that there was indeed missionary work early on in the Christian era.

Gradually, there are signs of Roman settlement being found in Jersey – although it was possibly only a dependency of Guernsey (a thought that will rightly appal Islanders today). St Lawrence Church has a pillar with a Latin inscription that seems to date from Roman times and there appears to have been some Roman settlement near the site of both Grouville and St Clement churches.

Romans came and Romans went, but Jersey remained very much in the centre of a Celtic world: Cornwall, South-West England and Wales, Brittany and the Côtentin were all Celtic lands that surrounded Jersey and there was constant traffic between them all. Missionaries came to the Channel Islands, such as St Branwaladr (Brelade) who built a simple mission station near where the St Brelade Parish Church now stands. At a later date, when the Church was being built, 'fairies' are reputed to have moved the stones at night while the builders slept, from the intended building site on the east (Ouaisné) side of the bay to the west side. Not content to give up with a struggle, the next morning builders moved all the building materials back to Ouaisné – but overnight the fairies moved everything back westwards. So the builders gave up and built their church on its present site – one might speculate that if there is any fact behind this legend, that there was still a vigorous Pagan opposition in the Island at the time.

St Marculf was another peripatetic missionary as was also St Sampson, who evangelised Guernsey and whom the Arthurian scholar Norma Goodrich equated, for some charming but obscure reason, with the historical personality that legend calls Sir Lancelot.

St Helier is the most famous Jersey saint, and his cave at L'Hermitage rock behind Elizabeth Castle is in modern time the destination of an annual pilgrimage near his Feast Day on 16 July. He seems, unlike his contemporary missionary saints, not to have been from one of the Celtic kingdoms, but instead came from the area that is now Belgium and was maybe called Helibert. The story of his life and martyrdom by 'pirates' is so well known in Jersey that it need not be repeated here. However, the end of the legend is of particular interest: his grieving friends put the body of the murdered Saint in a boat and straight away it sailed miraculously from Jersey to the port of Bréville near Granville in Normandy. An unbelievable legend, surely, similar to many hundreds of other hagiographical fantasies composed in the Dark Ages?

Some years ago, an Islander, who had been a keen leisure sailor, died. He had directed that his ashes be buried at sea, out in St Aubin's Bay that had been the scene of so many happy days pursuing his favourite hobby. According to one of the undertaker's staff, some mistake was made at the burial at sea: perhaps a miscalculation of the speed and direction of currents, or of the weight of the container in which the ashes of the body had been placed. It did not sink; it floated directly to Bréville.

—ooo000ooo—

FURTHER history and continued movements of people caused Jersey's eventual translation from the Celtic-Breton world to that of Normandy, the area of France with which the Island has always been subsequently associated. The 12 Island parishes were formed and in addition to the parish churches there were numerous chapels and small priories, of which the most famous was that of St Helier on the islet off the south coast now occupied by Elizabeth Castle.

Jersey was part of the Diocese of Coutances, a situation that existed until the end of the 1400s, when the Island's jurisdiction was transferred to England, although it took nearly 70 years after that before the episcopal link with Coutances was broken.

The Middle Ages in Europe was a time – perhaps the most pronounced time in the history of Christianity – when the practice of the Faith was also part of the warp and weft of daily life. In Jersey, the wayside crosses, the painted walls and images, the churches and chapels - they were a constant reminder of another country, more real and vibrant, of which this world was only a pale derivation. As everywhere in Europe, the lives of Jersey people were informed by the seasons of the Church's year: summoned by the bells of church and chapel they moved from feast to fast and back to feast again; holidays were holy days; fairs were held on feast days; chapels by the roadside gave an opportunity for travellers to stop for a few moments to pray and to allow for periods of reflection and quiet. Wayside crosses and statues and church and chapel steeples were omnipresent, reaching skywards to bring Jersey closer to the more real and more sacred country that lay supposedly above the clouds, where there were no feudal dues, no unfair laws, no war, plague or invasions and a banquet was spread ready and waiting for all good people.

But by the late 15th Century changing times and changing social attitudes had brought about a gradual disenchantment with the Church. It might seem curious that anyone might wish to swap a religious culture of feasts and fairs for a Calvinist regime, and to what extent this was true is open to question. However, the mind-set of Jersey's sober, hard-working and independently minded (or, as some might stay, 'argumentative') Islanders inclined towards a questioning of the religious status quo.

Protestantism came to Jersey from French sources via the teachings of Calvin and later, the influence of the Huguenots. Farmers found handy new uses around their farms for the fonts and piscinas and the building stones of former chapels. The Catholic parish churches became 'temples' and the colourful vestments of the Catholic priests were supplanted by the monochrome black and white clothes of worthy and circumspect Divines.

Catholicism is often said to have died out at this time; certainly there is no equivalent in Jersey of the Recusancy – an organised, underground Catholic community – that in England so aggravated the fears of the ministers and spies of Queen Elizabeth.

There are, however, just a few hints that the Old Faith was kept alive by a few faithful adherents - or at least that some popular Catholic practices survived for some time. For example, the 18th Century Tory writer and polemicist, John Shabbeare, comments that when Elizabeth came to the throne, 'very few people in Jersey abandoned their old religion', although he gives no grounds for this assertion.

There were strict Orders published by the Royal Court to put an end to all pockets of Catholic resistance, such as the Order of 26 May 1562, stating that all pious books and breviaries should be thrown into the fire by their owners. By virtue of this law, any Islander, who was found to be in possession of such religious books, would be made to pay for - and transport - wood to St Helier market, and burn them in public. Such an incident happened on 22 May 1563.

There are other instances of 'a Jersey priest' being fined for saying Mass in Castel in Guernsey, and for a long time after the Reformation had started, an annual pilgrimage to Trinity Church was still held on Trinity Sunday. In 1602 the Court decreed that this was 'a foolish superstition, derogatory to the true service of God and a scandal to the Churches', and threatened to impose a fine of 100 sols or imprisonment on anyone making the pilgrimage.

Certain inhabitants of St Ouen were punished for 'murmuring and grumbling' at the religious changes, so perhaps the statement by the Jersey historian Philippe Falle, that 'there was not a single Catholic in Jersey' needs to be taken with a pinch of salt.

Certainly Catholic Islanders were under immense pressure to convert and most did so – even if for some it was a conversion simply to keep themselves out of trouble. Those who remained faithful to the Old Religion would have kept the nature of their religious faith very, very private.

In England, it was the threat of Spanish invasion at the time of the Armada, reinforced 17 years later by the misplaced zealotry of the

Gunpowder Plotters, that outraged moderate English people of all faiths and cast a shadow over Protestant-Catholic relationships that would last for centuries. Were Catholics truly, loyally, English? When push came to shove, were their sympathies English or foreign? How susceptible were they to the influence of radical foreign clerics? From the perspective of our own time and analogous contemporary concerns, it all seems drearily familiar.

The 16th and 17th Centuries in Jersey were alive with conflict and religious controversy, but Catholicism played no part in any of that. There were evidently some individual Catholics – perhaps mostly Irish soldiers stationed at Elizabeth Castle – but no open Catholic community. In the Civil War the contenders were Anglican Royalists against the local Puritan sympathisers of Parliament and Cromwell.

Huguenots settling in Jersey after the Revocation of the Edict of Nantes in 1685 had little reasons to love Catholicism, and their arrival in the Island would have reinforced existing anti-Catholic sentiment.

In the less warlike 18th Century, any Catholics coming to live in the Island had to notify the Lieutenant Governor of their residency and, if allowed to reside at all, were permitted grudgingly and on sufferance. And if they wanted to marry a Jersey girl… that also had to be by special permission of the Lieutenant Governor.

John Wesley travelled to Jersey and preached in the Island in the mid-18th Century. Methodism became very popular and remained so throughout the 19th Century and well into the 20th Century.

But things were about to change – come the French Revolution. At the end of the 18th Century Jersey would be transformed and a population explosion of French people fleeing from the French revolutionary Terror would take place. Jersey entered a far wider and more cosmopolitan world - and Catholicism returned, and Jersey was about to have one of its own sons become a martyr.

—ooo000ooo—

Matthieu de Gruchy died as a Catholic martyr in revolutionary France in 1797. He had been born in St Saviour in 1761 and in 1776 decided to travel to England to broaden his horizons. From there he sailed on to France in a boat that was captured by French seamen. During his captivity he fell ill, converted to Catholicism and received his First Communion. Upon his release he stayed for some time with a priest in Angers and in 1782 travelled through the village of Saint-Mars-La-Réorthe in the Vendée, where he built a pulpit for the church. He started to study for the priesthood and in 1788 he was ordained and served a local parish as curate.

At the time of the Revolution he was forced to leave France and came back to his native Jersey in 1792. Jersey had not promulgated the Catholic Relief Acts passed by Parliament and so, finding that he could not practise his ministry as a priest openly, he worked for a farmer. He aroused Protestant hostility in the Island when he converted two young Island girls and as a result was hurried out of the Island. After a spell in London as a chaplain to Irish soldiers, he returned to Jersey the following year and was given 'a Bill of Tolerance' to practise his religion 'on condition that he did so prudently'. This is considered to be the point at which the Church was re-established in the Island.

He then returned to France and ministered again in the Vendée. While travelling to Nantes, he was recognised as a priest, betrayed to the authorities, condemned to death and executed in 1797.

Although Matthieu de Gruchy has not been canonised, the present church of St Matthieu at Coin Varin, St Peter, which was built 70 years later, was named to commemorate him.

As Tina Spencer-Nairn says in her book on Matthieu de Gruchy, the ordination of this Jerseyman as a Catholic priest became 'the germ of resurrection for Catholic life in the Island of Jersey'.

Stained -glass window by Roger Degas in the Parish Church of Saint-Mars-la-Reorthe depicting the execution of Matthieu de Gruchy in 1797

Chapter 3

A CATHOLIC RENAISSANCE

Catholicism from the late 18th Century to the mid-20th Century

A FASCINATING piece of oral history of a Jersey family came from an elderly gentleman, Bob Le Sueur, who at the time of writing is aged 95. He recounted that as a young man, he was often in the company of his old grandmother, and she, similarly as a girl, was the frequent companion of her own elderly grandmother. It is from this grand-mother's grand-mother, growing up at the turn of the 18th and 19th Centuries, that this story has been passed down:

When she was a teenager, at the time of the French Revolution, she would often walk across the sands with other children of St Helier to the old 'French Harbour' to see the aristocratic French emigrés arrive from France by fishing boat – at the time, apparently, this activity was quite a popular entertainment for the local youngsters.

As the road along the water's edge called 'Commercial Buildings' had not yet been carved out of the steep slopes of the Mont de la Ville (Fort Regent), the refugees disembarked and either walked across the sands or followed what in future years, would become Pier Road, uphill, laterally along the hillside path and then downhill into town.

The teenage girl watching them arrive observed their amazingly luxurious silk clothes and also the entourages of the more important families, comprising privileged servants, such as fencing masters and dancing masters, who had accompanied their employers into exile.

Of course, the French people arriving did not believe that they would be leaving their homeland for ever; in a few months, they thought, the disturbances would be over and they would be able to return home to resume the even tenor of their lives.

There was only one hotel in St Helier on the site of what would later be the British Hotel and is now Barclays Bank on the corner of Broad Street and Library Place. The owner of the hotel made so much money from the French refugees looking for accommodation that he was later able to add two more storeys to his premises.

The impact of all these arrivals from France had a transforming effect on Jersey and Jersey life. In the early 1790s, St Helier had only 400 houses. Many of the inhabitants hired out their homes as refugee accommodation while they stayed with relatives elsewhere. The pretty blonde girl referred to above witnessed the explosion both of population and of social events brought about by the influx of refugees. It was not too surprising that she attracted the notice of one particular young Frenchman whose attentions were regarded as somewhat suspect by her family; probably wisely, her father removed the whole family to another property he owned in faraway Trinity – and let out his house in town.

Such was the pressure of refugees, that emergency accommodation had to be built and the population of the town doubled almost overnight.

These refugees were mainly Catholic and wished to hear Mass while they stayed in the Island. More than 2,000 priests and five Bishops took refuge in Jersey; of these, two Bishops and, it is said, nearly 200 priests died during their exile in the Island.

Permission was given by the Governor for private worship in four chapels in St Helier and in three others in St Aubin, Gorey and Trinity. Low Mass only could be said until 1804, when the first High Mass was sung in commemoration of the Duc d'Enghien who had just been kidnapped from Germany and then assassinated on Napoleon's orders.

As well as the French refugees there were also the Irish soldiers garrisoned in the Island, who alone were given special permission to attend Mass. However, the Catholic chaplains were forbidden to evangelise or to hold public services. In later years, as the 19th Century progressed, many Irish labourers came to Jersey to work on the big construction projects of the time, such as the construction of Fort Regent, the enlargement of St Helier Harbour and what was to be the new harbour at St Catherine – and in addition there was an influx of several thousand refugees escaping from the Irish potato famine.

The two elements of the development of Catholicism in the 19th Century - and indeed, also into the 20th Century - would continue to be, on the one hand, French (migrant workers from Normandy and Brittany) and on the other hand, Irish immigrants.

—ooo000ooo—

RESUMING our story at the time of the French Revolution and Napoleonic Wars, the French chapels closed down after a few years as the wave of refugees either moved on to England or returned to France, but in September 1803 an old flour loft was rented in Castle Street and converted into a Catholic chapel dedicated to Saint Louis; it was commonly called Les Mielles, as was the area later flattened and landscaped to form The Parade. Access to the chapel was gained, apparently, by a ladder; perhaps the Mass-goers were all male, or maybe the 'ladder' was actually an outside staircase.

Relations were often uneasy between the French refugees and the local population; those 'foreigners' attending Mass in the chapel often had to put up with being shouted at and stoned.

'Les Mielles' served both French and Irish communities and was far too small to accommodate all the Catholics who came.

As is recounted in greater details later in the book, in the two chapters relating to the French Catholic community (St Thomas') and the Irish Catholic community (St Mary and St Peter's), the two nationalities did not mix well together and accordingly an 'Irish Mission' Chapel was built in Hue Street.

In the 1840s, when the congregation had outgrown that building, a new site was found to the north of the town, where the church of St Mary was built in the suburban lane that would become Vauxhall Street. It was known as the Irish Chapel.

The French Catholic community solved their own problems of overcrowding for a while by opening a fund to buy Albion Chapel, an Anabaptist chapel in New Street, which they dedicated to St Thomas, in recognition of the help and support received from Bishop Thomas Griffiths, the

Altar of the 'old' St Thomas' Church in New Street

Catholic Vicar Apostolic in the London District. It was opened for worship in 1842.

The number of Catholics in Jersey in the 1840s was estimated at around 4,000. The St Thomas' chapel could only contain a tenth of that amount and could not cope with the Sunday congregations of 1,500, even split over three Masses. But by this time the profile of the congregation of French-speaking Catholics had long changed from being aristocratic emigrés, as at first, to farmworkers and domestic servants and there were no financial resources for building a larger church.

Not only was a lack of space a problem, but also a lack of what would nowadays be called 'infrastructure', such as schools, education for Catholic children, presbytery – or money to fund any of this from the French workers who formed the regular church-goers. A dynamic Belgian priest, Père Jean-François Volkeryck, arrived in 1860 to lead the French Mission, and, to help sort out this problem, he arranged for a missionary order of Sisters, Les *Dames de St André*, to send some of their members from their mother house in Bruges to Jersey. The first three Sisters arrived in 1863 and set up the first Catholic school since the Reformation near St Thomas'.

At the same time, the Irish Catholics had also found that St Mary's Church too small for the ever growing numbers of Catholic worshippers, so it was decided to build another church behind it. This was opened in 1867, and the enlarged church was dedicated to St Mary and St Peter.

As the French – speaking Catholic community ran out of room in their own chapel, collections were made for a new church and in the 1870s an empty building plot was acquired in Val Plaisant. But there was little money available from the French congregation and by the time the French religious order of Oblates of Mary Immaculate arrived to run the parish in 1880 only the sum of £2,500 had been collected – well short of the £10,000 to £15,000 estimated as the cost of a suitable church building.

The services of a fellow Oblate were solicited: Père Donat Michaux, who was well-known in France as a fund raiser. In 1882 he was invited to Jersey to preach at a First Communion service and it was hoped that he would become interested in the congregation's problems and stay to help in fund raising. He accepted the invitation and stayed on in the Island to raise funds for the new church.

Père Michaux was able to repeat in Jersey his previous successes; money came in fast and the foundation of the new St Thomas' Church was laid in 1883. It was consecrated on 5 September 1893 to commemorate the centenary of the re-establishment of Catholicism in the Channel Islands.

The influence of French Catholicism and French clergy and religious orders was very strong in Jersey at the time. This has been chronicled in detail by Diane Moore in her book, *Deo Gratias – A history of the French Catholic Church in Jersey: 1790 – 2007*, and the reader is strongly recommended to read this admirable work for a detailed account of this subject in the 19th and 20th Centuries, a subject that lies largely outside the theme of this book and is accordingly only summarised here.

Shrine of Sacred Heart above the High Altar at St Thomas', later whitewashed and now behind the crucifix.

In this present short account of Catholicism before the modern age it need suffice in this chapter simply to refer to the Catholic clergy, both French Oblates, English clergy and French religious sisters, who led the Renaissance of Catholicism in Jersey.

The French influence persisted at St Thomas' (commonly called *La Cathédrale*) and the country parishes; French Catholicism continued its dynamic path in Jersey, serving the very sizeable French-speaking element of the Island's population. The centre of the Irish and English - speaking influence on Jersey Catholic life was St Mary and St Peter's – two churches, *'both alike in dignity'*, situated so near each other, but with a deep fault-line between them

In 1931, the Protestant editor of the magazine, *The Jersey Critic*, wrote a leader headed: 'Is Jersey becoming Roman Catholic?' At the time, it would have seemed a pertinent and reasonable question to ask.

THE wartime Occupation of Jersey is now slipping into history and there are very few Islanders left who were adults during that time. The privations, distress and troubles endured by Islanders and, by the end, by the Occupying Forces as well, were shared equally by the Catholic clergy, both parish priests and religious orders. There was a sense, according to a survey by Diane Moore and recorded by her in her book, *Deo Gratias*, of solidarity against the Occupier and as a result of this, denominational differences and internal disputes among denominations were both reduced - everyone was in the same boat.

At the FCJ Convent, in the weeks before the Occupation, the Superior, Madame Marie-Hélène Laverrie, authorised that all the Convent's available cash be spent on food supplies, and they gathered together as many tins of food as possible. These were concealed in spaces such as underneath the teachers' podiums. Two English Brothers from Highlands who were teaching at De La Salle were removed from the Island and sent to internment in Germany and at Highlands both French Jesuit staff and the pupils were ordered to return to France. Buildings at Highlands and the presbytery and convent at St Matthieu were taken over by the Germans. Practically the only person permitted to have a radio set in Jersey during the Occupation was Père Louis Rey, at the Maison Saint Louis Observatory. This was permitted because of his meteorological research and in order for him to set the time on the Island's clocks. Clandestinely, he also made tiny matchbox crystal radios for people to listen in to the BBC.

During the Occupation the Catholic Dean, Fr Richard Arscott, was a Guernseyman and his two curates, Fr Gerard Dwyer and Fr Donal Murphy O'Connor, had Irish passports. As a result, the three of them were not interviewed by the German authorities or sent into interment.

There was a German Mass at St Thomas' at 9am on Sundays, which was always well attended by German Catholics serving in the Occupation Forces. Their singing was of such high quality that Islanders would often attend just to hear them and to listen to the organ being played.

The Occupation years even saw the beginnings of a new church building: St Patrick's. In St Aubin, the new church of Sacré Coeur had been started before the Occupation and services were held there, although the church was not opened officially until 1947.

For a German perspective on Catholicism during the Occupation, the late Engelbert Hoppe, a young German soldier who came from a very principled Catholic background and who was also very anti-Nazi, wrote: *'My religious life was mostly private except for once a month when there was a Catholic Sunday Service at the Soldatenheim St. Brelade's, either held by Division Chaplain Father Quecke or by Father Martin Clar and Father Richard Grünewald who also did Red Cross medical duties as corporals. These two were part of the Oblate Order, OMI and both were 32 years of age and had been leaders of the Catholic Youth. To me they were men of the highest regard and exemplary in their belief and attitude. Father Richard was also a wonderful musician playing the piano, organ and trumpet. Occasionally we would meet in groups as Catholics at the Soldatenheim with one of the Red Cross nurses calling us the "black corner". I once overheard a nurse saying to her colleague while pointing at Fathers Richard and Martin, "Look at these two handsome and good looking corporals. Would you imagine them being in a monastery". I thought her to be rather keen on them. It was always a highlight walking or riding by bike to St. Brelade's Bay and the Soldatenheim, but it didn't happen too often.'*

One of the best-known and most tragic stories of the Occupation is that of the would-be escapee from Brittany, François Scornet. He was one of 16 young men who escaped from Brittany in December 1940 intending to reach England and join General de Gaulle's army. They mistook Guernsey for the Isle of Wight and landed, singing La Marseillaise. They were promptly arrested by the Germans and taken to Jersey, where they were court-marshalled. Four of them were sentenced to death and the others to long terms of hard labour. However, it was only the man considered to be their ringleader, Francois Scornet, who was executed.

François Scornet (courtesy of St. Thomas' Church)

Père Théodule Maré, the Rector at St Thomas', was contacted by a German officer one evening at his presbytery and invited to attend the Frenchman at the Prison early the following morning, before the execution by firing squad at St Ouen's Manor.

37

Père Maré recounted later: *'We were left together in a separate cell for more than half an hour. I had brought the Blessed Sacrament and after devoted preparation the young Breton received Holy Communion from which he drew the strength and courage to persevere to the end of his hard sacrifice, just like the Christian martyrs of the past.'*

Père Maré insisted on accompanying Scornet in the vehicle that took him to St Ouen's Manor. *'From then on, right until the very end, we talked and prayed together. Both the faith and the religious fervour of the young Breton were aroused. He lovingly kissed my Oblate Missionary Crucifix, recited and read the wondrous prayers of the Catholic Liturgy.'*

On arrival at the Manor, Père Maré continued to accompany him as they walked together some 400 yards to the place of execution, a grassy lawn near the manor buildings. Scornet was led to the foot of a large tree and tied by his middle to the trunk, the priest still standing beside him. The firing party made ready and the death sentence was read out once again in German and French.

'François Scornet shouted in a loud and clear voice: "Vive la France! Vive la France." These were his last words in public. I gave him the final absolution and a fraternal embrace, made him kiss my crucifix and moved a few paces away. A moment later his heart and chest were ripped apart by ten bullets. His body gave a slight start and then crumpled slowly to the right.'

After Liberation, on 24 August 1945, Scornet's remains were exhumed from their burial place in Almorah Cemetery and the coffin lay in state in a private chapel belonging to undertakers J.B Le Quesne covered with a Tricolor. On 18 September a Requiem Mass was sung in St Thomas' Church before his remains were transported back to his birthplace in Brittany, Ploujean near Morlaix, for reburial.

—ooo000ooo—

AMID the joy of Liberation, the Island faced a new and very different era, both politically and socially. In the decades that lay ahead, Catholicism in Jersey would also face many changes and challenges and many transformations in the brave new post-war world.

II. DRAMATIS PERSONAE

Chapter 4

THE DIOCESE AND THE BISHOPS

FROM very early times - certainly until the early Middle Ages when the Channel Islands were an integral part of the Dukedom of Normandy - the Islands were part of the French diocese of Coutances.

After the loss of Normandy, various attempts were made by the English Crown to transfer the episcopal administration to an English see, but none of these efforts ever had the slightest effect. In 1415, after the victory of Agincourt, Henry V declared that since he had conquered France, all alien Priories were now the property of the Crown, no longer that of their French mother houses. Many of Jersey's priories and chapels were closed at this point, and their revenues, in a foreshadowing of the English Dissolution of the Abbeys in the following century, were appropriated by the Crown. Nonetheless, the Channel Islands continued to remain faithful to the See of Coutances.

In October 1496, King Henry VII requested Pope Alexander VI to transfer the Islands to the See of Salisbury and three years later he asked to have them transferred to the Diocese of Winchester. The Pope did as Henry asked - but the Pope's Bull still had no effect. Right up to the reign of Elizabeth I the Bishop of Coutances exercised jurisdiction over the Islands.

Even after the Protestant Reformation the authority of the Bishops of Winchester continued to be ignored in Jersey, since Presbyterian discipline and church government had been firmly established in the Islands. The Islands had to wait until 1829 to receive the first episcopal visitation from their Anglican Bishop, Dr Charles Sumner of Winchester.

The penal laws against Catholics were no longer so strictly applied in the 18th Century and by this time the Catholic Church in England had been placed by Rome under the care of four Vicars Apostolic and the Channel Islands were looked after (nominally) by the Vicar Apostolic of the London District.

Bishop John Douglas who was Vicar Apostolic from 1790 to 1812, appointed in 1807 an English-speaking French priest, Père Charles de Grimouville, in charge in Jersey as Vicar General for Catholic Administration in the

Channel Islands; in 1817 he was nominated Bishop of the recently re-established Diocese St Malo, but he died the same year before being consecrated.

The post of Vicar General was not continued until it was revived during the Occupation by the appointment of Mgr Thomas Hickey as Vicar General of the Channel Isles – an appointment of which the Catholic clergy in Jersey remained ignorant.

When the English Catholic hierarchy was restored by Pope Pius IX in 1850, the Channel Islands were included under the Diocese of Southwark. That diocese was divided in 1882 when the new Diocese of Portsmouth was created out of the Southwark diocese's western part.

The new see was based in Portsmouth rather than the more obvious central town of Southampton. This was determined by the potential of St John's in Portsmouth as a suitable Cathedral, rather than St Joseph's, in Bugle Street, Southampton.

The Diocese started off with 55 chapels and 49 priests to serve a scattered Catholic population. At that time parishes were called 'Missions' and were served by Missionary Rectors. The first priority of priests and people was not the building of churches but of schools to foster the Catholic faith of children. From the pennies of the poor began Portsmouth's great diocesan school tradition.

Most Catholics in those days lived in towns, though there were a few country Missions where Catholic families had kept alive the old religion during penal times, in places like East Hendred and Tichborne. In Winchester itself there had always been a Catholic congregation, proud of its Elizabethan martyrs.

In the new diocese most Catholics were local folk, with immigrant or convert additions.

The Diocese of Portsmouth covers the Channel Islands as well as Hampshire, the Isle of Wight and parts of Berkshire, Dorset and Oxfordshire.

The episcopal see is the Portsmouth Cathedral and the Diocese remains part of the metropolitan Province of Southwark, which covers all of the far South of England as well as the Channel Islands. The estimated Catholic population in 2014 was just over 170,000.

THE BISHOPS

There have been a total of eight Bishops of Portsmouth to date.

The first bishop was **Dr John Vertue** (1826–1900). He was ordained priest in 1851 and worked first of all at Poplar in London's East End. He quickly gained a reputation for his theological and philosophical studies and was selected to preach a sermon in Latin before the reigning Pope, Pius IX. He was then offered the position of Secretary to the Papal Emissary to the United States. On his return to Rome he was made Monsignor and returned again to England in 1854 where he once again worked in the East End, this time in Hackney.

In 1855 he became the Catholic Military Chaplain at Chatham, before being posted to Aldershot for six years before being posted to Bermuda. After serving as priest and chaplain in England and Malta, he was selected to become the first Bishop of Portsmouth and was consecrated by Cardinal Manning in 25 July 1882. The new Cathedral of St John the Evangelist was opened a few weeks later.

One of the early appointments in his time as Bishop was the laying of the foundation stone of St Thomas' in Jersey in 1883 and the opening of the new church four years later in 1887.

The newly built Portsmouth Cathedral and his palatial Bishop's House, with its silver plate and ornaments, earned him the sobriquet 'John the Magnificent'. He did much to establish the diocese and to give it a fine start.

The second Bishop, briefly Bishop Vertue's auxiliary, was **John Baptist Cahill**. He was born in 1841 in London and was a man of intense energy and vision. Ordained in 1864, two years later he was at Ryde in the Isle of Wight, first of all as curate and then as parish priest. He always retained a special love for Ryde and was buried there following his death in 1910.

He liked the ritual and full ceremonial of Catholic worship. There were frequent litanies, processions, exposition, novenas and missions… everything connected with Catholic devotion. In short, he achieved much in strengthening the foundations of the diocese, though believing he came too late because of ill health and failing strength. He lived only ten years to enjoy his prelacy. His portrait in Bishop's House indicates that he certainly appreciated the grandeur of his office.

There are two achievements of Bishop Cahill from which Catholics in Jersey (and elsewhere) still benefit. First, he welcomed many religious communities expelled from France in the early 1900s due to the anti-clerical laws enacted there. Some were English exiles like the monks of Douai, who did Bishop Cahill a service in taking over his failing diocesan school at Woolhampton, making it their new monastic home. A community of monks from Solesmes near Le Mans settled at Quarr Abbey in the Isle of Wight.

In Jersey, four Carmelite convents, hundreds of Jesuits and other religious found a welcome sanctuary. French clerical exiles were also welcomed in the Island.

Although heavy handed in dealing with his priests, he was quite astute in dealing with Rome, especially when Pope Pius X led a reaction to modernist theology that appeared to undermine both the doctrinal and scriptural basis of Catholic faith. There was a search made, an enquiry of all Catholic Bishops to discern whether modernism existed in their dioceses. The clever reply of Bishop Cahill was that there was little danger of modernism being contagious in the Diocese of Portsmouth, as most clergy lived far apart and rarely met each other and, in any case, it was well known that his clergy never read books of theology.

Bishop Cotter with Altar servers and French priests including Père Theodule Mare, Père Eugene Meline, Père Alain Mao, Père Jean-Louis Messager, Père Pierre Gueret and Père Yves Jain.

Among the wave of Irish immigrants in the 19th and early 20th Centuries came many Catholic priests. To the Portsmouth diocese came priests from the Diocese of Cloyne, County Cork, among who was the third Bishop, **William Timothy Cotter**. After ordination, he was curate, and afterwards parish priest at Ryde, Isle of Eight, succeeding his predecessor, John Baptist Cahill, in the same parish and succeeding him as Bishop in 1910.

Bishop Cotter chose as his motto *Non Recuso Laborem*, loosely translated by his critics as 'never turn down a good job'.

An Irish nationalist, he also looked to Ireland for his supply of clergy, turning away vocations from within his own diocese. He has been much criticised for this, though he must have had his reasons - not least financial - as legend has it that all the diocesan finances were lost in the nationalisation of the Argentinian railways, in which they had been invested. This pro-Irish policy persuaded one student for the priesthood, a certain Derek Worlock, to test his vocation in the Westminster Diocese rather than his native Portsmouth. He was ordained in 1944 but eventually returned to the Diocese of Portsmouth in 1965 as bishop in succession to Bishop King.

In June 1934 Bishop Cotter created history by becoming the first British Bishop to fly to an official visitation, when rough seas in the English Channel prevented him taking the ferry and required him to fly to the Channel Isles.

Bishop Cotter died in Bishop's House in the autumn in 1940, just a few months before that residence was totally destroyed by enemy bombing.

The Cathedral was also damaged and other churches in the diocese suffered a similar fate.

The destruction of his official residence gave Bishop Cotter's successor, **John Henry King** (appointed in 1941), the excuse to stay in his beloved Winchester, where he had been Catholic parish priest since 1923. With the Cathedral of Portsmouth also damaged, St Peter's in Winchester became for many years the acting Cathedral of the diocese, a source of pride to all his successors in that church. With the home of the Army at Aldershot and the Royal Navy at Portsmouth, the diocese expanded very considerably during the turbulence of war.

Bishop John Henry King

The post-war period was a time of new immigration - Irish, Italian, Polish and Hungarian among many other nationalities. New churches, new schools - those were the days of a strong independent clergy and an easy-going, elderly Bishop allowing initiatives.

For example, the Clergy in the Cathedral were in the forefront of liturgical innovation, even before the Second Vatican Council. Alone of all the English Bishops, John Henry King received permission to absent himself, due to age, from attending the Second Vatican Council. However, in 1964, he was the first Bishop to take part in the new Rite of Concelebration at the Blessing of Aelred Sillem as Abbot of Quarr, remarking afterwards that he and his three fellow concelebrants should form a group like The Beatles.

With Bishop King we experience the first stirrings of ecumenism. Though steeped in the story of Catholic martyrs and recusant families, he had a great love of Winchester Cathedral and maintained a courteous relationship with its clergy. He once remarked that the Dean of Winchester had invited him to preach in his cathedral but he had declined as he feared his own clergy wouldn't let him do this.

The Bishop was quite a shy man, with not many apparent interests other than Church history, particularly in the time of the Recusants, on which subject he was quite an authority. He wrote a considerable volume of material on this subject and was for some time editor of the volumes of the Catholic Record Society, where much of his work is to be found.

In 1954, on the Golden Jubilee of his ordination as a priest, he was given the honorary title of Archbishop of Portsmouth by the Vatican. In 1960 a Coadjutor Bishop, Thomas Holland, was appointed to assist the now elderly Archbishop and from then on it was Bishop Holland who made episcopal visitations to the Channel Islands.

However, Archbishop King had a personal interest in Jersey: he had been ordained here. He had returned from his studies in Rome to be ordained and his Ordination was due to be carried out by Bishop Cahill. But the Bishop went ill and was unable to perform the ceremony. But it was realised that visiting the diocese was the French Vicar Apostolic of Nanking in China, who was staying in Jersey to ordain some of the Jesuits at the Maison St Louis – the building that one day would become the Hotel de France – and he agreed also to ordain the young John King. In future years, at receptions at the Hotel de France, Archbishop King would inform the guests in his speech that, years before, he had been ordained priest on the spot that was now the dance floor.

After the Occupation, during which time there had been no administration of the Sacrament of Confirmation, Bishop King visited Jersey in July 1945 to carry out a 'catch up' with many Confirmation ceremonies. He was also pleased to officiate at the opening of the Sacred Heart Church in St Aubin in 1947 and was also present during the official visit to the Islands by Cardinal Bernard Griffin, Archbishop of Westminster, in 1953.

In December 1965 following the transfer of Bishop Holland to the Diocese of Salford and the death of Archbishop King - and at the end of the Second Vatican Council - **Derek Worlock** came from Westminster to be the next Bishop. Half the age of his predecessor, he heralded inevitably a wind of change, promising immediately to implement all the programme of renewal proposed by the Second Vatican Council. He was true to his word and consistent in promoting the new liturgy and lay participation in the life of the Church, especially through establishing diocesan, deanery and parish pastoral councils.

Through Derek Worlock's initiative the first pastoral centre was opened in the South of England at Park Place, the bonds

Bishop Derek Worlock with his secretary, Fr Nicholas France

of friendship and support were developed with the diocese of Bamenda, in Cameroon, and the permanent diaconate was introduced with the ordination of Pat Taylor in Basingstoke in 1974.

Bishop Worlock was actively involved in promoting ecumenical relations with other denominations. His social conscience challenged the powers that be in the city of Portsmouth and he developed new social welfare structures for the diocese, although these were later not sustained. During these years parishes first became involved in the Pro-Life movement, and in CAFOD projects. To many Bishop Worlock seemed outwardly cold in personality, but others knew him to be inwardly a warm and emotional man, who loved his priests and scarcely lost one of them during those turbulent years.

He had a special love for Jersey and was always interested in the Island; he enjoyed his visits to the Channel Islands and was appreciative of the support from the Islands' clergy and laity. He set up the first Deanery Pastoral Council in Jersey, which was chaired by the late Jack Dupré. It was the first Pastoral Council in the Diocese. He also encouraged younger men, such as Dick Shenton, to stand for election to the States.

From 1966 until 1970 his chaplain (secretary) was Fr Cormac Murphy O'Connor, who would later become the Cardinal Archbishop of Westminster. In 1971 he was succeeded by a young priest, Fr Nicholas France – later to be the Catholic Dean in Jersey.

Fr France joined the Bishop's household, where the Cathedral Administrator was Fr David Mahy – who was later to be his predecessor as the Dean in Jersey.

The then Fr France first accompanied Bishop Worlock to Jersey for the Golden Jubilee of Père Jort, a former Rector at St Thomas'.

He recollected: 'The Bishop warned me that all the Catholic clergy would be out to greet us as we arrived. He was right. Canon Olney had hired one of the shiny black limousines from Curwood Motors and we travelled in state back to the presbytery.'

Bishop Emery

After Bishop Worlock left in 1976 to be Archbishop of Liverpool, Bishop **Anthony Emery**, Auxiliary Bishop in Birmingham, was appointed as the next Bishop. Older than his predecessor, without having the experience of attending the Vatican Council, it was hard for him at 58 to leave his beloved Midlands for the deep South, although he did come to love the diocese.

Bishop Emery promoted Catholic education both nationally and in the diocese and reorganised the catechetical formation. He supported the introduction of parish based sacramental programmes, the RCIA (Rite of Christian Initiation of Adults) and adult Catholic education.

He was less sure about other areas of lay involvement and some of the consultative bodies fell into abeyance. However, his support for his priests was without question and he was proud to celebrate the centenary of the diocese.

In Jersey, Bishop Emery laid the foundation stone of the new St Mary and St Peter's and the new community centre at St Thomas', later returning for the official opening of the former.

After his death in 1988, the next Bishop to be appointed was **Crispian Hollis**, who retired in 2012.

Bishop Hollis became an auxiliary Bishop in 1987 in the Birmingham Diocese. He lived in Oxford – a town he knew well as he had been a University Chaplain there for ten years and an undergraduate before then.

The Bishop was perhaps unusual among Catholic Bishops in having one Anglican Bishop as a grandfather, and another one as an uncle – they were respectively the Bishop of Taunton and the Bishop of Madras; his mother's father was also an Anglican Vicar. His parents both converted to Catholicism before he was born, and he was brought up as a Catholic.

His father, Christopher Hollis, had a varied career as a schoolmaster, author and Conservative MP. A prolific writer, he wrote on Catholic subjects, as well as on history and economics. An uncle was Sir Roger Hollis, the controversial director of MI5.

His father was one of a group of well-known Catholic writers and thinkers. Evelyn Waugh was a friend and neighbour, as was Monsignor Ronald Knox, who also lived in Mells.

The Bishop had a boyhood memory of Hilaire Belloc staying at their home: 'a big fat man in a black suit, with most of his lunch down the front of it.'

With a strong Catholic atmosphere at home, becoming a priest was an option in his mind from quite an early age. He was educated at Stonyhurst, where his father had once taught, and did his National Service in the Somerset Light Infantry, serving in Malaya. In 1956 he went to Baliol College, Oxford, to read Modern History, and after graduation took further his earlier interest in becoming a priest.

In 1959 he went to the English College in Rome to start his studies, and was ordained there in 1965. He began his priestly career in England the following year.

At the time the Second Vatican Council was just finishing, and the changes it wrought were permeating into Catholicism – at times, he admitted, with such lack of preparation for Catholics that many found these sudden changes to be alienating.

Bishop Hollis was installed as Bishop of Portsmouth in January 1989. He was chairman of the Catholic Media Trust and also chairman of the Bishops' Committee for Europe.

Bishop Crispian Hollis and Deacon Iain MacFirbhisigh

Among his many posts he was a member of the Pontifical Council for Social Communications in the Vatican, chairman of the Bishops' Conference Department of Mission and Unity and representative for the Bishops' Conference of the Churches Together in Britain and Ireland.

He was also a member of IARCCUM (International Anglican - Roman Catholic Committee for Unity and Mission) and was a keen exponent of ecumenism. He was also a close friend of the Anglican Bishop of Winchester, the late Bishop Michael Scott-Joynt. Together, they worked closely with other religious leaders and these relationships developed further following the establishment of Churches Together in 1990.

During his 23 years as Bishop of Portsmouth, Crispian Hollis frequently visited Jersey and was very supportive of David Mahy during his time as Dean. In response to a request from David Mahy the Bishop established a team to carry out a thorough Pastoral Review of the Church in the Island in 1994.

Later, during the years when he was Bishop and Nicholas France was Dean, he readily agreed to the amalgamation of parishes and financial resources, leading to Jersey becoming one Island Parish. Following the Diocesan Pastoral Congress in 2005 and the publication of the Bishop's Document *Go out and Bear Fruit*, the Church in Jersey fully supported these initiatives, especially in the development of lay ministries.

He retired at the age of 76, returning to his family home at Mells in the Diocese of Clifton.

Following his retirement, **Bishop Philip Egan**, who had been serving as the Vicar General of the Diocese of Shrewsbury, was appointed as the eighth Bishop of Portsmouth

Bishop Egan was born on 14 November 1955 in Altrincham, a suburb of Manchester. After classical studies locally at St. Ambrose College and at King's College London, he completed training for the priesthood at Allen Hall, Westminster, and at the Venerable English College in Rome. In 1984 he was ordained to the priesthood and for the next four years served as an assistant priest at Woodhouse Park, Manchester. From 1988 to 1991, he served as an assistant chaplain at the University of Cambridge. From 1991 to 1994 he served as parish vicar and chaplain at Arrowe Park

Hospital on the Wirral. From 1994 to 1995, he completed theological studies at Boston College in the United States, going on to serve, until 2007, as Professor of Fundamental Theology and Dean of Studies at Oscott College seminary in Birmingham. In 2008, he became a parish priest in Stockport before becoming, in 2010, Vicar General of the Shrewsbury diocese. Philip Egan was consecrated by his predecessor Bishop Crispian Hollis in September 2012. He made his first visit to Jersey the following February during the Year of Faith returning that summer to ordain David Cahill and Christopher Walters to the Permanent Diaconate and to carry out the confirmation of 150 adults and young people.

Bishop Philip Egan

Chapter 5

THE CATHOLIC DEANS

Fr John Cunningham

THE modern history of Catholicism in Jersey had a French genesis: the French exiles during the time of the Revolution and the French priests who served them. However, there was another strand of Catholicism that developed parallel with the 'French Mission' – and that was the 'Irish Mission'.

As described elsewhere in this book, the early French and Irish Catholics did not mix easily together; in 1821 Fr John Carroll arrived and it was agreed that new premises needed to be found for the Irish. These were obtained in a courtyard off Hue Street and a chapel was built by 1826; it was the first Catholic chapel to be built in Jersey since the Reformation.

As described in more detail elsewhere, a bigger church was needed, and a new church was built in Vauxhall Street, at the instigation of the Rector, Fr John Cunningham, dedicated to St Mary; it was known as 'the Irish Chapel' as opposed to 'the French Chapel'.

In August 1848 Fr Cunningham died. He had made an excellent impression on a largely Protestant Island, as this tribute in the *Jersey Times* of 28 August 1848 informs us: '...*of the late Mr Cunningham as a member of the Catholic priesthood, it is not for a Protestant journal to speak, but as a good citizen, and a kind friend, as a man of considerable and varied information, and extended and liberal views; as a warm hearted adviser, as a charitable reliever of the poor and unhappy, without distinction of nation or of church; as in fact – a man and a Christian, we would do violence to our sense of right no less than to his memory, and to the public estimation of his goodness of heart, his intelligence, his integrity of life, were we not to lay upon his bier this our humble tribute to the excellence of the late lamented Roman Catholic Minister in Jersey.'*

He was succeeded by his assistant priest, Fr Jeremiah McCarthy, who had arrived in Jersey two years earlier at the age of 22. He remained in charge for some 45 years and in 1850, upon the re-establishment of the English

Fr Jeremiah McCarthy

Hierarchy, Fr McCarthy was given the position and title of 'Dean of St Anne of the Isles.'

Because of the increase in the Irish population of the Island, Fr McCarthy proposed to build a new church that would hold some 2,000 people and be completed with a fine tower. This was duly built as an extension to St Mary: the extension was dedicated to St Peter.

In June 1893, Mgr McCarthy (he had been made a Papal Prelate - or Monsignor - on the completion of the church) died. He is buried in Almorah cemetery. The church was never completed as intended.

The next priest, Fr John Hourigan, came in 1893 to replace Fr McCarthy. He remained at St Mary and St Peter's for 38 years. He was appointed a Canon of the Diocese in 1916.

Fr Hourigan died at his brother's home in Ireland on Easter Sunday 1931.

These three priests – Cunningham, McCarthy and Hourigan - covered almost a century between them. They saw themselves as very much pastors to the Irish immigrant community. Inevitably, this was quite an inward looking community in which the priest was everything to his people. Parishioners used to call upon the priest even when they had physical illness (as they could not afford a doctor) and he would come round and give them some simple treatment – such as putting a poultice on a sprain.

Canon John Hourigan

During all this period 'Irishness' was by far the predominant character of the congregation at St Mary and St Peter's. At times there were meetings of the Irish Land League, the formation of a Hibernian football club, League of the Cross socials and the Brian Boru fife and drum band would parade the streets of St Helier on the eve of St Patrick's Day.

Canon Clifford Bailey succeeded Canon Hourigan as parish priest in 1931. He was no stranger to the Channel Islands having been for over 25 years parish priest of Alderney. He died in April 1940, just a few months before the Germans occupied the Islands. Two priests, Fr Richard Arscott and Fr Albert Lion, both Channel Islanders, were in the running for the succession. Bishop Cotter chose Fr Arscott, who remained in charge of the parish throughout the Occupation.

Canon Clifford Bailey

The Catholic administration of the Channel Islands during the Occupation was nominally in the hands of Canon (later Monsignor) Thomas Hickey, Parish Priest of St Joseph's, Guernsey, and Guernsey's Catholic Dean. He was appointed Vicar General of the Channel Islands by Bishop King. This fact was made known to Guernsey seemingly through Ireland and the Vichy government, but it appears that news of it did not reach Jersey until after the war.

The Rector of St Mary and St Peter's during the Occupation, Fr Richard Arscott, was a Guernseyman, who had only just arrived in the Island in 1940. He was a talented musician and composer whose works included his own settings of the Mass. He played the piano and held concerts throughout the Occupation. His two assistant priests were both Irish: Father Donal Murphy O'Connor and Father Gerard Dwyer – the former was the uncle of the future Archbishop of Westminster, Cardinal Murphy O'Connor.

It was fortuitous that during the Occupation all three of Jersey's English speaking Catholic priests were either from Guernsey or from Ireland rather than being English, so none of them were liable for deportation.

After the Occupation, all three priests left the Island – their time in Jersey having being rather longer and more strenuous than they might have imagined on their arrival. Fr Arscott gave a concert at The Playhouse on the afternoon before his departure, Friday 30 August 1946, to join the Catholic Missionary Society. A retiring collection was taken for the Little Sisters of the Poor: the grand total was £7 10s 6d.

He was succeeded by Fr [later Canon] **Albert Lion**, a Jerseyman, but who had spent much of his life as a chaplain to the Tichborne family, who lived near Alresford. He had been in the running for the post of Catholic Dean in Jersey in 1940 and after the war achieved his heart's desire of becoming it. Unfortunately, he became ill and his short time in the Island was not too happy.

One of his two curates was Fr John Devine, a former Army Catholic chaplain who had served in the 8th Army from El Alamein to Berlin. He was renowned, so he claimed, not so much for his scholarship or his holiness, as for being the best poker player in his regiment. He was mentioned in dispatches for driving an army lorry loaded with gin and cigarettes through enemy lines.

Canon Lion retired early in 1948 due to illness. He died in 1949 and was buried in Almorah Cemetery in Jersey.

Centre, the young Canon Arthur Olney in 1948, with his curates, Fr John Hickey (left) and Fr John Devine

Fr (later Canon) **Arthur Olney** arrived in Jersey in October 1948 to replace Canon Lion as parish priest of St Mary and St Peter's and Catholic Dean in Jersey.

He had been ordained as a priest in 1927; afterwards he served as a curate at St Joseph's, Aldershot, for 10 years, before becoming priest at the Church of the English Martyrs, Didcot. During his time there he was active in local politics, serving as a Member of Wallingford Rural District Council for nine years, part of this time as chairman of the Public Health Committee.

The arrival of Canon Olney in Jersey began a period of post-war stability for the local Church. He is remembered as a very good and conscientious priest. He was able to consolidate the post-Occupation Church in Jersey and developed all the local Catholic organisations that involved the laity - such as the Knights of St Columba and the Catholic Women's League - into a fine flowering in the Island.

Of course, it was only Canon Olney and his curates who were the diocesan clergy in the Island; most of the other parish clergy were Oblates of Mary Immaculate under the discipline of their own superiors. Canon Olney was a man of his own time and although he later built up excellent working relationships with other denominational leaders in the Island, he remained faithful to what might be called the 'un-ecumenical' atmosphere in Catholicism that preceded the Second Vatican Council. He was made a Canon of Portsmouth Cathedral in 1953.

During the 1960s, the Oblates of the French Province pulled out of all the Jersey parishes except for St Thomas', which remained with French Oblate priests until the departure of the last Oblate, Father Vincent Igoa, in 1999. The other parishes – including, surprisingly, St Matthieu, which had remained very much a 'French' church - were transferred to the Irish Oblates.

Jersey received a visitation from the Cardinal Archbishop of Westminster, John Carmel Heenan, in 1971, who stayed at the FCJ's new convent and school at Grainville. An open-air Mass had been planned in the Howard Davis Park – but it rained, so it was held instead at St Thomas' – by then already almost a century old, and looking its age.

Mgr France was in the visiting party and he recalled a lunch at the Pomme d'Or Hotel: 'I asked naively of the person dining beside me whether there had been many collaborators during the Occupation. He looked round and said "Well, there are five here in this room".'

In November 1973 Canon Olney was created a Prelate of Honour by the Pope, with the title of Monsignor, on the occasion of his 25th anniversary as Dean in Jersey and Rector of St Mary and St Peter's. Tributes were made by the Bishop Worlock and by Jack Dupré, the chairman of the Island Pastoral Council. Earlier, a special Mass, attended by about 400 people, was held at the St Mary and St Peter's Church, at the end of which the new Monsignor was informed about the honour.

In his speech, Mr Dupré said that he treasured his association with Arthur Olney, of whom he said 'he had led with kindness, firmness and humility: he can walk with kings and retain the common touch.'

He was respected and loved by members of all denominations and this had been shown by his appointment as chairman of the Jersey Council of Churches.

Recollecting him, the present Dean, Monsignor Nicholas France, described him as 'a safe pair of hands as Dean. He was a humble man, who cycled around the town visiting people and carrying out his duties – he did a lot of the work himself, rather than relying on his curates. I found him a reserved but most pleasant person.

'However, I doubt whether he received much in the way of official recognition as Catholic Dean.

'He would always take the Bishop to Government House to "sign the visitors' book" but I doubt if he was ever invited there in his capacity of Catholic Dean. For most of his time in Jersey due to Catholic rules forbidding joint services, he would not have been able to take part, for example, in the annual Cenotaph service.'

In 1975, at the age of 75, Monsignor Olney left the Island. He undertook then a number of different parish appointments within the diocese. He had served in the Island for 27 years.

His character was summed up by his successor as Dean, Canon David Mahy: 'He was a gentle man and people loved him dearly. He may not have been a dynamic figure, but he was a very good pastor.'

On leaving Jersey he moved to Hampshire but returned to Jersey in 1977 to celebrate his Golden Jubilee. He died in a nursing home in the Isle of Wight, at the age of 86, the year before the Diamond Jubilee of his ordination.

It was while Bishop Worlock was discussing the retirement of Monsignor Olney with his secretary, Nicholas France, that he suggested as a successor the name of Father David Mahy, the Administrator of Portsmouth Cathedral, who was a Channel Islander, if from Guernsey! The Bishop took up Father France's suggestion – and Father Mahy was duly posted to Jersey.

A quarter of a century later, Nicholas France himself was sent to Jersey as the Dean on David Mahy's recommendation. He joked that Canon Mahy had finally got his revenge!

David Mahy was a Guernseyman, but was born in Portsmouth in 1937, as his father was serving in the Royal Indian Navy; shortly after his birth his mother took him to India, where they were to spend the war years. His maternal grand-mother was from Jersey, so he had connections to both Islands.

After his father's retirement from the Navy, his parents – both of them Catholic – returned to the UK and then moved to Guernsey in 1948, where he was educated at Elizabeth College.

Although at one time he had thoughts of following his father into the Navy, he had decided, before leaving school at the age of 17, to train for the priesthood. Six years at St John's Seminary in Wonersh followed, and in 1960, at the age of 23, he was ordained in Guernsey as a priest.

After six years in St Peter's, Winchester, he was sent for by the new Bishop, Derek Worlock, who appointed him as an assistant priest at Portsmouth Cathedral. However, within months

Canon David Mahy

he became the Cathedral's Administrator, where he spent eight years. During that time he became chairman of the Portsmouth Council of Churches. Then came his move to Jersey in 1975, where he stayed for 24 years.

He came to Jersey as the new Catholic Dean, living with a curate in the presbytery of the old St Mary and St Peter's Church in Vauxhall; the presbytery was behind the church in Winchester Street.

On his retirement in 1999 he recollected, in the course of an interview for the *Jersey Evening Post*: 'When I first came to Jersey, it was very different from the Portsmouth urban parish in which I had been working. However, with my Guernsey upbringing, I did have some kind of insight into the Jersey way of doing things: there are, after all, certain parallels between Jersey ways and Guernsey ways – even though neither Island is likely to accept that as being true!'

A few months after his arrival in Jersey, he received a visit from Bishop Worlock, who was welcomed in great style. He installed David Mahy as Dean and his passing words to him as he left the Island were: 'I'll not forget, you, David. ' A couple of months later he had been appointed

Archbishop of Liverpool.

During his time as Dean there was a considerable reduction in the number of Catholic priests serving in the Island.

'At one time St Thomas' Church had eight priests and it was still being served by four priests when I arrived in Jersey. St Mary and St Peter's had two priests and then there was also the Chaplain at Sacré Coeur. '

Induction of Canon David Mahy as
Catholic Dean; Fr Nicholas France left of altar

(On his departure, the incoming Dean, Canon Nicholas France, had the pastoral care of the two town parishes and the Portuguese community – by himself.)

At the beginning of Canon Mahy's time as Dean, there were three priests at Sacred Heart, two at St Martin and three at St Matthieu's. Two church building disappeared entirely: St Anne's Church at St Ouen and St Joseph's in Grouville. In addition to the parish clergy, there were chaplains at the Sacré Coeur orphanage, Little Sisters, De La Salle College and Highlands.

There were regular meetings of all clergy and a good working relationship between the priests, both diocesan and religious.

Canon Mahy relates that the most significant events of his time in Jersey included the closing of FCJ's senior school and the redevelopment of the primary school, also the closure of the old St Mary and St Peter's Church in Vauxhall and its move in 1984 to the church's present site in Wellington Road. On the day of the opening Bishop Anthony Emery announced that he had appointed David Mahy as a Canon of the Cathedral Chapter. (On the same occasion he also appointed Nicholas France as a Chapter Canon. At that time he was parish priest of St Peter's Winchester and was among the guests of the Church's opening).

Another of David Mahy's strong memories was the visit of Cardinal Basil Hume, Archbishop of Westminster in 1988 - akin almost to a Royal Visit

- and the warm welcome he had received in the Island - it was a very happy pastoral visit.

The Cardinal celebrated Mass at an open-air service at Beaulieu and held an ecumenical celebration at FCJ School, an event attended by thousands of Islanders. He also opened an extension to de la Salle College, as well as visiting the church of Our Lady in St Martin, which was celebrating its 125th birthday.

In 1994 a pastoral review into all aspects of the Church in Jersey took place, the findings of which were published the following year. This involved a reappraisal of all church properties, education and social care, the Catholic Pastoral Centre and future re-configuration of the parishes. However, many of the recommendations were not implemented until after Canon Mahy had left the Island.

After leaving Jersey he was parish priest at Aldershot for 12 years and then became co-ordinating pastor in North-East Hampshire. He was also given the responsibility of being chairman of the Priests Retirement Fund. At the time of writing he is now retired – although still making visits to Jersey as a relief priest to cover absences of the parish clergy.

Canon **Nicholas France**, the next Dean, already had, on his arrival in 1999, memories of Jersey going back many decades. He had first visited the Island in 1949, aged six, staying with his parents at the Seabraes Hotel, St Clement (now the Shakespeare Hotel). They did not visit any churches, as far as he can recall, other than a touristic visit to the Glass Church. A much more vivid memory was the glut of tomatoes in the late summer – 1949 was a long and very hot summer and there was a very large crop. He observed the tomato battles that he saw 'bigger boys' enjoying on the beach near the hotel, one of whom, he discovered many years later, was the future States Member,

Mgr Nicholas France

61

Senator Frank Walker.

Born in Worthing, Nicholas France was the son of a bank manager who was an agnostic Anglican, and a Catholic mother. He was educated at Douai Abbey School and was a seminarian at St Edmund's College, Ware; he was ordained in 1968, aged 25, by Bishop Derek Worlock. Ordained alongside him was his fellow student, Peter Doyle, currently Bishop of Northampton. Nicholas France has always worked in the Portsmouth Diocese: his first two years as a curate were at Windsor and then for seven years served as chaplain (secretary) to Bishop Worlock and to his successor, Bishop Emery. He spent five years as parish priest at Aldershot in the civilian parish, where he developed an active pastoral council and the first finance committee. He was also much involved in the development of school buildings and in the renovation of the presbytery and the church.

In January 1983 Nicholas France was appointed to St Peter's, Winchester where he carried out a major re-organisation of the parish, both pastorally and materially with regard to the church properties which served the mission of the Catholic Church in that city.

At his recommendation, Bishop Hollis carried out a pastoral restructuring of the Catholic Deanery of Southampton and surprised him by asking him to go there as overall Dean with three sub-deans to assist him (Canon France was nicknamed 'Superdean'). He became involved in many ecumenical projects and in the development of the Apostleship of the Sea.

In 1999 Nicholas France was working with an ecumenical team planning the Millennium celebrations in Southampton, when to his surprise, he was asked by Bishop Hollis to move to Jersey.

Long before becoming the Catholic Dean in Jersey he had been present, during his years as Bishop's Secretary in the 1970's at some of the 'Catholic events' in the Island, including the induction of David Mahy as Dean and later, as already recorded, at the opening of the new St Mary & St Peter's church in 1984.

This familiarity with the Church in Jersey would stand him in good stead when he was appointed Dean in 1999.

He was also aware of the Review of the Island Church that had been produced in 1994 – two of his Southampton parishioners were on the Review team, so in many ways he was well prepared for his new job.

'A funny thing happened to me on the way to the Millennium: I was asked to move to Jersey,' he joked from the pulpit of St Thomas' when he was inducted as Dean on 28 September 1999 by Bishop Hollis, with the Lieutenant-Governor and Bailiff prominent guests in the large congregation.

He was referring to the surprise he had received when told by the Bishop about his appointment as Dean in Jersey. He had not expected the appointment and was at the time fulfilled in his work as the Roman Catholic Dean in Southampton, where he had had the job of combining two formerly independent Catholic parishes in the city centre – good practice, as it were, for his future role in Jersey.

As he said when interviewed by the *Jersey Evening Post*: 'I see my new job in the sense that I have not been given a benefice, but a role in the service of the church. I haven't come to the Island for career development or promotion, but to do a difficult job for the Lord.'

Father Vincent Igoa, the Rector at St Thomas' Church had left the week before Nicholas France arrived on 8 September and for the first time the new Rector of St Mary and St Peter's was also the Rector of St Thomas'. He was also responsible – contrary to his expectations - for the pastoral and worshipping needs of the large Portuguese community: a difficult task, he joked at the time, since the only Portuguese he knew was 'Mateus Rosé'.

In his *Jersey Evening Post* interview on his arrival he said: 'In my previous job in Southampton there was a 10,000-strong Sikh community, and more mosques and temples than churches, so I am not unused to a place being "a community of communities" – just as Jersey is, in its way.'

At the time he said he foresaw other parishes in the Island being combined, and stressed they would be 'enriched' by sharing resources with one another, both in terms of financial stability and of parishioners' help and skills.

'The days have gone when you had a parish priest for every little church and these days, with greater mobility, it's far less necessary to have a worshipping centre for small numbers of people when instead you can gather them together to give them a better sense of "church" in a larger gathering.'

His task was, he said, 'somehow to produce in the Island the right kind of new parish for the new century' – a task which would transform the traditional parish and church structure in the Island.'

During these years he concentrated first of all on uniting the two church communities in St Helier as one town parish, administered by him as a unifying figure. At the same time his aim was to allow diversity and subsidiarity within the two communities that had maintained a separate identity for 200 years. Only later on, as recorded elsewhere, was there a development towards Jersey becoming a single Island parish.

He believed that buildings could be the outward icon of the spiritual health and invisible soul of a parish. For this reason he began renewing the site around St Thomas' Church, the presbytery, hall and former school. Priority was given to providing a new centre for Catholic Pastoral Services, the Society of St Vincent de Paul and for the Portuguese and other immigrant communities in a Welcome Centre.

He took some years planning the renewal of the church with an architect, so that it could be the centrepiece, both pastorally and liturgically, that represented the face of the Catholic Church in the Island.

Canon France also undertook all the official roles, civil and ecumenical, expected of the Catholic Dean, at times having to argue for this principle until it was fully recognised.

In February 2008 he was created a 'Prelate of Honour' – a Papal honour that carries the title 'Monsignor'. Priests who are given this honour are considered to be members of the papal household and are listed in the Annuario Pontificio (the papal yearbook).

The honour, wrote Bishop Hollis at the time, was in relation to the work he had done in the Portsmouth Diocese, not least in the recent years he had spent in Jersey'.

Writing in the weekly Jersey Catholic newsletter, the new Monsignor France wrote: 'I am not sure that priests should have titles. Anyway, please continue to call me Father Nicholas! The greatest privilege is to be a priest.' However, he felt that that this title – and later, the bestowal of an MBE – was useful in raising the profile of the Catholic Dean and therefore of the Catholic Church in Jersey.

In June 2008 he celebrated the 40th anniversary of his ordination as a priest at a party held at the Living Legend, with some 400 members of the Catholic Church in Jersey from Poland, Portugal and South Africa as well as those from Jersey origins – an occasion to celebrate all the different cultures that make up the Church in Jersey in modern times.

In December 2009 Mgr Nicholas France was elected Provost of the Portsmouth Cathedral Chapter of Canons.

Mgr Nicholas France celebrating the 40th anniversary of his ordination
(Photo, Jersey Evening Post).

Chapter 6

THE MISSIONARY OBLATES OF MARY IMMACULATE

'He sent me to preach the gospel to the poor' (Motto of the Oblates)

THE Missionary Oblates of Mary Immaculate (OMI) is a missionary religious congregation founded in 1816 by Saint Eugène de Mazenod, a French priest born in Aix-en-Provence in 1782. It is composed of priests and brothers, usually living in community.

The founder was born into the French minor nobility and his family was forced to flee to Italy during the Revolution. They were political refugees for 11 years and during this unhappy and poverty-stricken time the marriage of his parents also broke down. Eugène determined to become a priest so as to help the poor and returning to France as a young man, he entered the Seminary of Saint-Sulpice and was ordained in 1811. In 1816, Father Eugène de Mazenod and four companions came together to preach missions in Provençal – the language of the local 'common people' -and to renew the Church in France after the Revolution. The *Oblats Marie Immaculée* was recognised as a religious congregation in 1826. Ultimately, Eugène de Mazenod became Bishop of Marseilles, dying in 1861. He was canonised in 1995.

The members take the three traditional religious vows of poverty, chastity and obedience, which are intended to make them totally available for religious service.

Today, the Oblates are active on five continents.

—ooo000ooo—

The first Oblate foundation in Britain was in 1841. In 1856 Fr Robert Cooke, a Dublin Doctor who had become an Oblate, training in the Oblates' Mother House in the South of France and ordained by Mgr de Mazenod, helped to set up the first Irish Oblate foundation. He became the London Provincial of the Order.

In 1880 Jersey was still part of the Diocese of Southwark. Its Bishop, Mgr James Danell, was aware of the needs of the growing Catholic Church in Jersey and called upon the Oblates to establish a Mission in the Island.

At the time, Jersey would have been seen as a deserving area for missionary work. Catholics in the Island were mostly French, poor seasonal labourers from Brittany and Normandy. Many of them were unable to attend Sunday Mass times. Owing to the often transitory or temporary nature of their occupations, their children had little opportunity for a settled education. The Catholic clergy in the Island were being swamped by the magnitude of the problems that they faced.

On 30 October 1880 Fr Cooke arrived in Jersey together with a French priest, Père Victor Fick, to set up the Jersey mission.

The young French republic was anti-clerical and some French Orders were forced to disband or go into exile. Oblate priests were obliged to leave France and Jersey became a destination for some of the priests who had been in Rennes and Limoges: Jersey was close at hand and there was missionary work they could do there to help their colleague, Père Fick.

Père Victor Fick

Père Fick was from Metz in Lorraine but had been working in England until he came to Jersey. Père Victor Bourde, who would eventually succeed Père Fick as the Rector of St Thomas', joined him from Limoges a fortnight after Père Fick's own arrival, together with another Oblate priest, Père F Guiller. It was soon very apparent that the Oblates were very much to the fore in Jersey Catholic life. Quoting from Diane Moore's book, *Deo Gratias*: 'The interaction between the Orders' [the newly arrived Jesuits and newly arrived Oblates] 'was strong, the Oblates actually strengthening the bonds through organised excursions, parish involvement, fêtes, bazaars, recruitment of new parishioners and community spirit. Looking through historical notes and records one can find a common message: the Oblates were becoming the driving force of the Catholic community.'

They took over the new parish of St Matthieu in 1882 and asked the *Dames de St André* to reactivate the school that had been established. Two years later the Catholic parish of Our Lady in St Martin was also taken over.

It had long been felt that a new, larger and purpose-built church was needed in St Helier. Père Jean-François Volkeryk, Rector of St Thomas' had foreseen the need and had started the funding process for it, but he had left in 1879, the year before the Oblates took over the parish. In 1881 Père Fick invited a fellow French Oblate, Père Donat Michaux, to preach at a First Communion Mass – and, as is detailed in the book on the chapter of the history of St Thomas, he accepted a commission to manage the fund-raising effort to build St Thomas's Church, which was opened and blessed officially in 1887.

The first Corpus Christi procession in Jersey since the Reformation took place in 1888, although this was held probably held in the grounds surrounding the new church building. St Thomas' was consecrated by Bishop Vertue in 1893.

—ooo000ooo—

Mention of the Corpus Christi processions is an opportunity to mention as well the role of the *Suisses*, the gentlemen in imposing uniforms who at one time headed Catholic processions, be it the procession of priest and altar servers to and from the altar at St Thomas' at the start and end of High Mass, or the massive Corpus Christi processions that were held from 1930.

The custom of having a *Suisse* at such events became established at St Thomas' during the early years of the 20th Century. In France, a *Suisse*'s role was usually limited to the Cathedrals; it suggests that the local status of St Thomas' as 'The French Cathedral' made it worthy to have a *Suisse* – a uniformed layman - at its celebrations and processions.

French kings had a *Garde Suisse* as part of the royal guard until the time of the Revolution.

The Suisse,
Jean-Marie - Francois
Le Fondre, leading a
post-Second World War
Corpus Christi Procession

Diane Moore in *Deo Gratias* explained the role of *Suisses* in French Catholicism: 'Churches and cathedrals of importance incorporated a uniformed layman into their services; he was neither a sexton nor a verger nor a beadle, but a man who would cover many of these duties whilst maintaining a unique role of his own. Dressed in a dark blue or red uniform and wearing a bicorn hat, he would lead the procession into church bearing a halberd in his right hand and a silver-topped staff in his left. This tradition also has emblematic roots at the Vatican, the Pope's own Swiss Guard, and it is thought that symbolically a *Suisse* in French cathedrals acted as a reminder of the papal guard.

'The *Suisse* in Jersey had two uniforms – a red one for Mass on Sundays and a dark blue one for more formal occasions.' A uniform used by the *Suisses* at St Thomas is preserved in a showcase at the Chapel of Relics at the back of the church.

There have only been three *Suisses* in Jersey at St Thomas': the first, although his name is not known for certain, was possibly a M. Le Fevre. The second, who led the first Corpus Christi procession to wind its way through the street of St Helier, was Jean-Marie Le Fondré who remained in this role until 1948. He was then replaced by Ferdinand Joseph Lecrivain, who was the *Suisse* until his death in 1971. At that point, no further *Suisses* were deployed.

—ooo000ooo—

A succession of French Oblate fathers lived in the Presbytery near St Thomas' throughout the late 19th Century and practically right through the 20th Century. There were generally about six to eight priests living together at any one time until the 1970s, when numbers began to drop until finally there were one or two – and then finally, one, Père Vincent Igoa, who described himself jokingly as 'the last of the Mohicans'.

It might be wondered, considering that the same church today has an establishment of only one priest, what exactly they all did during the course of the day. Of course, their duties were not just connected with the church, but as chaplains to Sacré Coeur Orphanage, De La Salle College, the Hospital, and Prison and the many duties now undertaken by Catholic laity. Each priest also had a 'visiting' district of St Helier.

In addition to the community at St Thomas' the Oblates provided priests for the parishes of St Matthieu and also Our Lady of the Annunciation (in St Martin), as well as, at the beginning of its existence, the Sacred Heart Parish in St Aubin.

At the start of their Mission to Jersey in the 19th Century, those Catholics in Jersey who were not Irish were mostly French or French speaking. But by the end of Occupation and the start of post-war prosperity in the Island, the demographics had changed completely. It made every sense for the Anglo-Irish Province of the Order to take over the Jersey parishes that had been served by the French Oblates.

That is indeed what happened, starting with Sacred Heart in 1946, then St Matthieu in 1952 and the St Martin parish in 1960. But St Thomas' remained 'the French church', continuing to be served by its French Oblates.

Père Maré – still remembered in the Island as 'the Priest in a wig', was the Rector of St Thomas' who had served during the Occupation and had accompanied François Scornet to his execution in 1941. He stayed on as '*Econome*' (or 'financial supervisor' and celebrated the 50th anniversary as an Oblate at St Thomas' in 1956. Forty-four of those 50 years had been spent in Jersey, arriving in the Island in 1912 to take up the post of *Econome* and Professor in the Oblate Juniorate of the Northern French Province, then at St Mary's House, Rouge Bouillon. He retired in August 1960 after a total of 48 years of service as an Oblate in Jersey.

By the 1960s, the number of French Oblates in Jersey was decreasing and the number of Anglo-Irish oblates was increasing. Furthermore, the Anglo-Irish Province was under less financial pressure than the French Province.

Jersey continued to change and by the late 1960s the great Corpus Christi processions had become a thing of the past.

For 15 years from 1967 (with a break of one year from 1975-1976) Père Jean-Marie Chuffart was the Rector of St Thomas'. With him in the presbytery next door were still around eight Oblate priests. However, although he had all these assistants, he did not use them to the best advantage, preferring to do most things himself.

Père Jean-Marie Chuffart

Mgr France found that many parishioners still remembered Père Chuffart and spoke fondly of 'Father Shuffart': 'He was so well loved – in the days before the Shelter he would invite homeless people to sleep in the hallway of St Thomas' Presbytery. He was a saintly man, but perhaps not very worldly wise. He burnt out, of course, before his time.'

On his retirement he moved to Pontmain, where he died 20 years later. His place in Jersey was taken by Father Vincent Igoa.

In 1980 were the celebrations of the centenary of the arrival of the Oblates. A Mass was held at St Thomas' in May 1980, led by Bishop Emery and with singing in Latin, French and English by the combined choirs of all the Catholic churches in Jersey. Fr Igoa wrote and published a booklet on 100 Years of the Oblates in Jersey.

By now there were four French Oblates serving at St Thomas'. The continuation of the French Oblates seemed ever less viable in an Island that had moved away from being a society in which French people or the French language played any significant part.

Perhaps the last act in the 120-year history of the French Oblates in Jersey was the effect of the Second Vatican Council and its teachings, which resulted in a radical re-ordering of St Thomas' Church. This is dealt with at greater length in this book in the chapter concerning the effects of 'Vatican II', but the effect of the changes, on the whole, dismayed the congregation at St Thomas'.

The 'new' ordering of the church, combined with linguistic and demographic changes, meant that the Church became a far less significant 'French' centre – and the writing was on the wall for the French Oblates in Jersey.

There was speculation that on Père Chuffart's retirement, a priest would be appointed from the diocese and not from the OMI. But instead, Père Igoa succeeded Père Chuffart.

In a newsletter in June 1992, he wrote that the Provincial and his council had decided that at the age of 66 it really was time for him to retire. He had spent 25 years in the Island.

At this time, a popular annual fund-raising event was initiated: the Continental Fête, which helped towards the considerable sums needed for restoring the roof and the external fabric of St Thomas'.

The Anglo-Irish Oblates also stayed on in their parishes until the late 1990s. Their intention of withdrawing was given in December 1994, two months after the publication of the Pastoral Review's report, when it was announced that they would leave by September 1997, after a presence in the Island of almost 50 years. Two parishes were affected: Sacred Heart and the churches served from there, at which Fr Liam Griffin officiated with assistant priest Fr John Mahon, and Our Lady in St Martin and the other two churches in Grouville, served by Fr Eamon Fitzgerald and retired priest Fr Tom Magee, who had been the parish priest there from 1974 to 1983.

The priests in the Sacred Heart parish left in September 1995; those in the East of the Island two years later. After leaving Jersey, Fr Griffin became co-ordinator of English language pilgrimages at Lourdes.

In fact Père Igoa at St Thomas' stayed on until 1999, leaving on 7 September, one day before Canon Nicholas France arrived to become Rector jointly of St Thomas' and also of St Mary and St Peter's.

As his Order, the Oblates of Mary Immaculate, was unable to find a replacement due to the shortage of priests, it had been decided that the time was right for St Thomas' to come under the jurisdiction of the Portsmouth diocese.

The Bishop, in a pastoral letter to both congregations, wrote: 'The inability of the Oblates of Mary Immaculate to replace him has meant that I have had to take a radical look at the pastoral and parish provision in St Helier. There are no spare priests available to take Fr Vincent's place, so the decision has had to be taken to merge the two parishes and place them in the pastoral care of one priest.'

When Père Igoa left the Island late in 1999, a long and edifying chapter in the religious life of the Island came to its final end.

III. A TALE OF TWO MISSIONS

Chapter 7

THE FRENCH MISSION

Redivivus: the story of St Thomas' Church: its triumphant birth, successful maturity, decline into grey and gloomy shabbiness – and its restoration to a more vibrant life

THE RISE

FROM the mid-19th Century onwards, the number of French Catholics in the Island continued to grow apace. But these were not the aristocratic emigrés of the previous generation. Agriculture was the Island's chief economic activity and Frenchmen from Brittany and Normandy flocked to the Island to work in the fields and farms and as domestic servants.

The first chapels that were built were soon far too small to contain the number of worshipers and even the purchase of an Anabaptist chapel in New Street proved to be only a temporary solution. This re-opened as a Catholic chapel in 1842, dedicated to St Thomas, in honour of Bishop Thomas Griffiths, the Vicar Apostolic in London. It is this building that gave its name to the present St Thomas' Church when the chapel, in its turn, became too small for its Sunday congregation of mainly French-speaking Catholics.

Père Jean François Volkerick

The French community saved and collected for a new church and in the 1870s an empty building plot was acquired by the Rector of St Thomas', Père Jean-François Volkeryk, in Val Plaisant.... but that was about as far as the project had got by 1880, when the French religious order of Oblates of Mary Immaculate arrived to run the parish, in the person of Père Victor Fick from Metz in Lorraine. Only the sum of £2,500 had been collected – well short of the £10,000 to £15,000 estimated as the cost of a suitable church building.

What to do? The answer came in the shape of a French priest, a fellow Oblate, Père Michaux, who had a great reputation in France as a fund raiser. In 1882 he was invited to Jersey to preach at a First Communion service. At the service, he said that he was grieved and horrified by the cramped conditions in the chapel, and that 'something must be done'. He was promptly invited to do it – and accepted. Père Fick's plan had worked admirably.

Père Michaux got down to work, assembling a fund raising team of French Oblates. Money flowed in, and not just from the Island's Catholics, for prominent and noble French families were also invited to subscribe. The French Revolution had taken place only some 90 years before and many of their grand-parents or great-grand-parents would have recounted to their descendants the hospitality they had found in Jersey during their exile from the Terror. Now these descendants were invited, as it were, to 'think of Granny' and give money to the appeal.

St Thomas' - how it looked originally

The foundation of the new St Thomas' Church was laid in 1883.

It has been said that the Oblates wished to dedicate their new church to the Sacred Heart – Le Sacré Coeur – hence the shrine above the high altar – but the Bishop ordered that the new church keep the dedication to St Thomas.

Bishop Vertue of Portsmouth came to Jersey for the occasion and he was met at the Harbour by the Island's Catholic clergy and by the band, L'Avenir, playing light march music. Together, they processed to Val Plaisant, where the site had been decorated with flowers and greenery. An altar had been placed on the spot where the future Tabernacle would stand, and this was solemnly blessed by the Bishop.

Four years later, in 1887, the new building was ready to be opened for public worship. It had been built in 13th Century Gothic style and looked – as it still does – like countless churches in France. This is hardly surprising, as it was designed by a French architect for a French (or French-speaking) congregation.

For the opening, the new church was decorated and the ceremony was arranged to take place on 30 October. In the preceding week the old chapel in New Street was closed (it became a Catholic social club, *le Cercle St Thomas*) and the parish clergy – now eight Oblates – moved into a new presbytery at 17 Val Plaisant.

Père Fick now takes up the story: 'Tomorrow we shall see a new era in the life of the mission. What progress, what joy, what hopes! We went to sleep with these sweet thoughts, but alas, our awakening was not so joyful! The devil must have shaken with rage. He must have understood that the new church meant war and all Hell seemed to rise against us.'

More prosaically, that night there was a violent storm and at about midnight it became so violent that everything shook. Houses were shaken, trees were uprooted and several people were buried under the rubble of chimneystacks and walls.

In the new church, the windows in both transepts were blown in and many others in the nave were loosened. The scaffolding around the spire was in dire danger of collapsing and of crashing down on the neighbouring houses. The fact that it didn't was judged to be a miracle.

Away in St Peter, at the convent beside the Catholic Church of St Matthieu at Coin Varin, a boiler fell through the roof. Two Religious Sisters disappeared beneath the rubble, but were dug out the next morning unscathed – another miracle.

Early the next morning the parish clergy surveyed the chaos left by the storm. The church was swimming in water and bits of glass lay everywhere. But it was decided that there was nothing for it but to go ahead with the original plans. As they worked frantically through the morning to get the church ready by the start of the ceremony at 10.30am, the wind diminished, patches of blue appeared in the sky and then the sun appeared. Yet another miracle.

The damage was repaired as far as possible and the altars were once again magnificently decorated. All was ready for 10.30am and the crowds arrived to fill the church. The procession formed up in the Sanctuary: 28 choirboys, 29 cantors, followed by the Cross. After them came the Jesuits, the Oblate priests of the parish and their own Provincial, delegated by the Bishop to bless the new church.

But it had begun to rain heavily once again, so the procession wisely stayed indoors, except for the Oblate priest celebrating Mass, Père Richard, and another priest were given the unenviable task of processing around the exterior of the church to sprinkle it with holy water. Then came High Mass, and at the conclusion prayers for Queen Victoria were sung in Latin.

The consecration of the totally finished church took place on 5 September 1893 to commemorate the centenary of the re-establishment of Catholicism in the Channel Islands.

And the final cost of the new St Thomas' Church? Unfortunately it was neither on time nor on budget. It cost a whole £30,000.

St Thomas' remained serving the purpose of what it had been built to achieve: to be the main church in the Island for French-speaking Catholics. Only 21 years later, in 1914, many of the parishioners had been recalled to France to be conscripted into the French army, often leaving behind wives and family in the Island. If, as was only too likely, they subsequently fell in action, the surviving dependants faced horrible problems without proper social security payments to help them.

The names of the fallen are recorded in St Thomas' in the Chapel of Our Lady of Lourdes.

The church building remained at the centre of Catholic life for the Island's French-speaking community – often being referred to as 'La Cathédrale'. It was looked after by a varying number of Oblates – usually about eight.

Only 22 years after the First World War, during which the Island had been used as a Prisoner of War Camp, the tables were turned when Jersey was itself invaded in June 1940.

The Rector, Père Maré, attended the would-be French escapee, François Scornet, as is detailed in Chapter 3. He stayed on after the Occupation before leaving to spend his retirement at the Oblate Home in Pontmain, Normandy.

Readers with long memories will remember the successful and optimistic years of the 1950s at the church, still largely unaltered from the time of its building and with the same interior decorations, some of them rather sugary-sweet in the best Victorian tradition.

This description of the Church is taken from a description of St Thomas' written by Père Jean-Louis Messager OMI, probably in the late 1930s, but which applies to the Church at any time until the changes wrought by the Second Vatican Council:

The Frescoes: the paintings represent St Michael and the Guardian Angels, angels playing musical instruments and angels singing....

The Pulpit: stands against the second pillar of the Nave, on the Gospel side. It is made of polished oak and beautifully carved.... The plan is hexagonal with panels containing the containing the figures of the four evangelists. The canopy in two storeys, richly designed with trefoiled and crocketed pediments and pinnacles with finials, is terminated by a spire in open work with a Cross as finial...The spire is supported by open-work mullions and four-leaved rose windows with flying buttresses or arch-buttants. The rail of the staircase is of an elegant open tracery with a moulded cornice decorated with a here-leaved ornament...

The Confessionals: These are of polished oak and of exquisite workmanship, with richly decorated doors and frontons and with slender shafts supporting the cornice with a crested parapet,..

Stations of the Cross: ...Each station is framed in a beautifully carved design of polished oak with two decorated shafts bearing angels on the summit...

The Communion Rail... is in a very artistic iron scroll work of long carved foliation and long stems with buds, while the kneeling stool running along the rail is of blue granite...

The descriptions continue with details of The Blessed Virgin Chapel, St Joseph's Chapel, St Michael's Chapel, the statue of St Theresa of the Child Jesus, the shield of the Holy Face, St Joan of Arc chapel, chapel of Our Lady of Lourdes and the Chapel of the Font.

It remained 'the French Church' – Mass was in Latin, of course, but sermons were in French. Even in the 1960s, as the Second Vatican Council was taking place, a High Mass at St Thomas' was still a special and uplifting experience – the decorated high altar, the chapels with their statues, flags and reliquaries, the imposing '*Suisse*' in his uniform and bearing his halberd – colour, music, sights and the transcendent glory of the sung Tridentine Mass helping the mind raise up and away from the mundane.

THE DECLINE

By the early 1970s, St Thomas' had become somewhat run down. A Mass for Cardinal Heenan's visit to Jersey in 1971 did not show the church at its best, with broken windows and stains on the decorated walls – but there was nevertheless still a very devotional atmosphere.

But one positive change a decade later was the construction of a new Community Centre and clubroom, for which planning permission was gained in 1982. It was built on the site of what had been a grotto of Our Lady of Lourdes, situated between the rear of the presbytery and the adjacent wall of the church. Until that time, the church's social club used premises belonging to the Sacré Coeur in Roussel Street and church meetings were usually held at Beaulieu Convent School. Apart from any more important reasons, the new premises by the church allowed people to meet for coffee after Mass.

In 1984 the church underwent much-needed and expensive repairs to the fabric of the exterior. At the same time, however, there was a radical reorganisation of the interior in keeping - as it was said at the time - with the liturgical directions flowing from the decrees of the Second Vatican Council. This involved a move away from devotional extras to the centrality of the Mass on a single altar in the central crossing of the Church. It resulted in doing away with the side altars, the old Stations of the Cross, the Confessionals, the beautifully decorated pulpit and the original High Altar. It also involved taking away the central aisle in order to bring all the benches together with direct focus on the altar. The Blessed Sacrament was placed somewhat obscurely in a small tabernacle in a side chapel. The decorated walls were repaired and covered with a lime finish that made the church seem somewhat grey and severe.

As the 1990's wore on, the building seemed to become even greyer and more dismal. It had become a victim of the contemporary, 'Conciliar' minimalist attitude towards religious art and architecture: only one altar, no need for distracting statues, everything as simple as possible. With the benches joined together and the central aisle eliminated, the church suggested a Methodist temple. Everything was about the Mass - and nothing else mattered. A committee was formed of parishioners who enthusiastically recommended this 20th Century equivalent of the Protestant 'Stripping of the Altars' in Reformation times.

St Thomas' - after the stripping of the interior

At St Thomas, what might have been austere and dignified at its inception had just become dark and dismal by the turn of the Millennium.

In May 1999 Canon Mahy's departure was announced by Bishop Hollis in the course of a pastoral visit to the Island. He also told Island Catholics that from the beginning of the following year, the communities of St Thomas' and St Mary and St Peter's would be combined.

The previous November it had been announced that the Rector at St Thomas', Père Vincent Igoa, would be leaving and returning to France.

The new priest – who was not named but was later announced to be Canon Nicholas France – was expected to arrive in September.

He duly arrived and was named as the parish priest of both the churches and Catholic Dean. Père Igoa had already left and it was with some trepidation that the new Dean took over 'the French church'.

He said: 'When I arrived, I thought, because of my surname, that people would come up to me and start talking to me in French – but no one did!

I then discovered it was Portuguese I needed. It may still have been, theoretically, the "French church" but even if the liturgy was in French, the appeal for money was always in English! Furthermore, Mass had ceased to be celebrated in the French language two years before Père Igoa retired.

'Before I took over, the congregation was still desperate to stop being 'taken over' by St Mary and St Peter's as they saw it and were anxious to find another stopgap to follow Father Igoa. The Bishop put his foot down and informed the congregation that the time was right for appointing one of his own Diocesan priests and uniting St Thomas with St Mary and St Peter as a single Catholic Parish for St Helier. Some parishioners opted out in protest but they soon returned.'

REDIVIVUS

Although the church needed significant refurbishment, it was obvious to Canon France that St Thomas' could still be the 'humming' centre of Catholicism in the Island, including the more effective use of the church hall and the former school at the north side of the church.

An extensive programme of restoration was initiated, beginning with the Presbytery, the state of which left much to be desired – it needed a huge amount of restoration work. Canon France thought it should be the home for the town priests, in the middle of St Helier rather than in the 'leafy suburb' of Westbourne Terrace, Wellington Road – a big house where he was now the sole occupant.

The value of the Westbourne Terrace had been enhanced by obtaining (eventually) planning permission to build four houses in its grounds.

The building had originally been a Carmelite convent for French Sisters expelled by the country's anti-clerical laws. Then it was used to house De La Salle brothers teaching at the nearby school. When the Brothers left the Island, Canon Mahy bought this house to replace the inadequate new presbytery next to the new St Mary and St Peter's Church.

At the same time, Canon France announced that Catholic Pastoral Services would move to the former Val Plaisant School building, beside St Thomas'. The new centre was blessed by Mgr John Nelson, Vicar General of the Portsmouth Diocese, at a service in November 2003.

Outside the Catholic Pastoral Services: Catholic Dean Mgr Nicholas France,
Deacon Tony Ward, Deacon Iain MacFirbhisigh, Fr Kevin Hoiles.
(Photo, Jersey Evening Post)

The new centre contained meeting rooms, a library, a quiet room and offices, as well as a bookshop selling a range of Christian resources.

It also had a new computerised library for use by Island Catholics and anyone interested in books on the Christian and Catholic faith, containing books for lending as well as for reference.

At the other end of this building a 'Welcome Centre' was developed as a place where Portuguese, Polish and other nationalities in the Island could be taught English in a friendly and welcoming environment. As Canon France said at the time: 'To empower people by teaching them the English language is one of the best things we can do for them.'

Although provided by the Catholic Church, it was to be open for use by anyone, irrespective of their origin or religion.

The venture, which cost over £400,000, was achieved by a fund-raising appeal led by the former Senator Dick Shenton and by Canon France.

The schoolhouse had been built in 1890 as the church school for St Thomas and was run by Religious Sisters and De La Salle Brothers.

In 1912 Catholic teaching in the school was forbidden and the States Education Committee took over the school, which then became Val Plaisant School. The local catchment area of the school drew on French-speaking and English-speaking families, many of them very poor. The school lasted until 1982, when it was closed by the Education Committee and handed back to St Thomas' Church.

The St Thomas' Sports and Social Club took up residence there following the closure of St Mary's House in Roussel Street. This club ceased functioning in 1997, after which date the rooms were used as a furniture storage area by the St Vincent de Paul Society.

On the scaffolding, Canon France visits the restoration work.

The conversion of the former school provided a meeting room for language classes, a counselling room and a café that in the summer opened up on to the terrace outside. There was also a gallery with the function of celebrating the varied cultural differences contained within the Island. It was named The Sir John Cheshire Gallery in appreciation of the support given to the appeal by the Lieut-Governor. The main meeting room was named the Shenton Room.

A new home for the Society of St Vincent de Paul was also provided in the same building.

The new Welcome Centre was opened in February 2004 by Sir John Cheshire. He called the Centre: 'a catalyst to help people to integrate in the Island, in friendship and in Christian community.' Canon France said 'it was for all who wanted to find a home, gather socially, learn languages, receive counselling and share in music and art.'

The week after the opening of the Welcome Centre, the first exhibition in the Sir John Cheshire Gallery opened, featuring the art of the Polish artist and Jersey resident George Kowzan.

By the following year (2005), the Welcome Centre was teaching English to over 200 Portuguese, Polish and other newcomers.

The restoration of St Thomas' church to some of its former beauty was an expensive but worthwhile project, turning the old building back into a Cathedral-like church. In September 2005 an Island-wide appeal was launched. The church was in need of a radical overhaul. Only the steeple clock seemed to be in good repair, thanks to a £3,000 donation by Senator Dick Shenton in April 2004. It had stopped the year before and had been stuck on midday ever since. For the Senator, it was a 'thank-you present' to the Island and voters of St Helier for putting him back in office at the last election. The bells, however, needed to be taken down and repaired as they had been silent for many years.

The details of the proposed restoration were twofold: first, the practical requirement to ensure that the church had adequate levels of heating and lighting and secondly, to make it once more a place of beauty to uplift the spirit.

Among the many changes that were on the restoration agenda were:

* The installation of partial underfloor heating to make it warm in winter;

* New electrics, with an audio system and visual system for the benefit of people in the side pews where the visibility of the altar was restricted;

*Better lighting to enhance the building and to bring out its considerable architectural merits, lighting the roof as well as lighting downwards into the interior space.

To meet the second requirement, included among the many other details were:

*The restitution of the central aisle;

*The repositioning of the Tabernacle in the weekday chapel behind the sanctuary to create a more devotional atmosphere; the Tabernacle and other panels from the original St Mary and St Peter's would be used;

*The French chapel of Our Lady of Lourdes returned, containing the memorials, formerly in the old French Consulate, to Frenchmen resident in Jersey who fell in the First World War.

*A Portuguese chapel, of Our Lady of Fatima, in traditional blue, white and gold Portuguese tiles, was created, as well as a Shrine of Our Lady of Czestochowa for the Island's Polish community.

*The sanctuary and aisles of the church were re-tiled and the carpet covering removed.

*A Chapel of Holy Relics was created to show off the historic reliquaries, church plates and vestments. It also displayed the uniform of the '*Suisse*'.

*A new set of Stations of the Cross were purchased from France;

*The font, formerly in the old St Mary's and St Peter's Church, was put in place in a prominent position near the entrance of the church.

*The main porch of the church was made more attractive and open, as befitting the church's chief entrance.

Returning the Church bell

*The church bells were re-hung (the church has the largest set of bells in the Channel Islands) and the grand organ was restored.

*The exterior approach area at the foot of the steps in front of the main doors was renovated and new iron railings put in place.

The sum needed for the restoration appeal was at least £900,000 – which itself was only a portion of the estimated cost. It was by no means an insignificant sum, but at least the appeal did not have to start from the ground. Some money (£230,000) was already in the restoration account because of the sale of the former St Mary and St Peter clergy residence at Westbourne Terrace and the sale of its garden for development.

The appeal was by the Lieut-Governor, Air Chief Marshal Sir John Cheshire for the restoration of St Thomas' Church, with an open garden event at Government House on 16 September 2005. Close on £12,000 was raised and around 1,500 people attended the event, much to the gratification for the Appeal Committee, which was chaired by Daphne Minihane.

The church closed in July 2006 and the repairs began. The parish accepted the loan of the Anglican Church of St Simon in Great Union Road for Sunday Mass, courtesy of the Vicar of All Saints, the Rev Geoff Houghton. It felt like home, as the church contained the former high altar from the old FCJ Convent School in David Place.

Inevitably the restoration work took longer than expected, about four months longer than the original estimate. The annual service of carols in 2006, normally held at St Thomas', was held at the Methodist Centre in Halkett Place, instead. The collection taken that evening raised a further £1,000 towards the restoration work.

Many local craftsmen and craftswomen took part in the restoration.

Louisa Humphries, a decorative painter used to working in private houses, worked full-time for three months on the intricate decorative details : gold-leaf gilding the roof bosses and painting murals on the main walls.

The Head of Art at De La Salle College, Mark Blanchard, painted two large oil paintings based on the Resurrection accounts of the Supper at Emmaus and the Appearance to Saint Thomas. Stained glass windows were restored by Neil Mackenzie.

Four Archangels were created – Gabriel, Raphael, Michael and Uriel – by Mark Blanchard and plasterers Jason Crump and Ben Mallet. The eight-foot plaster-cast angels were put into place on the four sides of the sanctuary. They were not 'cosy Victorian angels' in Nicholas France's words, but challenging figures of power,

Photo showing Louisa Humphries with Cardinal Murphy O'Connor and Canon Nicholas France at the reception following the rededication of St Thomas'

indicating the awe and majesty of God, surrounding the Holy of Holies, the altar of the Eucharist. The grey walls were re-painted a pale honey colour.

In total, the restoration cost £1,250,000. The church opened its doors for Palm Sunday, 2007.

A further successful fund-raising event took place in March 2008 when the soprano singer, Lesley Garratt, performed at a sell-out concert in St Thomas'. It moved the appeal a further £17,000 towards its goal, although there still £250,000 to pay off.

In the same month, relics and regalia belonging to the church were put into a special display area created at the back of the church. They included monstrances, reliquaries and vestments – as well as the uniform of the '*Suisse*' who used to officiate at Mass and head Catholic processions.

Before then, in October 2007 the Archbishop of Westminster, Cardinal Cormac Murphy O'Connor, came to celebrate a Mass of Thanksgiving and rededication. The newly-restored church looked its best and the congregation filled it to overflowing.

Photo of Cardinal Murphy O'Connor and the architect of the restoration project Gerard Smith

Concelebrants were Bishop Hollis, Nicholas France and Island clergy (both present and former) as well as the Catholic Dean in Guernsey, the Rev Michael Hore. The service was attended by the Lieut - Governor, Lieutenant-General Andrew Ridgway, the Bailiff, Sir Philip Bailhache, Chief Minister Frank Walker, as well as by representatives of other denominations in Jersey. Returning to the Island for the service were the former Catholic Dean, David Mahy and the former Priest of St Thomas', Father Vincent Igoa.

Quoting from Psalm 83 (sung at the service by the Church's Portuguese choir): 'How lovely is Your dwelling place, Lord God of Hosts' the Cardinal said, in the course of his Homily: 'How lovely is this church building, now restored'.

Canon France, talking about the restoration to the *Jersey Evening Post*, observed: 'Beauty is an aspect of God and we need to recover that sense of beauty to take us into something bigger than ourselves, into something far grander and into something "other" that is beyond our comprehension.

'In the restored St Thomas, the whole church is a tool for teaching about Christ and the faith. Indeed, it really is now like a Cathedral!'

Chapter 8

'THE IRISH MISSION'

The story of St Mary and St Peter's Church

AT the beginning of the 19th Century, the building of Fort Regent brought a considerable number of Irish labourers to Jersey. At first they were cared for spiritually by Père de Grimouville and later by Père Le Guédois, both from the French chapel of St Louis in Castle Street, although from 1811 to 1821 separate registers were kept from the French and English speaking communities.

Within a few years the numbers of Irish had grown so much in such a way that as to cause friction with the French congregation who shared the same chapel. Matters reached boiling point and a letter was sent to Bishop Poynter of the London District asking him to send one of their fellow countrymen as their priest.

The Irish and the French did not get on well together - perhaps it was a problem of language – each complaining that the 'others' would not make way for them.

In 1821 Fr John Carroll arrived and it was agreed that new premises needed to be found for the Irish. These were obtained in a courtyard off Hue Street and a chapel had been built by 1826 it was the first Catholic chapel to be built in Jersey since the Reformation.

The money was borrowed, but the mortgage could not be repaid, so the chapel had to be sold the following year. Father Carroll seems to have left the Island at the same time and for the next two years it seems that the Irish congregation went back to St Louis in Castle Street. In September 1829 Fr Matthew Ryan came to Jersey and the Irish Mission was re-established; Hue Street chapel was re-acquired and put to its original use.

Ten years later the chapel had become too small for the growing congregation and the 'Missionary Rector', Fr John Cunningham, decided that a bigger church would have to be built. A new site was found in Vauxhall Street – then at the outskirts of town - and the foundation stone of the church was laid on Wednesday 13 October 1841. Work on the new church continued swiftly and some 14 months after the foundation stone had been laid, the church was opened at the beginning of January 1843. A month later, it was consecrated by Bishop Thomas Griffiths of the London District and dedicated to St Mary; it was known as 'the Irish Chapel' as opposed to 'the French Chapel'.

In the years ahead there was a yearly increase in Catholics in Jersey – both Irish and French – from 2,000 to 3,000 within the 1840s. The number doubled in the two years between 1845 and 1847 because of the arrival of refugees from the Irish Famine.

Work on the naval harbours and breakwaters and labour was also needed: the government gave free passage; the work was constant and the wages good. From the district around Waterford alone came some 4,000 people to Jersey.

The congregation increased to such an extent that the existing church became completely inadequate for its congregation.

On Fr Cunningham's death in 1848 he was succeeded by his assistant priest, the Rev Jeremiah McCarthy, who remained in charge for some 45 years.

Year after year the number of Irish in Jersey was increasing. When the work on St Catherine's breakwater was finished, Irish workmen moved into town from the country and they were joined in town by compatriots who, having completed government construction work in Alderney, had come across to the larger island.

By 1860 it was clear that St Mary's, Vauxhall Street, would have to be replaced by something bigger. Plans were drawn up and construction work started behind the existing building. Fr McCarthy proposed to build a new church that would hold some 2,000 people and be completed with a fine tower. This church was duly built as an extension to St Mary's and joined to it by a large archway so that the entire congregation could be accommodated. The new part of the enlarged church was dedicated to St Peter – and the enlarged church was dedicated to St Mary and St Peter and consecrated by Bishop Thomas Grant of Southwark on 6 August 1867.

It was incomplete when opened – the intention was to complete it as soon as possible. But the project was interrupted and delayed by a grave financial and banking crisis that overwhelmed Jersey in the 1870s, just a few years after the opening, causing great distress and an almost entire

Interior of the original St Mary and St Peter's

cessation of employment. Many of the Irish congregation of the church – and other Islanders - had to leave Jersey and they emigrated to the USA, Canada and Australia. The church's congregation of some 4,000 was reduced almost overnight to just over 1,000 – with comparatively little work and greatly reduced wages.

Fr McCarthy did not lose heart, but continued to work for the good of the parish and the completion of the church. It took 24 years before the chancel and the transepts could be completed in September 1891. Two years later, in June 1893, Mgr McCarthy (he had been made a Papal Prelate - or Monsignor - on the completion of the church) died. He is buried in Almorah cemetery. The church was never completed as intended.

The next priest, Fr John Hourigan, came in 1893 to replace Fr McCarthy; he remained at St Mary and St Peter's for 38 years. He paid off the debt on the church by 1905 and so was able to have it consecrated by Bishop Cotter, then the Auxiliary Bishop of Portsmouth. He was appointed a Canon of the Diocese in 1916 and in 1925 he beautified the sanctuary of

The choir, St Mary and St Peter's, 1948

the church with a new altar. The former high altar was transferred in time to St Thomas', where it is still in place.

Canon Clifford Bailey succeeded Canon Hourigan in 1931 and was, in turn, succeeded by Canon Richard Arscott, who remained in charge of the parish throughout the Occupation. After the Occupation he was succeeded in turn by Canon Albert Lion and in 1948 by Canon Arthur Olney, who remained for 27 years.

The year 1948 was significant for a number of reasons: it was the centenary of St Mary's Church in Vauxhall Street, it was the year in which a new Dean would begin his appointment, it was the year that saw the sweeping away of one of the last restrictions on Catholicism in Jersey: from thenceforward a Jurat of the Royal Court would need no longer to be a member of 'L'Eglise Reformé'.

Canon (later Monsignor) Olney's time in Jersey, and that of his successors, Canon Mahy and Monsignor France, are described in detail on 53 - 61.

In the immediate post-war years there was a full round of repair and re-decoration work. In 1951 there was a minor drama when workmen, digging the foundations of an organ gallery support, came across a brick-lined grave and a lead lined coffin. There were remains of an iron plate on the coffin with traces of a painted inscription, but this was so eaten away by rust that nothing could be read. Inside was a body, clothed in a long coarse, woven garment, the original colour of which could not be known. About the head was what might have been a hood, or maybe part of the coffin lining. On the feet were shoes, the leather soles of which were still preserved. The body was by no means a skeleton, but without a proper dissection and measurement of the comparative size of some of the bones, it was impossible to say whether it was that of a man or a woman – although if it had been a woman, it was someone tall. The body, in its leaden coffin, was taken to Mont-à-l'Abbé cemetery and duly reburied.

The question is – whose body? It could have been that of Father Cunningham, since he was buried within the precincts of the church. On the other hand, it might have been that of a nun, since the building behind the church in Winchester Street that became the presbytery had once been occupied by a community of Sisters of Mercy. It is unlikely to be that of a lay person, because there were no signs of any other graves nearby, such as one would have expected had the ground been used as a parish churchyard.

The grave remains unmarked, but with modern DNA analysis one might hope that one day the likely identity of the body may be discovered.

By 1965 work was completed on the façade of the church. This involved taking down the original 19th Century Church (St Mary's), which had latterly been used as a hall, and building a new modern front at the west end of the main church, with a forecourt opening on to Vauxhall Street. Islanders with memories stretching back over the decades will remember how the church was set back from the road and appeared to be a modern building – the façade and porch disguising the traditional church behind.

It was the final completion of the church – which had been 98 years in the building.

In October 1966, 140 years of the separate existence of the French and English speaking missions came to an end with the territorial amalgamation of both parishes. A fault line continued to exist between the two communities, even if they were one parish. It was a fault line that would continue, really, until the turn of the Millennium.

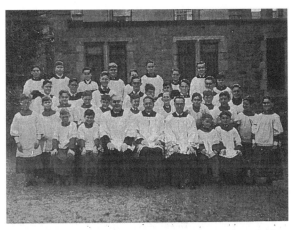

The altar boys of St Mary and St Peter's, 1948

But only 13 years after this final completion, further modifications had to be made: Mgr Olney's successor, Canon David Mahy, realised that it was necessary to dismantle the large concrete panels that had been added to the frontage of the church in 1965 because they had become unsafe. This was done in 1978 and considerable discussion took place concerning a necessary major restoration of the church, which was costed at £250,000.

In the end, it was accepted that a more economical solution would be to rebuild the church on a new site, while trying to keep, in the new building, some of its old treasures, such as the stained glass and much of the carved stone. However, no site was available.

Discussions continued into the 1980s. A description of the church in 1984 describes it as being: 'in desperate need of redecoration... the shining cross once on the front has been removed. The fibreglass canopy covering the porch is somewhat battered with wear. The porch, although clean, has mauve paint peeling off the walls but this is disguised either by posters of future events or brightly coloured cards stating 'Buy a Brick' (money collected for a new church).'

A new church appeared, in fact, to be the less costly option. The existing church would have cost too much to renovate and it would have been a burden on future generations, as money would always have had to be spent on it.

In May 1981 Canon Mahy was able to write to Bishop Emery: 'I have now received an offer from Beaulieu Convent of their car park site in Wellington Road... The site has the advantage of proximity to the two Catholic secondary schools. We could build a new church with a normal seating capacity of 400, designed to accommodate a further 200 in a narthex area. A presbytery could be incorporated. The site is near two housing estates and a number of hotels... We would propose to move off our present site and would ask the diocese to sell it so as to allow us to finance the new building.... It looks as though we have a solution to what has seemed an intractable problem.'

He later recollected: 'It had been a difficult searching of conscience to know whether we should bring the building up to standard or whether we should build something new. We took the latter decision partly because Vauxhall was so close to St Thomas'.

'It was an odd situation, having two big churches so close together.

We were very keen to renovate St Mary and St Peter's Church. The replacement frontage of 1965, in a modern style, hadn't been a good job, nor was it actually finished. At an early stage after my arrival in Jersey there arose the vexed question: "How are we going to raise money to bring the church up to scratch? It was basically a beautiful building, a very large church on which work had stopped once the nave had been completed; the south wall had been constructed mainly out of rubble and would have needed rebuilding completely. '

An option that did cross the minds of a few of us at the time was that we should close St Mary & St Peter's and use St Thomas' instead. It was not a popular suggestion and it was not pursued. In retrospect, it was an ironic decision, considering that both communities have since been merged.'

Angela Le Sueur remembers a meeting of the two congregations at which she put forward the idea of having simply one church and one parish, considering how close to one another the two existing churches were located. She was astonished and taken aback at the hostility caused by this suggestion.

However, at diocesan level, where the past history of 'French' and 'Anglo-Irish' Catholic factions in Jersey might not have been so easily understood, there was considerable support for making one church and parish out of the two communities. Bishop Emery arrived in Jersey to discuss this option and met with parishioners. Although in favour of the 'one church' option, he was dissuaded by Dick Shenton, who, in an eloquent speech, asked the Bishop whether he had no faith – an interesting question to put to any Bishop; did he not have the faith to see the possibility of creating a new St Mary and St Peter's Church?' The Bishop was persuaded.

Canon David Mahy amid the ruins of the demolished St Mary and St Peter's Church

It was suggested to Dick Shenton that if he was so much in favour of a new church, he should organise the fund-raising to make this happen – and in fact he did spearhead the fundraising campaign.

The foundation stone of the new church was laid 19 April 1983 and the final Mass was held at Vauxhall Street on 29 August 1984. For nine months afterwards, masses were held at the Hotel de France's 'Lido de France' while the new church was being built on the Beaulieu School carpark site. That, of course, was on quite a steep slope, so the church was constructed at first-floor level with churchgoers entering the building on the ground floor and then reaching the church on the first floor by means of stairs, lift or ramp.

The plans for the new church were drawn up by Bill Davies of Breakwell and Davis architects. He had originally been asked for his advice on the proposed renovation of the original church. When Beaulieu offered their site, Mr Davies found himself designing a new church instead of renovating an old one.

The new church incorporated the same number of people as before – about 600 people – but it was designed so that nobody would be more than 50 or 60ft away from the altar. The general effect was more like a cinema or theatre than a traditional church building, despite the fact that two of the existing windows from the old church, plus the pulpit, font and part of the altar were incorporated, in the interests of continuity.

The comfortable chairs led to some criticism by people who thought it was not quite right to be comfortable in church.

The whole project hinged on the sale of the existing church, presbytery and youth club in Vauxhall Street. That was accomplished, but did not cover the costs – an estimated £750,000, of which more than half had to be raised by donations.

At the same time, renovation work at St Thomas' Church was said to have cost in the region of £200,000, and a new church hall at St Bernadette's was estimated at costing £200,000. In total, the Catholic Church in the Island was facing a total bill of about £1 million.

That was by no means the end of the story, however. Within two years, major repairs were seen to be needed and questions were raised about design faults; it seemed that there was a problem with the concrete and other materials used.

It was in May 1999 that in the course of a visit to Jersey, Bishop Hollis announced from the pulpit at services at St Thomas' and St Mary and St Peter's that Canon Mahy would be leaving Jersey at the end of the year as part of a reorganisation, which would see the two Catholic communities in St Helier combined into one. Canon Mahy had spent 24 years in the Island.

The announcement followed another one the previous November that the priest at St Thomas', Fr Vincent Igoa, would be returning to France in the summer of 1999.

In a pastoral address sent to members of both congregations, the Bishop wrote: 'There are no priests available to take Fr Vincent's place, so the decision has had to be taken to merge the parishes of St Mary and St Peter with St Thomas' and place them in the pastoral care of one priest.' Canon Mahy's successor had still to be appointed.

The merger, of course, was not unexpected: the territorial amalgamation had happened in 1966 but the arrival of a new Catholic Dean in late 1999 was the final end of the independent 'Irish Mission', which had been founded because Irish Catholics going to Mass did not get on with the French Catholics.

One of the church's treasures, a set of stained glass windows depicting the Irish saints that had been designed by the eminent Irish stained-glass artist and book illustrator, Harry Clarke, were restored in 2008 with the help of a donation from the Allied Irish Bank and the property company, Dandara. The windows, which had been installed in the old St Mary and St Peter's Church in 1925 and transferred to the new church in 1985, are said to be impressive examples of the Island's Irish history.

In 2010, the 25th anniversary of the building of the new church was celebrated with a Mass, concert and flower festival. David Mahy returned to take part; it was also the 50th anniversary of his ordination. The restored stained glass window was also put up in the church to mark the jubilee and was illuminated at the Mass.

St Mary and St Peter's Church

Shortly before this book went to print, the 30th anniversary of the 'new' St Mary and St Peter's Church was celebrated on 27 September 2015.

A Mass was concelebrated by the former and present Catholic Deans, Canon David Mahy and Monsignor Nicholas France and prominent in the congregation were parishioners who had been at the opening 30 years before.

At the conclusion of the Mass to celebrate the 30th anniversary of the building of the new St Mary and St Peter's Church, former Chief Minister Terence ('Terry') Le Sueur was presented with a papal award, the Knighthood of the Order of St Gregory the Great. He is pictured with his wife, Angela, Mgr Nicholas France and Canon David Mahy

At the conclusion of the Mass, Fr Nicholas presented a papal award, the Knighthood of the Order of St Gregory the Great to Terence ('Terry') Le Sueur. This award was made in recognition of the outstanding dedication and Christian example of Terry as a member of the Catholic Church in Jersey. Everyone then enjoyed a happy celebratory lunch, hosted by the former and present Catholic Deans.

St Mary & St Peter's is nowadays a centre of activity every day of the week, with school activities, prayer groups, parish meetings, liturgies and Island events like the Parish Mission and the Called and Gifted conference held there recently.

As the Third Millennium is well under way at the time of writing, the churches of St Thomas and St Mary and St Peter's are united as churches in one pastoral area.

IV. THE PARISHES

CHAPTER 9

PARISH OF OUR LADY OF THE ANNUNCIATION AND THE MARTYRS OF JAPAN

The Catholic Mission, based in St Martin, to the East of the Island

THE Church of Our Lady of the Annunciation is the Island's oldest surviving Catholic church; it opened in February 1863.

However, the origin of the church and parish was in 1847, when a French priest from Bordeaux, Père E Hallum, settled in the Island staying at the house Carteret View, Faldouet, the property of Philip Falle. Although he had come to Jersey only for health reasons, he soon felt that he should do something for the many French and Irish people living in the East of the Island – estimated at the time as being around 350 French people and 250 Irish. These included Irish workmen employed on the Breakwater at St Catherine's Bay and French families working on the farms or as domestic servants. A trip to town to attend Mass meant a five to seven mile journey on foot for very many of them.

Père Hallum decided to help by building a small school and chapel which he called 'Notre Dame de St Martin', near the house at Faldouet. Although only in an unofficial capacity, he worked there for about eight years.

In 1851 a petition from 336 French Catholics in Jersey for an official Mission to be set up in St Martin was sent to Mgr Thomas Grant, the Bishop of Southwark. A similar letter, written by 200 Irish Catholics living in the St Catherine area, was also sent and Père Hallum wrote a report for the Bishop, which accompanied the petition.

Nothing happened, even when, a few years later, Père Hallum wrote a letter to the Bishop saying he was leaving the Island. However, a second petition, this time sent to the French Emperor, Napoleon III, proved more effective; in due course a French priest, Père Joseph Guimarand, arrived to take charge of the St Martin Mission of Our Lady. In September 1857 the chapel was officially blessed.

Within a few years, this chapel proved to be far too small for its purpose, and a new church was desperately needed. There was no money available to pay for it, so Père Guimarand started to raise funding by sending

High Mass at Our Lady's, St Martin in the 1950's

appeal letters far and wide - to all the French Bishops, for example - and collections were taken in most of the big Paris churches as well as in the Dioceses of Coutances. Even Queen Melia of Portugal was approached and sent £200. The Emperor Napoleon seems to have taken a special interest in this small Catholic community, and sent both a monstrance with the Imperial arms engraved on its foot, and also a set of Stations of the Cross.

In 1863 the church was opened and given the name of 'Our Lady of the Annunciation and the Martyrs of Japan.' The Bishop of Southwark presided and the Bishop of Coutances preached the sermon.

The 'Martyrs of Japan' were Japanese Catholics who had been converted by missionaries in the 16th Century and then martyred once Christianity was banned. The 26 martyrs were crucified at Nagasaki on 5 February 1597, beatified in 1627 and canonised by Pope Pius IX in 1862. The new church in St Martin was completed 12 months later and as the feast day of the Martyrs had been set for 3 February, the first feast coincided with the completion and blessing of the church, hence the dedication.

Père Guimarand worked there for 26 years until his death at the age of 89 in 1882. The Jesuit Fathers undertook the parish work until the arrival of the Oblates Fathers in September 1884.

Bishop Vertue of the newly-formed Portsmouth diocese approached the Provincial of the French Oblates with the view of obtaining a priest for St Martin's. Père Victor Bourde, the Superior from St Thomas', worked there for a short while before a new priest came from France. A succession of Oblate priests came and went; a Catholic school was established in St Martin and then another one in Grouville, which by 1909 had evolved into St Joseph's Church at the top of Grouville Hill. Meanwhile, a Mass Centre, dedicated to Our Lady of the Assumption was opened in Gorey Village in 1903 and replaced by a larger building in 1909.

After the Occupation, the church's wooden altar was replaced through the kindness of the Sister Superior of Sacré Coeur Orphanage. A stone altar was obtained from Angers in France that had been originally consecrated by the Oblates in 1923. It was brought to Jersey, reconstructed in St Martin and re-consecrated by Bishop King in March 1949.

The Church bell, which had been cast in Villedieu-les-Poêles in 1865, and had hung in the belfry since then, needed to be was melted down and re-made. This was undertaken by the old-established Croydon bell foundry of Gillet and Johnston. The new bell was blessed and re-hung on Palm Sunday 1949 by Père Pierre Jort, of St Thomas, and rung for the first time on the Holy Thursday. The bell's 'godparents' were Joseph Boléat and Rose Guégan.

Fifty years after the opening of the original chapel in Gorey, it was felt that this was now too small to accommodate the growing congregation and increased population of post-war Gorey. In 1953, Pere Méline, who had come as the parish priest in 1937 and stayed throughout the Occupation, brought a hall in Gorey Village called 'Badminton Hall', previously a nonconformist chapel and then a cinema, which he converted it for use as a church.

Père Méline had celebrated his 50th anniversary of his priesthood in September 1952 and decided to retire back to France. He left Jersey on 15 October 1953; the new church opened its doors for worship two months later on 20 December 1953.

Père Méline

The assistant priest at the parish was Jersey-born Père Albert Durand OMI who spent 14 years there from 1945 to 1959. His life story is summarised in Appendix D ('Home Grown') on page 269.

Another of Père Méline's initiatives had been to replace the plain glass windows of St Joseph's with stained glass, a project he completed with parishioners' generosity. St Joseph's also received a new High Altar from Maison Saint-Louis, given by the Jesuits upon their departure from Jersey. The gift was to commemorate the years of commitment they had given to the district, in particular the social club and the former school.

Père Méline was replaced by Père Constant Quinton. Nine months later, Bishop King solemnly blessed the new church at Gorey on 26 September 1954 with the title of Our Lady of the Assumption.

A week later, on 1 October, St Joseph received a new bell, Jeanne-Marie, donated by Denis Bérézat, a resident of the parish. The name of the bell was chosen in order to commemorate the centenary of the proclamation of the dogma of the Immaculate Conception and also in memory of the golden jubilee of Bishop King's ordination as priest. In the same year a new altar to Our Lady was placed in St Joseph's side chapel.

Père Quinton established a bilingual parish magazine, *Le Lien*, and made considerable developments to the social club at St Martin's, converting two rooms into a billiard hall and adding a rifle range. He retired as Rector in 1957 and he was succeeded by the last French Oblate priest, Père Henri Hélouët, who left in 1960. More English-speaking people were moving into the area and it was felt that the work of the Church should be handed over to Oblates of the Anglo-Irish Province.

A succession of Anglo-Irish Oblates now ensued. The third of these, Fr Donal Sorohan (1967-1973), rebuilt the old Presbytery and laid out the car park beside the church. The old organ from St Matthieu's was acquired, renovated and placed in the church in December 1969, and the following year the interior of the church was unpicked and modified in accordance with the requirements of the new liturgy.

Bishop Emery visited the Church on its 120th anniversary in 1988 and a new community centre behind the church was opened by Bishop Hollis in 1993. It was named the Berni Community Centre after its chief

St Joseph's Church

benefactor, Frank Berni and a plaque to this effect was unveiled at the opening ceremony by his daughter, Gloria Warner. About 160 members and friends of the parish's three Catholic churches were present, as well as the Catholic Dean, Canon Mahy, and the Constables of St Martin and Grouville.

In 1996 it was announced that St Joseph's would be closed as part of the church's rationalisation programme, due to the economic pressure on parishes everywhere. Many Catholics living in that part of the Island were upset by the news; for many of them it had been their own 'home' and much loved church. Furthermore, there had been reassurances expressed in the JEP no less than two years before from the Catholic Dean that 'while anything is possible, the Catholic Church in Jersey is not at present contemplating the St Joseph's site....I have already gone on record as saying that, even if we come to a situation where there are not enough priests to provide their present level of service to any of our congregations, there is no reason why a flourishing congregation should not continue to flourish... From where I sit, St Joseph's seems to be very much alive!'

However, the writing had been on the wall for St Joseph. In November 1994 the parish priest, Fr Eamon Fitzgerald, had told the JEP that it no longer made sense for members of the congregation to provide the funds for the maintenance, heating and lighting of the three church buildings in the parish when only two would be sufficient. At the same time, he said that the closure of any church was 'a painful thing, a kind of dying.'

The last Mass was held there on 24 April 1996. After demolition, the area was turned into a housing estate.

The closure also left a number of sports and social groups without a permanent home. In January 1997 it was thought that the church site could be developed into a sport and recreation centre through a partnership arrangement between the community, charities and the States. A steering group was set up, involving a number of States Members and representatives of the organisations that used the facility adjacent to the church building. They formulated plans to acquire the site, but the group was warned by the parish council chairman, Leslie Norman, that they would almost certainly have to pay the full market price.

The owners of the site – the Portsmouth Diocesan Trustees – had already applied to the Planning committee to develop the area for housing; obviously the value of the site was affected by that.

Solange Rebours, the president of St Joseph's Sports and Social Club, which had used the facilities there for many years, told the JEP at the time: 'We have few such facilities in the east of the Island and I believe the public would much prefer to see these retained and developed than see another housing development built on the site.'

The scheme had good political backing and a club representative met Bishop Hollis to argue the case for retaining the site for community use. They received a sympathetic hearing, and the group were invited to meet the Catholic Parish Council, the body which would have the final say.

But it all came to nothing: in the end the site was sold for housing development.

However, the money received for the sale of the site did help the parish, since the church needed repairs and the sale paid for a necessary complete restoration of the fabric of the church and sacristy and for the adjacent Berni Centre. The work began in July 2003 and cost £200,000.

In 1997, the parish priest, Fr Eamon Fitzgerald, died of a heart attack while swimming in the sea. He was succeeded by the last Oblate priest, Fr Ted McSherry, who served for a year. Then the first diocesan priest, Fr Brian Cousins, who was also the Catholic chaplain to the Prison and the Hospital, took over. But only 18 months later Fr Cousins died of cancer at the age of 62.

He was the last Parish priest of the St Martin parish, which afterwards was merged with St Patrick's and became for several years 'the Eastern parish'.

Fr Cousin's death in December 1999 caused a further shortage of priests following the departure, earlier in the year, of Père Vincent Igoa and Fr Philip Doyle, the priest of the non-territorial Portuguese parish of Our Lady of Fatima. Canon Mahy, who had just handed over to the incoming Dean, Canon France, had been about to leave the Island to become Parish Priest of Aldershot, stayed in the Island to help cover the Christmas services.

This was just after the amalgamation of the two town Catholic communities in one parish. The three churches in the east of the Island: Our Lady of the Annunciation at St Martin, Our Lady of the Assumption at Gorey and what had hitherto been the separate parish of St Patrick now all formed part of the 'Eastern Parish', under an incoming diocesan priest, Fr Robin Ellwood. However, he left after five years and in 2008 the Eastern Parish was itself subsumed in the all-Island Jersey Pastoral Area.

In June 2013, Bishop Egan celebrated Mass to mark the 150th anniversary of the opening of the Church of our Lady and the Martyrs of Japan; the celebrations were organised by Fr James McAuley and Mrs Sarah Pendergast. Two days previously, a regular worshipper at this church, Christopher Walters, was ordained to the permanent diaconate.

Bishop Egan with Mgr Nicholas France, Deacon Christopher Walters, Fr James McAuley after the mass to mark the 150th Anniversary of the opening of our Lady and the Martyrs of Japan.

Chapter 10

ST MATTHIEU

THE former parish of St Matthieu was geographically the largest Catholic parish in Jersey: 14 sq miles, or ⅓ of the Island. But that area was – and still is, largely - almost entirely rural.

In the 19th Century, as Catholicism drifted back to the town area, this was a vast area without either priest or church, and so it captured the attention of the energetic missionary Rector, Père Jean-François Volkeryck. He raised money and tried to get a site for a church at Carrefour Selous, but failed. Finally he obtained land at the present site of St Matthieu and started building.

The foundation stone was laid on 23 May 1871, and during the ceremony Père Volkeryck explained that the name 'Matthieu' had been chosen in memory of the Jersey martyr, Matthieu de Gruchy. One year later the church was finished and opened on 4 September 1872 in the presence of Bishop James Danell of Southwark and Archbishop Fêlix Fournier of Rennes. It was the first Catholic Mass in the west of the Island since the Reformation. At the same time a granite building to serve as a presbytery and a school was also built.

From this period until 1880, every Saturday evening, either the Parish priest or one of the curates could be seen making his way from St Thomas' to St Matthew's. He would sleep the night there, celebrate Mass in the morning, hear a few confessions, give the children their catechism session, administer any sacraments if necessary and then return to town.

The fact that there was no priest on the spot led to difficulties. Masses were only held infrequently and the buildings deteriorated; the parish was struggling. A chapel and a school were opened in St Ouen, dedicated to St Anne, but the difficulties in maintaining regular services and lessons there made things equally difficult.

When the Oblates arrived to take over St Thomas', they were also given charge of St Matthieu and Père Bourde from St Thomas took personal control of this western mission and of the school. *The Dames de St André* took over the school in 1884 and almost immediately purchased land opposite the church to build a convent and school.

Père Constant Le Vaçon took over the mission in 1886 and he bought a property in St Ouen as the site of a future mission church and school. He had also bought a plot of land at Hautes Croix in St John with a view to building another Chapel-of-ease and school.

In July 1911 *The Dames de St André* were replaced by another teaching order, the Faithful Companion of Jesus (FCJ). Eight years later, however, in December 1919, came the day when, by order of the States Public Instruction Committee, the schools at St Matthieu, Hautes Croix and St Ouen were closed (although it was re-opened again).

In 1922 the Hautes Croix property was sold and the following year a site was bought for a new church at Ville à l'Evêque, St John and St Anthony, which was opened in 1924 and the FCJ Sisters sold the convent at St Matthieu.

The sale was the culmination of an increasingly acrimonious relationship between the FCJ Sisters and the Oblates at St Matthieu. It began with small, even trivial issues, such as the alleged non-return of borrowed property, but escalated almost out of control until neither side, Oblates or Sisters, were speaking to one another. When the Sisters entered into a contract to sell the Convent building to the States for a Boys' Home, the Rector, Père Pitard, saw red. A Catholic convent building being sold to Protestants? Abominable! A letter was even drawn up and sent to the Pope – and this seems to have been effective, or at least the sale was stopped. The FCJ Sisters abandoned their convent – they left without saying goodbye to their neighbours, the Oblates and to take their place came the St Méen Sisters, a teaching order founded in Brittany.

In 1930 a field was donated by Dr Chichester and his wife at St Peter for a chapel. In the end, a small wooden chapel as built in 1946, named the Immaculate Conception. This was later transferred to the Sacred Heart parish. It had to be closed when extensions to the Airport necessitated clearing the site.

The old school-chapel of St Anne was rebuilt in 1938 and inaugurated on Good Friday 1939.

During the Occupation, the Germans took over the Presbytery and the priests had to find accommodation elsewhere.

The post-Liberation years saw changes at St Matthieu: the Rector, Père Messager, retired (he died in 1949). He is remembered as a 'big, cuddly teddy bear of a man, but who stood no nonsense from children in his catechism classes!' In his retirement as Rector of St Matthieu, he took pleasure in being on the megaphone during the Corpus Christi processions: he had a big, booming voice.

Père Le Bas took over St Matthieu in 1945. In his time, the St Méen Sisters decided that their aims would be better served by moving to town, which happened in 1950. This time the move happened without any of the drama that had occurred in 1924 when the FCJ Sisters had attempted to sell the Convent to 'Protestants'. The Occupation had brought many changes, many of them bad, but at least there was one beneficial effect: a greater mutual tolerance between the denominations.

The Convent building was sold to the furniture merchants, Fred Langlois and his family, who used the building as a depository. Mr Langlois, incidentally, was a Catholic who had loaned his boat to take back to France the body of François Scornet (the executed would-be escapee). The body was accompanied by Père Yves Jaine, the Oblate priest from St Matthieu who generally ministered at St Anne's. He was also the cousin of Père Alain Mao, who had been Rector of St Thomas' from 1920 to 1933.

Very much later, the St Matthieu convent building then became the property of David Hick, who used it for storage. It was sold again in 2015 to be turned into flats.

It was very much the end of an era: two years later, in 1952, when Père Le Bas retired, the parish was taken over by the Anglo-Irish Province of the Oblates and he was succeeded by Fr Teddy Maher.

Fr William Hughes, Parish Priest of St Matthieu, 1953 - 1967

Although St Matthieu's worshipping community remained vibrant, various pressures forced the closure of St Anne's Church in 1985. Included in these were greater mobility on the part of the local people, deterioration in the state of the building, and a reduction in the number of priests available. The land was sold for housing development and the church demolished.

In February 1981 the Oblates withdrew from St Matthew's Parish and Diocesan clergy assumed responsibility until May 1989, when The Holy Ghost Fathers (The Spiritans) took over from the Oblates.

The parish priest was Father Tom Friery, a former Missionary priest in Africa and English Provincial for the Holy Ghost Fathers. (See pages 227 - 228).

A successful fund-raiser, he raised funds for improvements to the church, and for Uncle Tom's Cabin, a charity shop in former stables behind the presbytery. He found £60,000 to replace the leaky and unstable bell tower and funds to establish a coffee room to benefit CAFOD. He retired in the spring of 2003, after a long period of ill health and moved back to the Liverpool area, where he died shortly afterwards.

He was succeeded by Fr Peter Glas, the first diocesan priest for the parish. He was Polish and had come to Jersey in late 2002 as assistant priest to Nicholas France. He had grown up in southern Poland and after ordination was one of the country's first military chaplains after Poland threw off Communism. He was later sent to the UK to help the large Polish communities who had settled there, working in Manchester and Southampton for ten years before being sent to Jersey by Bishop Hollis.

St John and St Anthony at Ville-à-l'Evêque

In June 2003 Bishop Hollis announced the closure of both the Ville à l'Evêque chapel and the Millbrook Mass centre of Our Lady Queen of the Universe. In a pastoral letter, he wrote: 'These measures are being implemented to establish the kind of pastoral structures that are needed for the missionary situation of our Church in the 21st Century, which are so different from the needs of the 19th or even the 20th century.'

The Ville-à-l'Evêque chapel was put up for sale in 2005 following the granting of Planning permission for a five-bedroomed house with garage. The building became a private property. Its stained glass windows were removed, although initially the Planning Department were against the idea and wanted the windows to remain in place. However, Nicholas France wrote to Planning asking them to reconsider their decision, saying it was a bit like 'sacrilege' if the windows, some depicting French saints, were to remain in the building when it was converted into a house.

'Some people would be unlikely to want the saints looking down on them in their living room,' he said.

The decision by the Department to insist that the windows be retained in the building was overruled by the committee president, Senator Philip Ozouf. The windows had already been removed and were being kept at St Thomas's Church for future re-use, but the decision meant that they did not have to be re-fitted. However, the committee insisted that other features, such as the crosses on the roof, were retained.

St Matthew Parish was soon afterwards absorbed into the Sacred Heart parish and which later became part of the Catholic Parish of the West. Fr Petr Glas served as the priest of the new parish, serving Sacred Heart, St Bernadette and St Matthew churches.

The Western Catholic Parish was itself amalgamated into the all-Island Parish of Jersey in 2008. At the time of writing, the western churches are served by Fr Kevin Hoiles.

Chapter 11

THE SACRED HEART PARISH

THE Sacred Heart church in St Aubin has one of the most picturesque sites of any church, overlooking the sweep of St Aubin's Bay. In recent years, with the accent on less formality, there have been weddings that began in the church, followed by a beach party on the sands opposite.

There had been a chapel-school in St Aubin since 1900, served by French Oblates from St Thomas. Before then on Sunday mornings a special train had been laid on to take St Aubin and Beaumont residents to town for Mass at St Thomas'. Because of the perceived need for a more local place of worship, a property called Jubilee Hall on Mont Les Vaux was found and acquired by the Oblates and converted into a chapel and school. It was dedicated to the Sacré Coeur and opened in February 1900 by Père Louis Legrand; it was the first Catholic ceremony in the south-west of the Island for some 300 years. In September a small school was opened in the building, run by Les *Dames de St André*.

Until 1919 the chapel was attached to St Thomas' parish; Père Mao became Rector of St Matthew in that year and asked for St Aubin to be re-annexed to the St Matthew parish. He had a great fondness for St Aubin, and a new, beautiful church in St Aubin became a life-long dream and ambition.

Since 1911 he had longed to enlarge the Catholic church facilities in the area. In 1912 he was already in contact with Julien Barbier (1869-1940), a noted Paris architect specialising in religious architecture who had designed at least nine churches in France in an attractive neo-gothic style. Barbier's plans for the new church were already drawn up by 1912.

Sacred Heart Church, St Aubin

Bishop Cotter laying the foundation stone of Sacred Heart, 1 November 1937

Why did nothing then happen? In an obituary of Père Mao written following his death in 1937 by a French Oblate colleague, Père Lemius from Paris, he simply wanted the church to be a masterpiece: *'He could easily have built it if he had wanted a chapel or an ordinary church. But he wanted it to be beautiful, worthy of the Sacred Heart, worthy of the Island of Jersey.'*

Père Mao's unattainable dream was to create in Jersey a smaller copy of the famous Parisian church, the Sacré Coeur in Montmartre. He had a special devotion to the Sacred Heart and he went on collecting funds for 'his' church throughout his life. In retirement in the early 1930s he went every day from town to St Aubin. He died in February 1937, months before Bishop Cotter laid the foundation stone of Sacred Heart the following November; its first Rector was Père Louis Choinel. By the 1930s, the long drawn-up plans of Julien Barbier and Père Mao were finally realised and building started in 1937; it was not the Montmartre Sacré Coeur, but it was a building of great architectural merit. Père Choinel played a major part in the construction. It should have been completed in 1939, but war broke out – the Occupation began the following year and so the opening of the church was delayed until after Liberation; it was finally opened in 1947. However, Père Choinel often held services in the uncompleted church during the Occupation.

The old chapel at Mont Les Vaux was still used until the new church was ready enough to use for holding Mass; it was also now used as Catholic social club; the school there remained in use after the Occupation and was run for a number of years by the 'Beaulieu sisters' (The Sisters of St Méen Le Grand).

Following the morale-boosting British naval victory of the sinking of the German battleship Graf von Spee in December 1939, the design of an anchor was integrated in the stonework of the still unfinished church building by Breton-born local stonemason Joseph Le Guyader, working shortly after the Occupation had begun. It was seen both as an act of defiance and of religious resistance.

Père Choinel was the first French Oblate parish priest, but he was also the last: it was obvious that in post-war St Aubin there were many more English-speakers than French-speakers, so in 1946 the church was handed to the Anglo-Irish Oblates; Fr Francis O'Connor was the first Anglo-Irish Oblate Rector. A new parish was also created for the St Aubin area for the church to serve.

The church finally opened and was blessed by Bishop King on 8 June 1947. The Lieut-Governor and Bailiff were both in the congregation with their wives. On the same afternoon the Bishop led the Corpus Christi procession, in which around 2,500 to 3,000 Catholics took part.

In the procession were a couple of hundred Polish soldiers who had been sent to the Island to help with the defence against the Colorado beetle depredations on the Jersey Royal crop. They were accorded a place of honour immediately behind the canopy protecting the Host.

Two days later, the Jersey Morning News commented on the church: *'It is a credit to all concerned and a showpiece of architecture, of which the R.C community and the Island as a whole can feel proud.'*

There is a story that cannot be confirmed that the American film star, Bing Crosby, was approached for a donation for the new church. He declined, but sent his cigarette case to be auctioned, and the proceeds paid for the Tabernacle.

The clock face on the exterior of the church was finally installed in 1990 – 40 years later than planned.

Two other chapels of ease formed part of the new Sacred Heart parish. The first of these was a small chapel dedicated to the Immaculate Conception and built in a field near the Airport. The eight-vergée field, Le Clos du Chemin Vert, was given to the Oblates for a Mass Centre. Popularly known as 'the Airport Chapel', it was demolished in November 1968 as part of a runway extension scheme. A number of religious artefacts from the Chapel were re-housed at St Theresa of the Child Jesus - a new place of worship that had been opened in 1950 at La Moye to serve parishioners at the far end of the parish.

Yet another church was built at Millbrook in 1956: Our Lady, Queen of the Universe. It was built, on what had been a vacant, condemned piece of bog land that had always been shunned by builders because of its tendency to flooding. This danger never materialised for the new church, due undoubtedly to improved drainage and a new reservoir at the head of Waterworks Valley - and, as the JCR magazine suggested, to the blessing of Our Lady.

Our Lady,
Queen of the Universe

The church replaced a Mass Centre at the First Tower Institute that had been served from St Mary and St Peter's. One of the rooms at the Institute (a social club) was used. The chairs hung from hooks nailed into the wall, from which they were taken down for Mass and put back again afterwards. A trestle table was kept there, which had a hole cut in the middle, into which an altar stone was inserted before Mass and removed from it afterwards to be taken back to St Mary and St Peter's by the priest.

The priest who usually served there was Père Christian Burdo SJ, who had originally come to Jersey to study at the Bon Secours Novitiate and returned to the Island in 1924 to keep the Observatory at Maison Saint Louis, which he did for eight years until he retired as Director. A year later, it was taken over by Père Charles Rey. He was also a keen archaeologist and excavated at La Cotte in St Brelade.

To quote from the *Jersey Catholic Record* (December 1959): 'Père Burdo went out (after an early Mass at the Convent) to say Mass and preach [at the Mass Centre].Until he got his auto-cycle, he would often cancel the taxi for the return journey and walk back (*before* breakfast), carrying the bag with the vestments and chalice. With the advent of the auto-cycle, he declined a taxi altogether, and it was a familiar sound outside the Presbytery [of St Mary and St Peter's] on a Sunday morning, to hear the engine chug-chugging away, while Fr Burdo came in for the vestments, chalice and notice-book.' He returned to France in November 1959.

Our Lady Queen of the Universe quickly became part of the Sacred Heart Parish. This was served from 1951 to 1961 by Fr Lawrence Hargreaves, who was the first editor of the new Island Catholic magazine, the *Jersey Catholic Record*. One former parishioner described him as 'a gentleman priest' who had his own boat moored in St Aubin's Harbour and was a keen amateur sailor.

Cardinal Heenan lays the foundation stone of St. Bernadette's, Jersey with Fr. James O'Regan O.M.I, Canon Olney and the architect with his wife.

This post-war period was the high water mark of Catholic building in Jersey. After the closure of the Airport Chapel, St Theresa's was closed down in 1972. But there was one more substantial church still to be built: St Bernadette's Church at Les Quennevais was opened and blessed by Bishop Worlock in September 1972. It was built to cater for the needs of the growing estate development in that area: this was now the centre of population in St Brelade. It was constructed in a modern style with plenty of car parking spaces. The relics in the altar stone were of St Sixtus (a 2nd Century martyr) and St John Southworth, a Lancashire priest martyred during the Reformation.

In later years a new hall was built which enabled St Bernadette's to become a focus for pastoral and social activity.

Father James Carling CSSp was the first Holy Ghost Father to serve as Rector of the Sacred Heart parish after the departure of the Anglo-Irish Oblates (see page 228).

It had been suggested in the 1994 Pastoral Review that the Sacred Heart Church at St Aubin might be among those that should be closed in a rationalisation of Jersey's Catholic parishes. This view caused quite considerable alarm – even outrage – among parishioners, and the threatened closure never happened. However, by the mid-1990s it was showing signs of disrepair, and Fr Carling told a parish annual general meeting in February 1997 that the cost of repairing the Sacred Heart building could run to several thousand pounds. The whole structure needed repairing – roof, walls, basement, central heating and woodwork.

Heritage groups regarded the building as architecturally significant, but the repairs to Sacred Heart might have meant the loss of Our Lady of the Universe at Millbrook – and thus the loss of another church for the Catholic community, which had only recently heard with sadness the loss of St Joseph's.

It was the same old story: in his words – 'It is unfortunate that we are faced with declining congregations and a static income' and that was the reason why one church of the three might have to close.

The parish needed £96,800 just to break even during the forthcoming year, of which £46,000 would not be covered by church collections or other regular income. The expected deficit per week would be £900, and Fr Carling suggested that parishioners might care to consider doubling their weekly church collection money to £4 per person, a suggestion received with - politeness.

Fr Carling said that no-one wanted to close either church, but with declining congregations and insufficient income, the total amount to be spent on the three churches of the parish could be in excess of £300,000 within 18 months.

Another meeting in April – an Emergency General Meeting – agreed a plan for repairs, while at the same time trimming parish expenses and raising the weekly collection figure if possible. A sub-committee was formed, chaired by a parishioner and former Save Jersey's Heritage chairman Deputy Alastair Layzell. Its purpose was to examine ways and means of maintaining all three churches within the parish.

An anonymous benefactor offered to match donations to a building fund on a pound-for-pound basis up to £30,000 to help prevent any of the three churches within the parish from having to close. Deputy Layzell urged the parish to adopt the plan, offering every hope of raising £60,000 for repairs. If the plan failed after six months, serious consideration would be given to leasing out one of the church buildings, probably Our Lady of the Universe, to help maintain the other two churches.

The report was adopted by a substantial majority, although six speakers spoke against the plan, taking the view that it would merely postpone the inevitable closure of the church.

Our Lady Queen of the Universe was also in a bad way: there was damp penetration and a major long-term problem that the roof was covered in asbestos sheeting, which would be difficult to replace. It was agreed to put into action a plan to raise money for necessary repairs and this did stave off the evil day for a few years, but in 2003 both it and the St John and St Anthony chapels were closed as Mass centres and the sites sold for property development. The sale of Our Lady Queen of the Universe church raised £878,000. It was sold in 2007 after Planning consent to build six three-bedroomed houses.

The large Crucifix on the front of the church, originally donated by Fred Langlois, was relocated to the front of the new St Mary and St Peter Church.

The Holy Ghost Fathers left the Parish in 2003; since then it has been served by Diocesan priest and in 2006 it became part of the Island Pastoral Area.

The ordination of a parishioner, Brendan Flaxman to the diaconate provided additional leadership to this community. He was ordained on the 22 June 2012 by Bishop Crispian Hollis, shortly before the Bishop retired as Bishop of Portsmouth.

Chapter 12

ST PATRICK'S CHURCH AND PARISH

This section on St Patrick's is partly from an article by Mr W Troy that appeared in Fr Francis Isherwood's 'Jersey Church History' supplement to the Jersey Catholic Record magazine in 1974

'THE sight of a father cycling into Mass along a windswept country road, one little child on the cross-bat on front of him and mother in the carrier behind, set up a train of thought in an onlooker which eventually led to the church of St Patrick.

'The time was mid-way through the German Occupation. The scene was the Samarès Inner Road, and the principal actors were two Catholics well known at St Mary and St Peter's – Messrs Bob Troy and Fred Knight. The former was the father on the cycle, and it was Freddie, who on seeing him, thought it was time that the Mass was brought out to Samarès. When he made this idea known to Bob Troy, the latter acted quickly and told the priests in town about his idea. They agreed and a former army hut, which before the Occupation had been turned into a couple of tiny cottages, was rented, and, with the permission of the owner, was very quickly gutted.'

[The site of this hut was opposite the present church]

'By the time the late Mr O H Griffin had interested himself in the project, and Messrs Richard Troy and Fred Hidrio gave valuable assistance in the work of transforming the old hut into a temporary church.

Friends from the town also helped, and it was an enthusiastic band that carried the hundred and one tasks necessary before the little building could be turned into a fitting House of God.

His Lordship The Rt. Rev. Mgr. J. H. King laying the foundation stone of St Patrick's Church, Samares. (Photo Evening Post).

'The work was eventually accomplished and all the necessary fittings and furnishings provided. The Beeches loaned an altar, a generous donor supplied a small organ, Bert Young helped with the furnishings , and, whenever any little difficulties presented themselves, Mr Griffin would be there with a word of encouragement, a cheery smile, and, so very often, another pound or a few shillings more from a pocket not over full.

'He was undoubtedly a wonderful example.

'So we justified the confidence our parish priest, Father Arscott, had shown in us, and we delighted the curates who helped us in every way they could.

'The chapel was opened on the Sunday within the octave of St Patrick,1943, a fitting date for the church in the foundation of which so many of Irish descent had played a prominent part, and for which the name of Ireland's patron saint had already been chosen.

'It soon became evident that St Patrick's fulfilled a long felt need in the district, for the congregation grew steadily. With the liberation of the Island came thoughts of a larger and more permanent church, and this was followed by the formation of a building fund committee.

Steady progress was made, plans were invited and discussed, and it was not long before the advent of one who showed himself to be a great friend that the whole project really began to move forward. Mr George Boudin, although not a Catholic, was the husband of one of the helpers. George came along with his wife and in a short time all the team were fired with his enthusiasm, and from that day on there was something in the nature of a triumphant success. £1,000 was raised in the first year, largely the result of a wonderful bazaar.

'Inspired by the first year's success, plans were prepared for a permanent church, and, with the permission of the clergy, they were laid before His Lordship the Bishop of Portsmouth.

'Warm approval was given for the work to go ahead, and on 27 September 1948, the foundation stone of the new church was laid by the Bishop who had flown specially over to the Island to perform the ceremony. 'The church was opened on 20 March 1949. It became a chapel of ease to St Mary and St Peter's, only becoming a parish in its own right in November 1968. (Fr Anthony Moore was the first Parish Priest).

The new church had a fine granite altar and matching altar rails enhanced with sculptured Celtic crosses, the font (also in granite) is of very pleasing design. The stained glass window (erected 1953) over the main door is the work of the Harry Clarke Studios (Dublin), being of compatible design with the splendid 'Irish Window' in St Mary and St Peter's.'

A hall and presbytery were added later to the new parish church and later, in 1982, 12 new stained glass windows. These depicted the seven Sacraments of the Church, Faith, Hope and Charity, motherhood and St Patrick himself. They were designed and made by two Benedictine monks from Buckfast Abbey in Devon, Fr Charles Norris OSB and Fr Paulinus Angol OSB and commissioned and later brought in his van from England by Fr (later Canon) Peter Turbitt during his time as Parish Priest.

Father Colin Ward was the longest serving of the parish priests of St Patrick's, serving on three separate occasions for a total of 16 years. He retired early at the age of 60 because of illness.

He was a student at university when the nominal Catholicism of his childhood deepened into active faith – until one day it dawned on him that he wanted to be a priest.

In his own words, he has been, at times, a turbulent priest. 'I get up people's noses something chronic' he observed to the JEP on his retirement from active ministry in October 2000. For the first two years he served as assistant priest to Canon Mahy, before moving from St Mary and St Peter's to become the parish priest of St Patrick's.

After his retirement, St Patrick's became part of the new Eastern Parish before that was in turn subsumed into the Island Catholic parish.

The church was closed for five months from August to December 2009 for a £150,000 renovation project, transforming the rather dark church into a bright, newly carpeted, freshly decorated and structurally sound building. £100,000 was given by the diocese and the remaining £50,000 found by the church through fund-raising events.

Chapter 13

THE OASIS OF PEACE

Cardinal Murphy O'Connor dedicating the Oasis of Peace in October 2007.

THE Oasis of Peace was established in 2007 in the former Presbytery at St Matthieu's with the aim of being a visible sign of the unity of the Catholic Church in Jersey as one parish and the implementation in Jersey of the Diocesan Pastoral Plan.

Its purpose was to be an Oratory – a place of prayer and reflection. The interior of the Presbytery was altered to create a small prayer room on the ground floor. It was envisaged that once occupied, morning and evening prayer would take place there, open to all. It would be a centre not only for the Catholic community but a place where the Catholic Church could put into practice its mission to all and it would be available for all who wished to have some time to spend time with God or to find some peace in their life.

It would also be a place of study, available to be used by school groups, private groups and organisations – to lead members of the Island community to develop their faith and also be another centre that could assist in the formation work of Catholic Pastoral Services.

Deacon David Cahill, after his early retirement as head teacher at Grainville School, became the director of the Oasis. He said that the Oasis was aimed at being a resource for all Island Catholics to utilise: 'Many of our community have talents that they can share with others but not the resource from which to share those gifts. The Oasis can be that resource.

'It will be a place where people can give of their time, talent and treasure to help others and the Church. In short it should help people to put the call to stewardship into practice. As the Church teaches: "If the Christian life is to mature all aspects of it must be cultivated: prayer, liturgical life, moral formation, belonging to community and missionary spirit." The aim and hope of the Oasis is to help our Island Parish community to reach this maturity.'

In 2007 Cardinal Cormac Murphy O'Connor dedicated the Oasis of Peace during his visit to the Island to bless the recently restored St Thomas' Church. The following year, in 2008, the vision for the Oasis was presented at the Island assembly for the Catholic Church. One of the elements seen as being essential for putting this vision into place was to attract a Religious community to oversee the work of the Oasis. There was a danger that the vision was stalling as the great efforts made to attract a community did not seem to be bearing fruit. The decision was made that it was more important to have 'an Oasis for the community rather than a community for the Oasis.'

It was opened on 26 September 2009. The principal concelebrant at Mass at St Matthieu was the Vicar General, Monsignor John Nelson. After the mass the Oasis Centre was open for the afternoon to allow people to visit.

The first event at the Oasis took place the same evening, when the Prayer Room at the Oasis was open through the night from 11pm until 7am and a prayer vigil took place.

A management committee was formed to administer the Oasis, chaired by Maureen Corrigan and comprising David Hick, Andrew Wintour and Robert Killen. At the time of writing Maureen Corrigan remains as chairman, and the committee is made up David and Mary Cahill, Andrew Wintour, Nick Touzel and Paula Foster.

Deacon Cahill and his wife, Mary, live in a flat on the top floor of the old Presbytery building. There had been no interior maintenance of this part of the building since the Occupation, when the building had been used as a German army billet – and it looked very much as if that was the case! The whole house was refurbished during 2012, with the cost being covered by the diocesan 'Living Our Faith' appeal – the Oasis was Jersey's parish project.

As a result of a donation from a St Matthieu parishioner, Martha Moser, in memory of her husband, Charles, the garden was landscaped to become a 'prayer garden'.

Deacon Cahill is also the Chaplain at the Prison and in that capacity has become aware of the extreme difficulties suffered by prisoners' families who have to travel to the Island to visit their incarcerated relatives. The price of hotel accommodation is often far beyond their means, so there is guest accommodation at the Oasis for their use – and an understanding, non-judgmental reception during the time they spend in Jersey.

The heart of the Oasis is a chapel in which there is a model of a well, relating to the Gospel story of Jesus asking the Samaritan woman to draw water for him:

Jesus said: Whoever drinks of the water I give will never thirst' (Jn 4:14).

Deacon Cahill said: 'In this conversation with the Samaritan woman as she came to draw water at Jacob's well, Jesus shows us that He comes to meet us wherever we are on our spiritual journey. The hope is that having spent time at the Oasis of Peace in the presence of Jesus, lives will be transformed like the woman of Samaria who met Jesus at Jacob's well, so that all who come to the well at the Oasis will be similarly moved to have Jesus and his Gospel message at the centre of their lives.'

V. THE LAITY

Chapter 14

THE CONTRIBUTION OF THE LAITY

INSPIRATIONAL leadership from lay Catholics in Jersey was perhaps stronger in the past than it is even today.

In the field of education, States' government, social care, charitable action and Catholic organisation, active Catholics were prominent and so Jersey was well prepared for the Decree on the Role of the Laity, as promulgated by Pope Paul VI and the Bishops at the Second Vatican Council.

After the Second World War, perhaps empowered by the greater sense of common purpose achieved during the German Occupation, many Catholics in Jersey were ready to show their initiative not only in building up their own Island and local Catholic communities but in working where possible with like-minded spirits for the common good.

Early after the war the clergy fostered not only the spiritual and devotional life of parishioners but encouraged them to participate in Catholic Action through lay confraternities, societies and organisations. The Eucharistic Crusade promoted, for example, frequent reception of Holy Communion (not possible except at early morning masses due to the fasting from midnight law).

Children of Mary, 1948

The moral protection of children was ensured through local branches of The Children of Mary (with the Children of St Louis as a section for younger girls, at least at St Thomas'). There was also the Third Order of St Francis, the League of the Sacred Heart, and the Apostolate of Prayer. The work of the wider apostolate was promoted through the Confraternity of the Propagation of the Faith (APF) in support of the missions, the Conference of the Society of St Vincent de Paul and the Ladies of Charity, the Knights of St Columba, the Catholic Women's League, and the Legion of Mary. Later, in 1954, the Catholic association, The Catenians, was established. In more recent times, supported by the Knights of St Columba, the Apostleship of the Sea has been established in the Island. As recorded elsewhere, Caritas Jersey has also been established and is now the foremost social justice body of the Catholic Church in the Island.

Knights of St Columba, 1948

More social, but with the raison d'être of providing healthy entertainment in a Catholic milieu, was the Cercle Catholique de St Thomas and each of the churches probably had dances and other gatherings during which it was hoped that young men and women would find Catholic partners for marriage. This was a time when 'mixed marriages' were much frowned on due to the test of faith they would demand. In those years Catholic church communities were self-contained and provided not only a social milieu for local people but a harbour for those entering the Island seeking not only a church in which to worship, a priest to offer pastoral and sacramental care but parishioners to offer a welcome hospitality, social activities and friendship.

Each church community hosted its own Social Club activities, in an era before the television had become the centre of the living room. In so many people's lives, there was a social and sports opportunity at 'The Club'. There was a League and inter-club competitions were held throughout the year, with trophies for table tennis, darts and snooker. These clubs provided social and sporting opportunities for young people who vied with their seniors for team places and were supervised by parents with regular participation - and even had some sporting tuition from the Priests.

For immigrants entering Jersey after the Second World War, St Mary and St Peter's, the 'Irish Church', soon became the spiritual home of the Italians who came here seeking work particularly in the hospitality industry. Later for the Portuguese, coming in increasing numbers from Madeira, St Thomas' Church became their focus of activity and the place where their statue of Our Lady of Fatima, their country's patroness, found a home.

In the years since the Second Vatican Council there has been more emphasis in developing consultative church councils and finance committees, prayer groups and scripture groups than in promoting traditional organisations. In particular, consultative church councils have evolved slowly and continue to develop in response to need. This is firstly because of the structure of the Island as one parish, following the days when it consisted of many parishes. Secondly, it has come about in response to the call of Bishop Egan to develop Evangelisation Strategy Groups to concentrate on ways in which Catholics can better share their faith, not only with those outside the Church, but with many within who have no proper understanding of a Catholic ethos.

—ooo000ooo—

It is invidious in a book of recent history of the Church in this Island, to select lay individuals for special mention and to ignore others who might thus feel their own contribution or that of family members has been undervalued. Yet, some, particularly those who received diocesan or papal awards, can be seen as good examples among many Catholics who were outstanding in their particular field or in things that they inaugurated.

With regard to those who served their fellow citizens:

* in public office in the States of Jersey, Senators Clarrie Dupré and Dick Shenton stand out. Senator Terry Le Sueur was first elected as a Deputy in 1987 and following various re-elections he was elected Senator in 2005. He was appointed Chief Minister in 2008 and completed his distinguished service in 2011. In 2015 he was made a Knight of the Order of St Gregory the Great for his services to the Catholic Church in Jersey.

* in Catholic education, John Sankey;

* in service to the community, women's issues and the foundation of the Catholic Women's League, Floria Hebden;

* as promoter of The Guild of St Stephen and an altar server for nearly 80 years, Tony Pezet;

139

* in concern for the aged and in fundraising for many projects and causes within and without the Catholic community, Daphne Minihane;

* for leadership of the Deanery Pastoral Council and as a member of many pastoral and finance committees, Jack Dupré and Ron Satchell.

In the mid-1960s, Bishop Derek Worlock, echoing what priests in the Island had probably been saying since the war, spoke strongly of the need for Catholics to be involved in public life, especially through standing for office in the States of Jersey. The purpose was not only to represent the needs of the Catholic community but to be seen as Catholics committed to the common good of all the people of the Island.

In recent years many practising Catholics in the States have retired and have not been replaced.

Mgr France commented: 'There is current need for Catholics to commit themselves to this form of public service, including members of our more recent immigrant communities, especially the Portuguese who make up 10% of our Island, but have failed to put forward anyone for election to the States.'

Deacon Iain MacFirbhisigh, looking back on his time as an active young Catholic shortly after his arrival in Jersey from Ireland as a young man, said: 'The social side of being a members of the Catholic Community was also part of our way of life - the Social Clubs attached to all the Churches and overseen by the Priests assisted by lay Adults, provided a stable and good example. Through this we were eventually recruited into more "active" Catholic life, in my case the Society of St Vincent de Paul, which remains a hugely important part of my life to this day.'

Bishop Crispian Holliis blessing a group of lay people involved in various ministries' in St Thomas' Church in 2002. In the foreground can be seen the late Deacon Louis Omer.

Chapter 15

CATHOLIC ACTION

The road from the Jersey Catholic Association in 1951 to today's Catholic Pastoral Services and 'Caritas'.

THE post-war history of lay 'Catholic Action' starts with the foundation of the Jersey Catholic Association in 1951. There was still some suspicion and prejudice against Catholics and Catholicism in the Island, especially in rural parishes. At the turn of the century, a small boy of Methodist parents living in St Peter was told to cross the road whenever he saw a Catholic Priest walking towards him for fear of being bewitched. Anti-Catholicism was combined up with a feeling of 'too many French workers' and anti-French sentiment. There was still a residue of this prejudice half a century later.

The solidity of denominational barriers in post-war decades was such that a Catholic child, who had been taught by the Methodist music teacher, Amy Lobb, was asked by her to sing in the choir at her wedding in a Methodist Church– but she was not allowed to do so, being a Catholic. At a celebration of boy scouting, young Catholic boys could not join in at a service for the Scouts held at an Anglican church, but had to have their own service at a Catholic church.

In the political world, there was still some opposition to the Catholic, Dick Shenton, when he was the first Catholic to stand for Senator in 1969. The election campaigns of the Catholic, George Troy, as Constable of St Helier, and of Stan Morel as Constable of St Ouen both ran into difficulties because of the 'anti-Catholic' vote, despite both candidates being personally well-liked.

This 'anti-Catholic' element in Jersey politics has disappeared completely, largely due to the ecumenical policy of all Churches in the Island.

The same girl who could not sing at Amy Lobb's wedding was invited by her, when she was at a pupil at the FCJ Convent, to join the 'Holmchase Choir' – a choir that included both Amy Lobb's Methodist Sunday School choir members and Catholics from the FCJ School choir. When the choir sang at her own wedding in 1968 at St Mary and St Peter's, the organ was played by Amy's brother, John.

In the 1980s, the leaders of the three major denominations: the Catholic Dean, David Mahy, the Anglican Dean, Basil O'Farrell, and the Methodist Superintendent, Donald Lee, worked collaboratively on many issues and were often jokingly referred to as 'the Three Wise Men'.

Reverting back to the 1950s and the start of the Jersey Catholic Association, there was an element of self-defence in its formation of the JCA, but it was most largely influenced by educational concerns and in providing a free schooling with a Catholic ethos for Catholic children. Indeed, this subject was seen as a priority.

Quoting from the first issue of the *Jersey Catholic Record* in June 1956: '*In 1951, a few people, enthusiastic for work in Catholic Action, and perhaps inspired to some extent by the work in England of the Catholic Parents and Electors Association, decided that the time was ripe for the inauguration of some similar organisation in this Island.*

'*With the co-operation of the clergy and with help from the Dioceses of Portsmouth's branch of the C.P.E.A (Catholic Parents Education Association), who sent two speakers to explain the work done by their organisation, a meeting was held in the Town Hall under the chairmanship of Mr Gerard Reeve* [later Fr Gerard Reeve]. *The Town Hall was crowded by representatives from all the Parishes and very lively discussion ensued.*

'*Two facts came out very clearly as a result of this meeting; the first was that there was a very substantial body of feeling in favour of the formation of some body which would help to co-ordinate Catholic Action in the Island. The second fact was that it was very clear that the Catholics of Jersey did not wish to become involved in the formation of anything that might savour of a definite Catholic political party.*'

That, the magazine pointed out, had never been the intention of the sponsors. To avoid any appearance of that, it was decided to call the organisation the Jersey Catholic Association.

'*It was decided that the organisation should be divided into Parish Units with a Central Committee made up of delegates from each Unit to co-ordinate the work and to sponsor Island efforts.*'

The objects of the JCA were given as:

(1) To promote and encourage Catholic Educational interests;

(2) To acquaint parents with their rights, duties and power;

(3) To promote and encourage Catholic representation on public and educational bodies;

(4) To give attention to the needs of Catholic Youth;

(5) To further the application of Christian principles to all essential questions of the day, especially as they affect the family;

(6) To deepen the spiritual life of the members through the practice of Family Prayers and other methods.

Continuing in a theme that could have been written at any time up until the present moment, the article continues: *'A few minutes thought will show that the ultimate aim is thus to help to build up, with God's help, an informed, active and educated Catholic community within this Island, which, unfortunately, in common with so many much larger countries is fast losing hold of Christianity as a factor in the life of the people. …*

'Today, we all stand in danger of being chilled by this cold indifference to religion which confronts us on all sides and if the Jersey Catholic Association can do something to combat this state of affairs it will have more than justified its formation.'

The remainder of the article was given up to the committee's study of the deficiencies of Catholic education in the Island.

The days of the Jersey Catholic Association came and went. Subsequent issues of the *Jersey Catholic Record* detail the slow defeat against apathy and lack of interest: annual general meetings at which it was difficult to raise a quorum, fund raising initiatives that ran into the sand, requests for some degree of States-funded education that went unheeded.

—ooo000ooo—

THE story picks up again after the Second Vatican Council and the formation of pastoral councils, parish and deanery, and parish finance committees.

One of the themes of 'Vatican II' was increased lay participation in the Church and in accordance with this Bishop Worlock set up Parish Councils and gave considerable latitude in such areas as ecumenism and education. In practice, the members of these councils found it easier to discuss the practicalities of parish life and events, such as who would play Father Christmas at the Parish Christmas party or the organisation of the Summer fete, than more conceptual subjects concerning the development of the Faith, such as ecumenism or catechesis. Some priests were not too sympathetic towards these councils anyway, having become used to running a parish as a one-man show and some active parishioners were not impressed with them either: 'We do the work, they do the chat.'

Thus in many places the parish councils died out; those that remained evolved into Pastoral Councils, concerned with pastoral issues.

This is what has happened in Jersey. The first Deanery Pastoral Council, established in 1967, was headed by Jack Dupré. There is now a flourishing 'Stewardship Group' at St Mary and St Peter's that deals both with practical issues and larger questions. It has not proved possible to do the same at St Thomas', because of the disparate nature of the congregation and the various different communities – Polish, Portuguese etc – and the different congregations formed by the times of the Masses.

There are also stewardship groups for the east and the west of the Island respectively and also finance sub-committees as well as an Island Finance and Property Committee as required by Canon Law.

Another difficulty has been the one common to all associations or clubs in the modern age: the increased attention to work expected by employers and the consequent reluctance to do anything with leisure time than to spend it at home.

—ooo000ooo—

There was Catholic opposition as part of a more general Christian opposition to the legalisation of abortion by the States in 1996. Prominent among those States Members who opposed the legislation was the Catholic, Deputy David Crespel.

Out of this opposition arose the foundation of the Causeway Association – a hostel to give a home and security to pregnant women who had nowhere to go and to give expectant mothers a choice other than abortion (although Causeway is not a religious organisation as such). The first chairman was the Methodist minister, Rev Derek Poole. The first hostel was opened in Lemprière Street and later one in Belmont Road, with accommodation for nine women and babies.

—ooo000ooo—

One of the most important expressions of lay leadership within the Church in Jersey can be seen in the development over many years of Catholic Pastoral Services. This began in the days of Père Jean-Marie Chuffart, when he was rector of St Thomas'. He welcomed Yvonne Callec and Karen Blampied, former teachers at Beaulieu, who left teaching to become coordinators of catechetical and liturgical formation for children and adults within the community of St Thomas'. At first these two were based in a room within St Thomas's Presbytery, later moving into the upper room of St Thomas Community Centre when their activity was recognised as a Pastoral Centre for the Island with a growing number of parishes offering association and support.

Gradually the work developed with a social justice dimension in partnership with the Society of St Vincent de Paul. Support for the Portuguese community was offered when Zinha Powell joined the Centre. Nicky Thompson was another member, responsible for youth formation. There was a management committee, first chaired by Angela Le Sueur and later by Alicia Rainbault. This committee sought to integrate the Centre with the mainstream objectives of the Deanery Pastoral Council. Inevitably there were certain tensions, which were seen as creative.

Angela Le Sueur said: 'The work was productive and a lot of good things came out of our work, such as the CPC initiating the adoption in Jersey of the UN's Eradication of Poverty Decade (1996-2006) movement, in relation to the causes in Jersey of poverty, such as deficient housing. This subsequently became an Island-wide movement, chaired in turn by Jurat Tim Herbert, Deputy Maurice Dubras and Constable Iris Le Feuvre. I also like to think that out of the many meetings we had at that time, the

Community Bank started. So I think we did have some influence and that was a good thing in itself.'

However, in 1994, Bishop Hollis had to intervene in a dispute over the use of the Catholic Pastoral Centre at St Thomas' Community Centre. This had been built for the Parish in 1987, on the site of what had been previously been a grotto of Our Lady of Lourdes. The ground floor was used – as it still is in 2015 – for church activities, with the Jersey Pastoral Centre operating from upstairs, carrying out youth, welfare and religious education work. For this work there was a £60,000 annual budget, partly funded by a trust.

The management committee of the Pastoral Centre was made up of priest and lay representatives from the Catholic parishes, together with officers of the Trust and other officials. It had four full-time representatives working in welfare, youth and training activities, along with a counsellor and volunteers.

The issue developed over the use of the first floor hall, which Père Igoa and his parish council said was needed for parish and community activities. Moreover, when the Centre had moved there, it had been assumed that this move would not be permanent.

In Père Igoa's view, the Pastoral Centre had grown too large and although he did not disapprove of what they were doing, some of the welfare work carried out by the centre was duplicating what was available from other agencies for those in need, especially the work of the Society of St Vincent de Paul.

All of the five parishes involved in the Centre's work had to pay an annual sum based on the size of their congregations, with St Thomas' (the largest) paying in between £6,000 and £7,000 a year.

Because of the amount St Thomas' were required to pay, and the fact that the Centre was occupying the premises rent free, Fr Igoa asked for the situation to be reviewed as, in the parish council's view, St Thomas' contribution was disproportionate compared to what was being paid by other parishes.

When they failed to gain support to have this system of payment reviewed, the St Thomas Parish Council gave the Centre a year to quit the premises and withdrew their annual donation.

The Centre team denied that their work was duplicating what was available elsewhere and said that their efforts to help those in need involved working alongside and co-operating with other agencies. It was their contention that it was vital that their work was allowed to carry on from a central town base and that if the use of all the facilities on the St Thomas' site was reorganised, there might be enough space for everyone.

A year passed and the Pastoral Centre members were still in place at the Hall with no indication of moving away from it. However, the parish council agreed to leave the status quo until the Pastoral Review findings had been published.

The 1994 Pastoral Review highlighted the problems existing between the Jersey Catholic Pastoral Centre and St Thomas'. It suggested that one possible solution might be the relocation of the centre's youth and education work to St Joseph's Church Hall in Grouville, while the welfare work remained on the St Thomas' site. But this recommendation did not appeal to either side, because the parish wanted the centre team to leave completely, and the centre team believed it would be inappropriate to split them up – it also was imperative to have a town centre base from which to operate.

By November 1994 stalemate had been reached. Père Igoa was talking about the parish taking legal action to remove the Pastoral Centre from St Thomas' Hall and that the situation was likely only to be resolved by an independent intermediary.

The Bishop was so concerned about the impasse reached over the problem that he wrote to both parties inviting three members of each side for a meeting on 3 January 1995, at which, he said, he wanted the matter sorted out. He told them if necessary he would arbitrate and although he did not wish to impose a decision, he would do so for the benefit and good name of the Catholic community.

The upshot was that, through the good offices of Mr and Mrs Terry Le Sueur, alternative premises were found. The CPC moved out of the Community Centre, first of all into premises into Clarendon Road, then half moved to Winchester Chambers, a building on Val Plaisant opposite St Thomas' church and the other half into the presbytery attached to the new St Mary and St Peter's Church.

In 1999 and early 2000, three members of the Catholic Pastoral Centre resigned, subsequent to the appointment to the Centre of two religious sisters, Sister Loretta Madigan FCJ and Sister Joan Tierney UJ as Pastoral Assistants.

Sister Loretta was a former headmistress of the FCJ School, from 1969 - 1981 and Sister Joan had been working in Scotland.

The two full-time workers were Religious Sisters supported professionally by their own Orders and performed a wide variety of deanery functions in an ancillary role to the Island's parish priests as part of what had become 'Catholic Pastoral Services'.

The re-naming followed a debate on the future of the Centre that had been instigated by Canon France in his first year as Dean as a follow-up to the 1994 Review. It was decided that the new name better reflected its outreach service to the parishes - no longer a 'centre' to which people came, but a 'service' that reached out to them.

In October 2003, Catholic Pastoral Services moved down the road to join the new Welcome Centre next to St Thomas' Church.

When Sister Loretta left the Island to take on the position of national promoter for justice and peace in the British Province of the FCJ, she was replaced by Sister Hilary Brown UJ; later another Sister briefly succeeded Sister Joan Tierney.

Following the withdrawal from the Island of the religious sisters, and another minor pastoral review, five Jersey women formed Catholic Pastoral Services. Maureen Corrigan was appointed coordinator and manager, with Mary Cahill coordinating youth ministry; Evelyn Maloret had responsibility for spiritual development, Martina Wintour for catechetics, ecumenism and family life and Joan Copp for promoting the work of States' Schools Catechists.

At the time of writing in 2016, the team consists of Delia Hardiman as manager, Mary Cahill as Coordinator of Marriage and Family Life Ministry, Sarah Wakeling as Coordinator for Youth Ministry, Paula Andrew responsible for Safeguarding, co-ordinating States Schools Catechists and the weekly newsletter, and Diana Richmond, administrator for marriage formation and Confirmation.

Mgr France commented: 'Jersey is fortunate in having Catholic Pastoral Services as an amazing resource, a cause of envy in many parishes in the mainland of the Portsmouth Diocese.'

—ooo000ooo—

Most recently, from the perspective of the publication of this book, in 2013 a three-week all-Island Mission rook place, led by the Sion Community from the UK, after nearly two years preparation.

Previous missions had taken place in the Island before; two of them by the same Sion Community had taken place in the Sacred Heart parish in 1983 and 1993.

The 2013 Mission took place in early autumn and involved 50 of their wider membership in visiting all the homes of known Catholics, holding mission services, giving talks on prayer, on growing old gracefully and understanding the Faith better and on how to pass it on. A youth team worked daily with young people and children in both school and after school.

'Only God can assess the effect of the mission, but it really got noticed and touched many,' commented Nicholas France afterwards.

The final Mass in Fort Regent was attended by over 2,000 people, at the end of which was launched publicly CARITAS JERSEY as a branch of the international charity of the Catholic Church.

In addition to promoting and supporting current social action in the parish, Caritas Jersey's aim was to research any needs in the Island that were not being met by either the States of Jersey or other Christian charities, especially the needs of immigrant families, most of whom were Catholic.

—ooo000ooo—

CARITAS JERSEY had been established the year before the Mission. It was the first parish branch, within the Portsmouth diocese, of the

Catholic Church's official international organisation in the area of social justice, Caritas Internationalis.

Based on the Catholic Social Teaching and best professional practice, Caritas Jersey. Its website is: *www.caritasjersey.je*. It was set up as a 'social welfare and action agency', an umbrella charitable organisation to integrate existing and well-established bodies together with some new initiatives starting up to meet current and future needs within the Island. These related to poverty (as broadly defined) and the aim 'to build justice and inclusion', among a number of issues that have been or are still to be identified and scoped out, to be applied to all residents in need.

A discussion document was prepared by the Caritas Think Tank in autumn 2013 before the General Election and sent out to every address in Jersey in the hope that it might inspire the public to raise matters of concern with election candidates concerning the future of Jersey.

It was the first publication of what was intended to become a series of public documents and reports, either in response to open consultations or as a stimulus to public debate on matters of particular interest to the general public of Jersey.

In the foreword, Monsignor France wrote: 'Caritas Jersey has decided to spend some time thinking about important issues which have a long-term impact on all residents of this Island, regardless of social and economic background and which seem to be 'core' to the future well-being of our community. Our aim is to offer some questions you might like to ask candidates, with comments to explain the thinking behind the question. These are questions about social and moral issues which touch the very heart of Jersey life and the long-term common good of all the people of our wonderful Island.

'We want to accentuate the positive and give all prospective candidates, both those now in the States of Jersey and anyone new willing to put their names forward, a challenge!

'We are neither promoting any particular election candidate nor are we publishing a political manifesto or some Catholic propaganda. Rather, we are aiming to raise awareness and address the much wider and more fundamental issue of what is basically and morally right and just for each of us living in Jersey.'

Chapter 16

SPREADING THE WORD

The Church and media communications

AT the beginning of the post-war period, 'the media' as a word hardly existed. On the one hand there was the Press, and the BBC; at parish level the notices were read out from the pulpit before the Sunday sermon and some parishioners would subscribe to Catholic newspapers. Nationally, there were some religious programmes on the wireless: the war-time broadcasts by C.S Lewis and the radio plays of 'The Man Born to be King' by Dorothy L Sayers were innovative and ground-breaking. Television was in its infancy and not generally available.

The attitude of the modern 'media' to matters religious was a thing as yet undreamt of; the whole modern edifice of Internet and social media and the novelty forms of communication that comprise it would have been regarded as pure science fiction to anybody growing up in any of the earlier decades before its invention.

In Jersey, a few years after the establishment of the Jersey Catholic Association in 1951, a monthly magazine was created by and for Catholics in the Island: the *Jersey Catholic Record.*

The first issue saw the light of day in June 1956. It was edited originally by Father Lawrence Hargreaves, the Rector of the Sacred Heart Parish. The original magazine committee consisted of the editor, 'Mesdames F A Page and C Brine and Mr M Lakeman and Mr E Gough.' It was printed by Bennett Brothers, whose printing works were at Charing Cross, St Helier.

In the introduction to the first issue, Fr Hargreaves wrote: 'It is nearly five years since the Jersey Catholic Association commenced its great work of uniting the Catholics of the Island, and this little magazine will consolidate that union... In it will be mirrored the Catholic life of the Island with all its faith and vigour.'

Those who decide to publish magazines are not generally aware of the pitfalls that lie ahead, especially the difficulty in securing advertising revenue to help fund it. It was not long before the editors' articles saw pleas for parishes to send in their news – and for contributors to observe deadlines.

The magazine changed and became more colourful with the passing of the decades and advances in print technology.

In the early 1970s, the editor was principally Canon Olney's curate, Father Francis Isherwood, who also produced a series of booklets titled 'Jersey Church History'. As the name implies, the series covered the two millennia of history of Catholicism in the Island.

Fr Isherwood became joint editor in 1970 with Angela Le Sueur and sole editor in 1972. Despite the many people in the Catholic community who wanted the 'Record' to continue, the manifold problems of production never diminished. A special meeting of the Jersey Pastoral Council, chaired by Canon Mahy, was held on 7 January 1976 to discuss the situation.

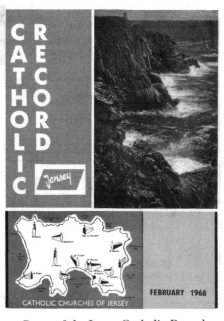

Cover of the Jersey Catholic Record

He said that despite being a relative newcomer to Jersey, he understood that the survival of the Record had been discussed ad nauseam, but it had now reached a very critical stage. It was decided to continue publishing it until May, when Fr Isherwood was due to leave the Island.

It was agreed that the Record was a useful and worthwhile publication, but there was a private loan of £500 to repay and 270 unsold copies of Jersey Church History at £2 each. Furthermore, Fr Isherwood was due to leave the Island at the end of May and so a new editor would have to be found. The problem was talked around until the end of the meeting without firm any conclusion being reached. The last issue was in May 1976.

From Jersey Fr Isherwood went for six years to the Bamenda Diocese in Cameroon, West Africa, which was twinned with the Portsmouth Diocese. On his return he became Diocesan Financial Secretary to Bishop Emery. He subsequently became parish priest of St Joseph's, Portsmouth.

BBC Radio Jersey and Channel TV both had religious content in their programmes during the 1970s and 1980s, such as daily epilogues before going off-air; a religious element to broadcasting that seems to have been lost in more modern times.

The 1994 Pastoral Review recommended that at deanery and parish level, there to be competent individuals who take special responsibility for developing relationships with the news media, as well as providing a creative religious input to the press and to broadcasting.'

The idea of a weekly 'Faith Page' in the *Jersey Evening Post* was suggested to the editor, Chris Bright, by Canon France and that has become a regular feature of the newspaper, covering news and relevant interviews across all the denominations in Jersey. Messages at Christmas time via all the local media have also become normal practice.

The Catholic Church in Jersey's link to on-line publishing was represented by a website, most recently re-launched in 2011, aimed at enhancing communication with its parishioners and the wider world.

It was designed by Oliver Baudains at Level Media and featured everything from information on the various Catholic churches in the Island to Mass times and events and information about marriages, baptisms and first communions. There was also an option to sign up to receive a weekly newsletter by e-mail and links to local faith schools and to the Diocese of Portsmouth.

In the past decade, two books have been published about the history of Catholicism in Jersey: *Deo Gratias*, by Diane Moore, concentrates on the French influence that has been a feature of the local Church since the time of the French Revolution until the departure of the last French Oblate, Father Vincent Igoa, in late 1999 and that has been followed by this present book on the history of the Church in Jersey in modern times.

VI. THE 'VC II' EFFECT

Chapter 17

THE WATERSHED

'Today, new Catholic churches and Mass Centres are being opened in the Island, whilst other denominations complain of poor attendance and consider the closure of chapels' – T W Attenborough, writing in the Centenary booklet for St Mary and St Peter's Church, 1948)

THE Second Vatican Council held in Rome between 1962 and 1965, has been a milestone in Church history. It matched any of the Councils of the Early Church, or the Council of Trent held in the 16th Century that embodied the Counter-Reformation and set the Church's course for the following 400 years.

The nub of any discussion on modern Catholicism, be it in Jersey or the wider world, is the effect the Council had, both at the time and subsequently until the present time, half a century later.

In Jersey, the modern history of Catholicism could be divided, like Gaul, into three parts: first, the re-establishment of Catholicism at the end of the 18th Century; secondly, the arrival of the Oblates in 1880; thirdly, the effects of the Vatican Council in the mid -1960s and its effect on Jersey since that time to the present.

The aim of 'Vatican II' was to address and renew the relationship between the Roman Catholic Church and the modern world. Observers were invited from Anglican, Protestant and Eastern Orthodox Churches and it was hoped that Catholics would be encouraged and renewed in their faith. As Pope John XXIII said, in a much quoted remark, it was 'time to open the windows and let in some fresh air'.

The council became known for its renewal of Catholic doctrine and for its increased emphasis on ecumenical dialogue with other churches and religions. Increased participation in and understanding of the Church liturgy was another major aim, hence the encouragement to use vernacular languages rather than Latin.

The most noticeable changes resulting from the Council, especially from the perspective of the ordinary Catholic going to church on Sundays, was the widespread use of vernacular language in the Mass; a greater involvement by the congregation in the Mass; more greater use of more modern music; the change by which the priest at Mass now stood facing the congregation rather than facing away from it and the so-called 'stripping of the altars' – a reformation in church decoration and artifacts from the ornate to the minimal, concentrating much more on the altar and stripping away everything that might distract the mind from the Sacrifice of the Mass enacted there.

Some Catholics saw this as an evolution, others as a 'revolution' – and like all revolutions, contained much that was good and much that was flawed. It created divisions in the Church that are still very much alive half a century later and an extreme range of different opinion about the merits or otherwise of the reforms. Although many Catholics did indeed feel renewed and encouraged in their faith, others were either dismayed or simply confused. It always used to be said that, unlike members of the 'broad' Church of England, that at least 'Catholics knew what they believed in'. Now, there seemed to be less certainty and more doubt about that.

Archbishop King and his secretary Fr. R. Lawrence watching the opening on television of the 2nd Vatican Council by Pope John XXIII

A priest talking to the author a year or so after the end of the Council remarked to him that whereas before the Council he felt that the Church was like an old carthorse that shambled sleepily along, now it was more like being astride a thoroughbred that was raring to go. There was certainly great excitement at the time of the Vatican 2: never before had there been so many Bishops come together from so many parts of the world. The exception was Archbishop King, Bishop of Portsmouth, who was too frail to attend.

As part of that 'excitement' or feeling of a new beginning, there were such reforms or innovations as a greater tolerance of mixed marriages

(Catholics marrying someone of another denomination), Concelebration of the Mass (by more than one Priest) and a greater emphasis on worshippers participating in the Mass to make it more of a community event – instead of (as often happened) saying their rosaries or reading their missals to the backdrop of what was sometimes called 'the sacred mutter of the Mass'.

Reform, it is safe to say, would gradually have come in any event; Vatican II accelerated that process of reform – quite possibly, at times, at a much quicker rate of evolution than was appreciated by 'Catholics in the pews'.

Mgr Nicholas France was ordained in 1968, a year of political riots and revolution in Europe and America, let alone being the aftermath of the 'revolutionary' Vatican II. He said: 'It was quite a time to be launched into the church as a young priest, especially when so many were abandoning the priesthood in a revolutionary spirit.

'On reflection, I believe that many of our problems following the Vatican II can be attributed to the crisis in society where not only was everything questioned, but authority in parliaments, the universities, social society and the Church was challenged. Catholics had always been obedient and observant, especially towards Rome. For the first time both clergy and laity questioned the authority of their leaders and the manner in which the teaching of the Church was being expressed.

'Also, if the Church felt able to change the rules in reforming and changing the liturgy, in removing the abstinence ban on Fridays etc, why could not other things be questioned, especially when the laity believed it was in their sphere of experience, as in the field of sexuality.'

At the other extreme of reaction to 'VC II' there was a feeling that the Council had been, as a Benedictine monk once said jokingly to this author, 'the most prominent interference of the Devil in the affairs of God and Man since the Temptation of Eve'.

However, it was often the diverse interpretation of the teachings and decisions of the Second Vatican Council that caused the greatest offence to some Catholics, rather than the Council's decisions themselves. The Acts of the Council, if properly researched, are not half as revolutionary or extreme as some of the interpretations of it taken at diocesan or parish level in the so-called 'spirit of the Council'.

Suddenly there was not only change but a rending of that seamlessness that hitherto had marked Catholic liturgy and practice throughout the world. Now there were differences from one country to another; from one diocese to another; from one parish to another. The Church may indeed have continued to be 'universal' in everything that was truly important, but from the pews it often looked as if it had lost its universality and was throwing away much that was good along with the accretion of religiosity and practices that it wished, justifiably, to discard.

For many Catholics, all of a sudden their local church building now seemed alien to all their long-term familiar habits of devotion. The change in the language of the Mass from Latin to the vernacular was very much a case in point. Often the sublime and devotional liturgy of the Tridentine Mass (although at times often expressed as a hurried mutter) seemed to be replaced by that of a Nonconformist prayer meeting.

Mgr France commented: 'There was a great enthusiasm for the reforms of the Council in the Portsmouth Diocese. But I can see now the arrogance of us clergy who were sometimes trying to act like the Protestant reformers of the 16th Century, even if with the best of intentions. I now regret that.

'The changes often broke the hearts of ordinary folk, as it did in Jersey at St Thomas', the sort of people who loved their devotional church or favourite statues and painted walls. Lots of things were destroyed in this iconoclastic mood of the times, in which everything should be simple, minimalist and austere. The programme of modernisation removed a lot of the church's treasures, the forms of devotion that had helped to uplift people from the ordinariness of their own lives. .

'Fortunately, nowadays there is a move back to recognising the need for beauty in worship and in church buildings.

'Before the modern restoration of St Thomas' I met an old couple sitting in the church who hadn't been there for some years. In fact they told me that they hadn't been since "the church had been destroyed". It had been a place of great devotion, entertaining celebrations and processions (in the days before television) and even though some of the statuary and wall paintings were rather sentimental in a 19th Century kind of way, the building belonged to the people who were not interested in taste but in it being their spiritual home, as it had been for their parents and grandparents.

'Similarly, the new church of St Mary and St Peter had a primary emphasis on the altar. It had a cross but not a crucifix and the tabernacle was in the side chapel. All very simple but a little bare and empty looking when the congregation had returned home.

'Everywhere, Catholics were deprived of devotions such as the Rosary and Benediction services. The traditional teaching of the Catechism was replaced by modern catechetics, where everything was less definite and more relative. As a result, many Catholics drifted away from their spiritual roots. The effect can be felt today.

'I was in charge of the Diocesan Liturgy Commission for a period of years following Vatican II. We were all a bit sold on the desire to make things simple and focus on the Eucharist alone, so I should not criticise! As a young priest, I had been delighted when Bishop Worlock stripped the Cathedral in a similar way, "in the Conciliar spirit". The focus was just on the altar and on little else. To many it seemed that these reforms were rather Protestant and not truly Catholic.

'God is beauty and a beautiful church enhances the faith of people who may have come from simple homes or from unimaginative office blocks or workshops.'

—ooo000ooo—

IN 1982, the Rector of St Thomas', Père Jean-Marie Chuffart, sent his parishioners a lengthy 1,200 worded letter informing them of the forthcoming changes planned for the church. He explained that the emphasis of the changes would be a new main altar, situated at the centre of the cross formed by nave and the two transepts. Although this did not cause too much concern, the statement that: *The centre nave will be reserved for the congregation in order to give as many people as possible the chance to see the altar'* did cause unease, since this meant the re-arrangement of the pews so as to abolish the central aisle. It also meant that processions, be they bridal, funerary or simply the everyday procession of priests and altar servers to and from the altar could no longer take place down the centre of the church, but would have to happen up and down the side aisles... part of the minimisation of 'pomp and circumstance' that was part of the Conciliar spirit.

The final wording of the letter read: *'Of course, we your priests, realise that this brings a noticeable change in our church and that changes are sometimes hard to accept, but we will ask of you an act of trust in the new plan as we feel quite sure that we will all be very pleased with the beauty of the final result.'*

The plans were duly carried out and the Church was re-opened on Good Friday 1983. The congregation saw the church transformed: the lack of a central aisle; many of the old artefacts stripped away, including the magnificent old pulpit (although this had been riddled with woodworm) and the murals on the wall had disappeared as had all the side chapel altars and shrines. The changes were not universally popular.

In her book, *Deo Gratias*, Diane Moore wrote that she had conducted a survey among St Thomas' parishioners: *'Very few of them said they were satisfied with this new look for their Cathédrale, and many feel that the whole purpose of Vatican II was distorted by the new redesigning of their church. Some said that it led to fewer parishioners actually attending Mass at St Thomas' after the refurbishment, and that, coupled with the linguistic and demographic changes in Jersey, it inevitably led to the departure of the French Oblates and a need for change.'*

Tony Pezet, the longest serving Altar Server at St Thomas' reflected on the changes that Vatican II had brought to service at the altar: 'Everything has changed so much since I first started serving at the altar. Lots of things have gone, especially the pomp and ceremony of the old form of Latin service, which went out after Vatican II. Before, there used to be a much stronger sense of ceremony and lots of different "jobs" for the altar servers to do during the course of Mass. Suddenly, all that changed as well, and it was necessary to re-think the form of altar service.'

Not only the form of altar serving needed to be re-thought, but the new world of 'Post-Vatican II' suggested that it was high time that altar serving should no longer be a male preserve. In May 1968 a call for greater participation by women in the Mass was made at the first meeting of the new Diocesan Pastoral Council. The proposition was put forward by Dick Shenton – this was before the start of his career as a States Member – and called for the ban on women and girls serving at the altar to be completely lifted.

A parishioner of the Sacred Heart parish, he told the Portsmouth Diocesan Pastoral Council that his daughters as well as his sons should be allowed to read the Epistle and to serve at Mass. He asked: 'Why have two of my children privileges that the other two have not?'

Another Jersey delegate, Mrs W Madely, asked: 'If I can go on to the Sanctuary on a Saturday to arrange flowers, why am I barred from it on a Sunday?'

—ooo000ooo—

Mgr France commented: 'Obviously one of the most striking things in the last 70 years has been the reduction of the number of the priests, mainly due to the religious orders withdrawing from Jersey. Female religious have also declined – and this decrease in vocations is often blamed as a confusion and lack of direction in the Church caused by Vatican II (although cultural and social changes in society are equally responsible).

'On the other hand, as St Mary and St Peter's has always been the only diocesan Parish in the Island, then there are no fewer diocesan clergy today than there ever were, especially when including our deacons.

'However, a compensating factor has been a corresponding rise in lay ministry - and we also have Deacons to assist us. I cannot think how we could contemplate a single priest looking after two communities in St Helier without this assistance.

'We priests do not have to behave as if the world rested on our shoulders. Sometimes people feel sorry for us - it's true, we do lead busy lives – but the Church doesn't depend on priests alone.

'It has been very heartening to see increasingly how lay people in the Island have taken on Church responsibilities. Even before I came to Jersey that spirit was already alive and well and was much promoted by my predecessor, Canon David Mahy. Jersey has been, in some ways, a pioneer of the lay Ministry.

'Having fewer priests is by no means an over-riding issue: it's the strength of people's life of faith that really matters. This is what is now developing rapidly in the Island, through God's grace.

'Strongly encouraged by our Bishops, lay people have been encouraged to use the Grace given to them in Baptism to share in the mission of the Church and in the pastoral care of local worshipping communities.

That is certainly a more positive effect of Vatican II.'

—ooo000ooo—

THE stresses and strains caused by Vatican II and its interpretation by clergy throughout the world caused the foundation of the 'break-away' Society of St Pius X (SSPX), which was a reaction against this – although its members would, with some justification, claim that it was not themselves who had broken away from the Church but vice versa.

Archbishop Marcel Lefebvre headed this organisation of traditional Catholics with an 'Old Believer' mind-set until his death in 1991; Bishop Bernard Tissier de Mallerais succeeded him as secretary-general of the Society. In their churches in London, Paris and further afield the unreformed Latin Tridentine Mass continues to be celebrated and regularly attract full to overflowing congregations.

The society is not yet in communion with the Catholic Church, but this, at the time of writing is an on-going story with little relevance to the story of the local Church in Jersey.

An old retired missionary priest, Father Arthur Amy, although ordained later in his life and after the Vatican II reforms, used to say 'the Old Mass' on a weekday morning at St Thomas – although in his final years no-one who was not standing directly beside him would have known actually in what language he was speaking.

For many years in the late 20th and early 21st Century, 'the old Mass' was also said in a private chapel in Jersey or at the private addresses of members of the SSPX, this has largely carried on with little or no publicity other than on one occasion in 2007 when a more 'militant' SSPX member advertised in the media for a celebration of the Tridentine Mass at the Sacred Heart Church. Jersey Catholics were requested not to attend, although the combination of advertisement and injunction had, of course, the effect of filling the church on both occasions. Afterwards, the person who had caused the publicity moved away from Jersey, and the sudden flurry of excitement and curiosity passed away again.

Nevertheless, an Apostolic Letter from Pope Benedict XVI issued on 7 July 2007 titled *Moto Proprio*, stated that it was possible to celebrate the traditional Latin Mass as an 'extraordinary form of the Liturgy of the Church. This was a major change of attitude on the part of the Vatican, which had distanced itself for over 40 years from the traditional Latin mass and from those organisations that offered it. It was seen as a bridge-building move towards those Catholics who had a preference for the old style of Mass rather than for the new form of Mass and of worship. The change of Pope since then to Pope Francis has created yet more question marks about what is and what is not authorised – and the story remains on-going (but not, fortunately, in Jersey at the time of writing). In 2015 a notice appeared in the Island parish weekly newsletter that Catholics were not permitted to attend any Mass said by an SSPX priest, wherever it might be held, as the SSPX was not in communion with the Pope or the Church.

Masses using the authorised 'extraordinary form' (i.e. the Tridentine Mass) have been said on various occasions in the Island in recent years, such as by a representative from the Priestly Fraternity of St Peter in 2011.

In 2012 Fr Phillip Pennington-Harris arrived in Jersey as an assistant priest and held regular Tridentine Mass services, mostly weekly, at Our Lady in St Martin, which were attended by a small group of like-minded Catholics. These liturgies ceased when he returned to the UK on a new posting a year later.

—ooo000000ooo—

THE 'Vatican II effect' described above might seem somewhat negative, but that view also needs to be balanced with some undoubted positive results, among which prominently should be placed the rise of an ecumenical spirit in the Church.

Jersey has shown that ecumenism is at its best at a local level. There has been, from the time of Vatican II and before, a pleasant and friendly relationship between leaders of the different denominations in Jersey.

The Catholic Church in the Island belongs to 'Christians Together in Jersey', the organisation that has evolved from the Jersey Council of Churches, and of which Canon David Mahy was president for two years and Canon Nicholas France for five.

However, gone are the days, immediately after Vatican II, when there was an excited supposition that Christian reunification – at least in Britain – would happen 'by the end of the century'. Doctrinally, the denominations have grown further apart, although there is far greater collaboration than ever, certainly in terms of joint projects relating to social justice or joint representation at civic events. The Island's government looks with approval at – and makes time - for the joint representations of the leaders of the Anglicans, Catholics and Methodists.

—ooo000ooo—

Commenting on the overall effect of the Vatican Council, Mgr France said: 'At the time of writing, 50 years after Vatican II, its effects, particularly in Jersey, can be broadly categorised as positive. This can be seen in new ways of thinking about how to be a Catholic Church for the 21st-century despite the radical reduction in number of priests since 1945.

'The practical effect of this has been the creation of one Island parish with seven churches, sharing personnel and resources, with a common mission focused outward towards the "New Evangelisation" and a real social concern for those on the peripheries, as symbolised by the creation of Caritas Jersey. In addition to this, there has developed over time greater lay pastoral involvement in the mission and maintenance of our island churches, particularly within the liturgy. Ecumenical cooperation and mutual respect at local level is now taken for granted.

"Following a misinterpretation of the Council's Decree on the Sacred Liturgy, some of the churches, which were full of statues and side altars, were too radically reordered and oversimplified - this lead to the loss of some of their devotional characteristics. In the last decade all the churches have been renewed and restored to much of their original devotional appearance.

'The vast majority of people have come to value and accept the reformed liturgy of the Church and many Catholics cannot remember the day when it was not celebrated in their own language. Inevitably, there are those who regret the passing of the Tridentine Latin Mass, often idealised at its best as a High Mass - that was rarely celebrated in any parish.

'Another positive factor has been the closer links between Deanery and Diocese. In part, this has been as much a product of the quicker and more convenient and links between Jersey and the UK. It has enabled the Church in Jersey to feel more integrated with the mainland of the Diocese.

'While to some the Second Vatican Council has indeed been felt like a revolution in the life of the Church, others agree with Pope Benedict, who preferred to see it correctly as an evolution and continuation. It is, of course, a natural wish for people to desire stability and permanence in their daily lives; the desire to experiment and create new things is an equal aspect of the human condition. Neither side brings totally positive or totally negative results. The Church has to be seen as being in this world if not of this world, so inevitably the changes in culture affect it.

'In a radically changing world the task of any leader – secular or ecclesiastical – is surely to try and balance both strands and keep the boat on even keel. This surely was achieved, in particular, by Pope St John Paul II. Some ill-considered implementation of reform in the Church in the 20th century has been counterbalanced in more recent years. Currently, under the focus set by Pope Francis, Catholics have been encouraged to be concerned, less about conservative or progressive agendas within the Church, and to look outward to serve "the peripheries", as the Pope has called them, in imitation of Christ who came "not to be served, but to serve and to give his life as a ransom for many".'

VII. FROM SEVEN PARISHES TO ONE PASTORAL AREA

Chapter 18

MISSION NOT MAINTENANCE

From seven parishes to one pastoral area

THE history of the Church in Jersey since the Second World War – as in most other places in the Western World – might be summed up as: 'Twenty years of expansion, followed by a half century of consolidation'.

Some would describe this rather as an ascent to a peak and then a steady decline, due to the way the Second Vatican Council's decisions were interpreted in dioceses and parishes.

The Council might or might not have been a contributory factor to the decline of the Catholic Church in Europe and North America, but unarguably the modern way of living, the atmosphere of moral relativism and the side-lining of religious faith in all aspects of daily life have had considerable effect on the lack of priestly vocations and the lessening commitment of the laity to attending Sunday Mass.

As a result, a re-arrangement of Catholic parish boundaries in the Island had been mooted for decades. In a letter from Bishop Emery to Canon Mahy in October 1980, he wrote about recent correspondence between him and the Oblates' Provincial, Fr Ciaran Dillon: *'We should take this opportunity of re-arranging the OMI parishes and to redress the imbalance of Diocesan Priests.'*

Within an area of 45 sq miles, there were in Jersey at this time seven Catholic parishes – six parishes with geographical boundaries and the Portuguese Parish, which was personal rather than geographic in its boundaries. The six parishes had 11 church buildings, six presbyteries and several halls; the Portuguese parish had no property of its own.

The pastoral care of these communities was entrusted by the Bishop to Diocesan and Religious Clergy. The diocesan clergy were only at St Mary and St Peter's and at St Patrick's.

The Oblates of Mary Immaculate of the Anglo-Irish Province were at Our Lady of the Annunciation Parish in St Martin, with Mass centres at Gorey and Grouville (St Joseph's) and at the Sacred Heart Parish, St Aubin with centres at Millbrook (Our Lady of the Universe) and Quennevais (St Bernadette).

171

The French OMI clergy were at St Thomas' and the Holy Ghost Fathers were at St Mathieu's Parish, with a centre at Ville à l'Eveque. The Holy Ghost Fathers also had pastoral care for the Portuguese chaplaincy.

In addition, by the 1990s there were two Deacons, a number of parish pastoral assistants, the team at the Pastoral Centre and a number of religious communities.

It did not seem feasible that all these arrangements would or could continue in the long-term. In September 1992, Bishop Hollis received an invitation from Gio Pollano, who at that time contributed to an occasional paper, produced every few months through the Catholic Pastoral Centre to disseminate news and views among the Catholic community in Jersey.

He told the Bishop: *'The next edition will take as its theme the effect on parishes of the present shortage of priests and the role of the laity in this situation.*

'It is generally felt that Jersey is fortunate knowing that its churches and parishes are at present well looked after with sufficient clergy. Whether this situation can, with the present shortage of priests, continue, is, of course, a matter for discussion and the occasional paper would be interested to hear and publicise your views on the subject… particularly concerning the role of the laity in the future running and administration of parishes both in Jersey and in the wider Diocese and whether a "rationalisation" of parishes will prove necessary.'

Bishop Hollis duly obliged and his article is worth quoting in full:

Jersey at the moment has seven parishes, one of which is the non-territorial parish for the Portuguese.

'The number of priests serving these parishes is 11, of whom only three are diocesan priests.

Five of the parishes are therefore served by priests from religious orders. If any of these orders should decide to discontinue their presence in the Island, it would be virtually impossible for the Diocese to replace them.

'I do not want to scaremonger because none of the religious communities have given any indication of their intention to withdraw, but the statistics do represent a reality which cannot and should not be ignored.

'In the worst of all possible scenarios, therefore, Jersey could find itself having to be served by, say, 5 priests. This would entail a massive change in attitudes and an

acceptance of the need to travel reasonable distances in order to attend Mass.

'You are very well served for Masses at the moment, but that could change and with it will have to change your own attitudes.

'It is very difficult to predict either whether or when this could happen, but it is no good waiting until it does or hoping that it will not. We need to plan now and to build on the involvement of lay people in the parishes that is already taking place in significant ways.

'I certainly would not want to close down any of our parishes on the Island but you may find yourselves becoming Catholic communities without a resident priest. There may not be Mass every Sunday and the lay communities may have to take upon themselves the responsibilities that go with the day to day life of a Church community. This means that the visiting and caring of the sick and housebound, the catechising of children, the preparation of children for sacraments, the celebration of the Word and the prayer of the community will need to be part and parcel of the Christian life of members of the community. Simply because there is no priest does not mean that this life cannot go on. The catechetical and pastoral centre which is based in St Helier will, I believe, have a very important part to play in these developments.

'This is a serious prospect and one which the Island has to face but it need not and should not be seen as a potential disaster. You are faced with a number of challenges:

* Training for Lay Ministry
* Even more active commitment by all to the life of the Church
* Openness to change
* Active assumption of pastoral responsibilities by lay people
* Untiring work and prayer for vocations to the priesthood

'These challenges are common to the whole Diocese and are not particular to Jersey. They are the basis for the Agenda of the Diocese for the foreseeable future and I believe they represent not only a challenge but a unique opportunity to develop and enrich the whole notion of what it means to be a Catholic Christian in the Church of today's world.

'We do not belong to a priests' Church, nor is our Church a lay Church. We belong to the Church of Christ in which priests and lay people are called to serve one another and the world, to work together in partnership and collaboration and to proclaim together the Good News of Jesus Christ.'

This philosophy has informed all the changes in the Church and its parish boundaries in the Island since then.

The Jersey Catholic Pastoral Review

Within two years of the Bishop's article appearing, a pastoral review was established by the Bishop in 1994 at the request of Canon Mahy.

As the Bishop made clear in writing the foreword to this report: *'The process which led to the setting up of this review began with an invitation to me from the Island Pastoral Council to consider the future shape of the Catholic Church in Jersey.'*

He detailed the factors that had led to the request being made: *'Not least among these factors was the prospect that the number of priests in the Island will be reduced, particularly as the Religious Congregations, who serve a number of the parishes, review deployment of their members, (Coupled with this, there was also felt the need to rationalise the considerable resources of the Island in order to maximise our effort towards mission and evangelisation.)'*

The Review team was made up of members from outside the Island who took an objective look at everything that was going on and *the Review represented their view of the Island Church's situation.*

He asked Island Catholics to discuss, evaluate, prioritise and implement the report and asked for a general response by Christmas. By Easter he wanted a detailed response, because by September/October 1995 he wanted to be in a position to put the first elements of the Review into place.

He concluded: *'We are being faced with a God-given opportunity to transform the face and image of the Church in Jersey.'*

The full texts of the foreword and of the Report's recommendations are contained in Appendix C of this book on page 257.

The report constituted probably the most fundamental review of Catholicism in Jersey in modern history. It was the result of six month's work by a team of nine people, all of whom met with a wide range of individuals and groups. Surveys were carried out and the results taken into account.

The review team included the Dean of Guernsey, Canon Gerard Hetherington and it was headed by Canon Declan Lang from the UK (subsequently made Bishop of Clifton). A list of the team members and their areas of responsibility is detailed in Appendix C.

Among the issues was a review of the use of buildings and the deployment of pastoral resources, including the possibility of the laity playing a greater role in the Church as a result of fewer priests entering the ministry.

At that time there were 14 Catholic priests in the Island, three of them retired and two semi-retired. In comparison to other countries, Jersey was well served in terms of numbers of priests – Malta was the only country in Europe to have a greater percentage of priests to its Catholic population than Jersey.

One of the key recommendations of the report was that the number of Catholic parishes in Jersey be reduced to three – one in the East, one in the Centre and one in the West, with the Portuguese parish to remain as it was.

It also suggested that the Sacred Heart Church in St Aubin should close. But that recommendation was not acted upon – it was far too popular a building.

Concerning the Island Pastoral Council, the report said that its membership was too big for effective communication or decision making other than the hearing of reports. It should look at ways it could encourage the emergence of new lay leaders on the Island and it had the potential to become a more effective and collaborative group.

At the time, the Pastoral Council consisted of five lay representatives from each of the Catholic parishes, all the parish clergy and one representative from each Catholic lay organisation. It met three times a year.

The report recommended that the IPC should become a decision-making body in its own right and that its size be radically cut down; the Catholic Pastoral Centre would be responsible to the Council.

Members of the Island's Catholic community were invited to the presentation of the report at the Hotel de France on 21 October 1994.

The main thrusts of the report were summed up in a Jersey Evening Post headline the following day: *Four Catholic Churches to close in major reshuffle?'*

175

It continued: *Four Roman Catholic Churches could close in the next three years as a result of a wide-ranging review which proposes reducing the number of church parishes from seven to three.*

'The report, published last night, also suggests greater co-operation with other denominations, an examination of whether the Catholic schools could become ecumenical and more attention to social issues such as drug abuse and racism.'

In addition to closing four churches because of a decline in the number of priests, the recommendations included the closure of three presbyteries and three church halls.

The buildings concerned were: the Church at Ville-à-l'Evêque; the Sacred Heart and its presbytery; Queen of the Universe, Millbrook; St Joseph's, Grouville, with its hall and outbuildings; the presbytery and hall at St Matthieu's; and the presbytery and hall at St Patrick's.

It also recommended that within three years the parishes should be reduced from seven to three, with the Portuguese parish also being retained.

Unsurprisingly, parishioners of the churches threatened with closure did not take too kindly to the report.

One of the first fruits of the rationalisation process that got under way was the announcement in 1996 of the closure of St Joseph's Church. This was despite fierce opposition from some parishioners who had a deep affection for this old-established church and worshipping community.

The closure of St Joseph's had been considered before the Report was published. There was a joint congregation of about 350 attending the three churches served from Our Lady in St Martin, with roughly one third of that number attending each church. The parish priest, Fr Eamon Fitzgerald, commented in the JEP in November 1994 that it no longer made sense for members of the congregation to provide the funds for the maintenance, heating and lighting of the three church buildings when two would be sufficient. At the same time, he was quoted as saying that the closure of any church was 'a painful thing, a kind of dying'

Parishioners at the Sacred Heart were also up in arms, but by virtue of its location and the intrinsic architectural merit of the building, they were luckier and this recommendation was not acted upon.

Further changes came with the arrival of Canon Nicholas France as Catholic Dean at the end of 1999. Although he was new to the Island, his knowledge of it went back many years and two of his parishioners in Southampton had been members of the Review team, so he was quite aware of all the issues before he arrived in Jersey.

With the departure of the previous Dean, Canon David Mahy, and also the priest in charge of St Thomas', Père Vincent Igoa, it was easy (in principle) for Canon France to combine these two town parishes.

He recollected that one of the most confusing things for him to come to terms with on his arrival in Jersey was the plethora of saints' names in Island life. Various saints' names were suggested for the combined town parish, but for the sake of convenience, it became simply 'the Catholic Parish in St Helier.'

When, in July 2000, he was interviewed by the Jersey Evening Post about how the new town unification was going, he said: 'Like a marriage. Two have to become one, while at the same time retaining their individuality, respecting one another's differences and not standing in each other's shadow.

'On the whole, it has gone quite well and I haven't forced the pace. Although people now know that they form one parish, they probably still feel that they are members of one or the other of the two churches.

'There are differences in the nature of the two church buildings just as much as there are differences in the ways each of the former parishes does things. There will always be a need for the individuality of different traditions.'

He also signalled the future of the Mass centres at Millbrook and Ville à l'Eveque: 'In these times when mobility is no problem, bigger Catholic parishes that have bigger resources help to make people realise that there is a bigger world than the place from which they come.

'Everywhere in the Island local shops or post offices are closing as people realise that a better choice or better service can be obtained from a larger outlet elsewhere. Catholic churches do not exactly sell consumer items, but the same could be said to apply. If you have a bigger church or a bigger community, you get more choice.'

A little while previously, in May 2000, Catholics in the east of the Island had been told they were to become members of one united parish, a combination of St Patrick's, Our Lady (in St Martin) and the Church of the Assumption in Gorey. The combined parish was to be under the one priest, Fr Robin Ellwood, who had previous experience in Jersey before his ordination in 1991 and he would be assisted by Deacon Tony Ward. The parish priest of St Patrick, Fr Colin Ward, was retiring at this point and Fr Brian Sandeman, who had assisted him, was appointed Hospital chaplain.

It was, said Canon France at the time that a sharing of resources in a time, when there were fewer vocations was sensible and in this respect the unification was making a virtue out of necessity.

The parish of Our Lady in St Martin had lost its priest on the death of Brian Cousins in 1999 and he had only replaced the previous parish priest, Fr Eamon Fitzgerald, a short time before then. In a pastoral message to the two eastern parishes, Bishop Hollis said that the two deaths, together with the poor medical condition of St Patrick's parish priest, Fr Colin Ward, meant that he had had to think carefully about the pastoral care of these parishes: 'Ideally, I would like to have a parish priest in both your communities, but I am afraid that is no longer going to be possible.'

The Mass Centre at Gorey Village, Our Lady of the Assumption, was also closed and at the time of writing the Church is attempting to sell the building, although some local residents – not Catholic – have objected, one of them even writing to the Pope about their concerns.

The two western parishes continued independently of each other for the time being, although unification had been discussed for a number of years. In any case, both of these western parishes – Sacred Heart with St Bernadette's and Queen of the Universe, and also St Matthieu's - were both now being run by the Holy Ghost Fathers. When they left in 2003, all the churches in the Island became diocesan churches served by diocesan priests and a new combined 'Western Parish' was created.

The sale of Our Lady of the Universe Church in Millbrook and St John and St Anthony at Ville à l'Evêque took place in 2004.

Announcing their closure in June 2003, Bishop Hollis said in a pastoral letter: 'Due to the decline in the number of Catholics attending Mass and the reduction in the number of our clergy, we are facing the challenge of the future by clustering or uniting parishes, rationalising parish properties and developing new pastoral structures to meet the needs of the Church in our diocese at this time. This is happening across the whole of our diocese.'

Both of these chapels of ease were Mass centres rather than parish churches and neither chapel had a parochial community, hall or presbytery attached to it. They were not places where pastoral or social activities happened.

In Bishop Hollis' words: 'The small chapels were established in the 19th Century or the first half of the last century to meet the needs of that era, especially when people were less mobile. Four of these chapels have already closed during the last three years. Now we must consolidate the Church in larger community groupings, with available facilities that are necessary for catechetics, children's liturgy and social meetings and functions.'

In the past, he said, the church had been very much 'priest-led'. In one sense that was still the case, but Catholic worship now involved a whole host of lay people: 'We are emerging from a period in our history when we were a very clerical Church. We can't be now – we haven't got the clergy. But that is not entirely a bad thing, because actually it draws people into ownership of their own church. More people are now involved, one way or another, than before with their own church or parish.'

Mgr France recollected: 'At a meeting in about 2001, someone said: "One day, Jersey will be all one parish." We all laughed.'

But that is exactly what happened: from 2005 it was decided that Jersey should become one pastoral area.

The development of larger pastoral areas rather than parishes with distinct and limited boundaries was one of the main features of the Portsmouth Diocesan Pastoral Plan. A party of 18 Catholic clergy and laity from Jersey, led by Canon France, attended in July 2005 what was the largest diocesan gathering ever to have been held. It took place at the campus of Reading University and was attended by 800 diocesan priests and lay people.

Nicholas France said on his return: 'Too often we have had parish boundaries and traditional parish structures and gradually those boundaries are going to break down as we share more together.

'I see it as turning from a 20th Century institutionalised church to being a 21st Century missionary church.'

'We are very conscious that Europe is mission territory and that a secularised, de-christianised Europe needs a missionary church, not a church with perhaps all the old structures, that somehow meant that we did not share personnel and resources together when needed.'

The plan, he said, had evolved from what Catholics in the diocese wanted, not something that was being imposed downwards through the church hierarchical order.

The following September, a pastoral letter from Bishop Hollis detailed that the Catholic parishes in Jersey would be clustered together into one large pastoral area. The letter also stated that a new priest would not be appointed to replace Fr Robin Ellwood in the east of the Island: pastoral care for the eastern parish would now be provided by Canon France and his assistant priest, Fr Michael Marett-Crosby, working in partnership with Fr Brian Sandeman and Deacon Tony Ward.

The purposes of the new changes would be to share more equitably personnel and resources, according to Nicholas France, who was interviewed by the Jersey Evening Post.

The letter stated that in the near future the diocesan pastoral plan would be applied to Jersey and that the total 'pastoral area' of the Island would be served by five priests and three deacons.

A few weeks later, on 24 October, the Bishop visited Jersey to discuss the future of the Church in the Island at a special meeting called at St Mary and St Peter's Church. The meeting was an opportunity for the Bishop to explain more fully and specifically the way in which the Diocesan Pastoral Plan would apply in the Island.

Roughly 250 Catholic Islanders came to the meeting, which was addressed by the Bishop as well as by the Vicar-General with responsibility for Jersey, Mgr John Nelson, and by the diocesan head of pastoral formation, Nicky Stevens. There were no surprises for Catholics, all of whom were already aware of the changes. A further meeting was held just over a year later in November 2006, attended by about 100 Catholics and again had little to concern those attending.

Yet a further meeting took place in June 2009, when Bishop Hollis travelled to the Island to hear about the progress made over the previous few years. A meeting – 'the Jersey Pastoral Area Assembly' was held at St Mary and St Peter's in which over 400 Catholics of all ages, together with their clergy, celebrated the many number of ways in which the Church in Jersey was served.

Deacon Iain MacFirbhisigh commented at the time to the Jersey Evening Post: 'While we may have fewer religious sisters and brothers and priests we have more people involved in ministry than ever before in the Island. That is what the Church is supposed to be about. The Catholic laity are taking up their proper roles.'

One effect of the changes became apparent in March 2006 when a letter was handed to Catholics attending Sunday Mass. It had been signed by the chairman of the Catholic Deanery and West of Jersey finance committees, Ron Satchell, and by Catholic clergy and finance committee representatives. The letter stressed that running costs of churches should be met by parishioners in their weekly contributions to church collections and through covenants.

The letter said: *'It would be altogether wrong to seek to avoid this responsibility and instead rely on being subsidised from the patrimony we have inherited.*

'While expressing a natural loyalty to our own particular place of worship, it is important to remember that we are Catholics, not Congregationalists, and should have a Christian regard for the needs of our fellow Catholic communities in the Island, as well as a wider vision of the needs of our diocese on the mainland. We must also never forget our responsibilities for fostering and supporting missionary and Cafod projects in developing countries.'

The letter gave a picture of the then financial situation of the Catholic Church in Jersey. The sale of St Joseph's Church had raised £800,000, about half of which had been spent on St Patrick's Church and on Our Lady in St Martin. The sale of the clergy residence in Westbourne Terrace had raised around £1m, of which £750,000 was spent on repaying loans to the dioceses for the major repairs to St Mary and St Peter's Church and also on completing the renovation of the St Thomas' Presbytery as the current clergy residence. The residue of £250,000 had been designated for the restoration of St Thomas' church.

The sale of the Millbrook church, Our Lady Queen of the Universe, had raised £878,000 and although the sale of the Ville-à-l'Evêque chapel had temporarily fallen through, it would be marketed again. Money from the

Millbrook sale had been assigned firstly to the needs of the Western Catholic Parish and then to the St Thomas Restoration scheme.

The Centre parish had raised £71,000 to date in fund-raising for St Thomas' restoration and aimed to raise a further £120,000 in 2006.

Looking back ten years later on the changes from parishes to one pastoral area, Mgr France said: 'I pushed ahead with that policy – I was very conscious that we needed to share financial resources: for example, the parish priest in St Martin had £800,000 in the church bank account, because St Joseph Church had been sold, so they had less work and more money. It seemed wrong to me that at the same time the Sacred Heart parish was in debt. I wanted to be certain that if properties were to be sold in the future, then the proceeds would be shared to benefit all the Jersey Catholic churches.

'So it seemed then to make more sense for Jersey to be one parish - it was a workable arrangement. '

The plan made sense in so far that although the division of the Island into three separate parishes in 2003 was then seen as the culmination of all the previous changes, this was upset by the unforeseen departure of Fr Robin Ellwood. So, it was decided to transform the three parishes into three administrative areas: Town, East and West. The priests were working as assistants to the Dean, but were fairly free in both the East and West to do most things themselves and there were - and are - some things that are shared out between all the clergy.

Mgr France: 'It was proposed and accepted at the Diocesan Pastoral Congress in 2005 that in order to share personnel and resources more effectively parishes should come together in pastoral areas. These would then develop into a new kind of parish where clergy with different gifts and skills – and even the retired – could work together in shared ministry and mission. Because of the clearly defined geography of this Island it appeared appropriate that Jersey should be one of the first parts of the diocese to develop this new type of parish, rather than stay as three parishes in one pastoral area.

'I soon recognised that it was harder to be a parish priest of this kind of newly defined parish than being just in charge of the town. It has called for greater subsidiarity and sensitivity from me in leading this new type of team parish. In addition, I have continued with my role in both the civic and ecumenical spheres as Catholic Dean in the Island. This involves me in representative work on important Island occasions as well as being the first port of call for the media at any time. I also have diocesan commitments arising from my pastoral responsibilities.'

At the time of writing there are now no parish boundaries in Jersey, just one Island parish, administered in three areas, East, West and St Helier. The number of churches has been reduced over the years to maintaining only seven, as being sufficient to meet our liturgical and pastoral needs.

As can be seen from the 1994 Pastoral Review (Appendix C) the rationalisation of church buildings is hard to determine objectively, as parishioners are inevitably biased in favour of a place of worship long associated with themselves or their families.

One might argue that St Matthieu's church has no natural congregation as it is not situated in a village. However, it serves the north-west part of the Island, has a Catholic cemetery and is the home of the Oasis of Peace in the former Presbytery. In town, two churches are only half a mile apart, yet both are used on a daily basis. In addition to St Mary and St Peter's being used frequently by Beaulieu Convent School and occasionally by De La Salle College during weekdays, the Polish priest and the Portuguese speaking Sisters use it on many evenings, together with the Wellspring Prayer Group , outside organisations and the St Mary and St Peter's Pastoral Stewardship group.

The 1994 Review, of course, was not just about parish boundaries and church buildings. Recommendations for the development of Parish Councils were implemented as far as possible, parish catechesis – and especially school catechesis – has also developed, with many more helpers spending an hour or so regularly at States primary schools. A Youth Officer was appointed, but some years after the Report was published.

The Church in Jersey has worked closely with the States Overseas Aid Committee and has been involved in many social issues over the years. The Pastoral Centre evolved into 'Pastoral Services' – more than just a change in name, it reflected a change of emphasis from being a place to which people had to come, to a service that went out from the Church to the public. This change came in tandem with a change of personnel, leading in due to course to the present Catholic Pastoral Services office in the Welcome Centre at St Thomas', to which the St Vincent de Paul Society also moved.

The 1994 Pastoral Review report had stressed the importance of 'Mission' as opposed to 'Maintenance'. In that respect, the Church in Jersey halfway through the second decade of the 21st Century has been able to maintain many of its own buildings, but not at the expense of a sense of mission.

Only the passage of time will be able to pronounce on the continuing success, or otherwise, of both of these elements.

VIII. THE CHURCH INCLUSIVE

Chapter 19

'A TWO-TIER SOCIETY'

The Church and social exclusion

JERSEY as an Island tends to have a self-perception that at times seems Panglossian: 'everything in Jersey is wonderful because ours is the best society in all possible worlds'.

It has been a remarkably persistent view in the past, and although this might have been eroded in recent decades, the rose-tinted vision can still persist, even these days Jersey people are apt to think of their Island simply as a green and pleasant land.

It is not exactly a description which Canon Nicholas France would have recognised in the months following his arrival in the Island.

For him, his daily routine was in the seedy part of town around St Thomas' Church, the Jersey of lodging houses, bedsits and a rootless population – many of them from the big British cities and from Portugal – with more than usual susceptibility to severe social and housing problems.

Ten months after his arrival to minister in the Island, he told the JEP: 'I've had more dealings with people with social problems in Jersey than I have had anywhere else. My first funeral service in the Island was of someone who had taken a heroin overdose. Since then there have been other funerals of young people who have committed suicide.

'I've got young parishioners in prison or awaiting trial for carrying or selling drugs. Ecstasy seems to be the popular drug - maybe it's part of Jersey's culture today – get your ecstasy now. The Church's offer of ecstasy in Heaven for eternity must seem to them to be too far off and rather too remote.'

People came to the Island, he said, in search of full employment, but found that housing conditions were very poor. For the lack of housing qualifications they could never settle in the Island fully, so they were limited to living in single rooms, eating take-away food and making the pub the centre of their social lives. If they married and had children they would not be able to afford to live in the Island at all.

'Heavens above! Seems there's more than a little dust under Jersey's carpet!'

JEP cartoon by Al Thomas, 2001

At that time Jersey's Housing qualifications were only obtainable after a period of 20 years residency and he blamed these regulations for causing the Island's less well-off immigrant population to be susceptible for severe social problems.

It was hardly surprising then, he said, that some people fell for the apparent escape route of drugs. 'It's a very difficult social problem and I can see some of the personal sadness that comes from it. Of course, "ecstasy now" is not only unlawful and sometimes anti-social, but it often leads on to other problems – the death of someone living almost opposite St Thomas' Church only a week or so ago shows the danger of that.

'I've seen people around the back of St Thomas' injecting each other or themselves; it's more blatant and open than I ever expected.'

In short, he added, there was a far wider division between the 'haves' and the 'have nots' in Jersey than he had experienced in his previous parish in central Southampton.

188

In March 2004 an unprecedented open letter was signed by Church leaders and clergy in St Helier, claiming that there was still no equal society in Jersey because of the two-tier system of housing. This, they said, prevented those without qualifications using their earned income to purchase a property of their own – something that was a natural human right.

The letter was a response to the social issues and concerns raised by people who lived in town listed in the ecumenical 'Springboard Project' that had taken place the previous year.

The letter was written jointly by Canon France and by the Vicar of St Paul's Church, the Rev Paul Brooks.

They wrote: *'The Churches have listened to a wide variety of people who are "stakeholders" in St Helier. They have been inspired by what has been achieved. Yet the Church leaders now respond to all they have heard and, in certain situations, seek to be the voice of the voiceless.'*

In particular, the clergy noted that that many social problems arose from poor or inadequate housing, especially for those without housing qualifications and they questioned the lack of law to protect the unqualified from unfair rents or eviction.

The letter called for rent control for all in unqualified and rented housing, such as was already enjoyed by qualified tenants. The two-tier system led to a two-tier society, they said – something that was not good for the Island.

The letter was signed by Canon France and by the Church of England Dean of Jersey, the Very Rev John Seaford, as well as by clergy representing the Methodist, Baptist and Immanuel Churches and the Salvation Army.

The letter stated that they were 'very disturbed' by the 'apparent unjust rents inflicted on so many by landlords'. They appreciated the aim of the Housing Committee to lower the qualifying period and recognised the committee's hopes that rents would reduce as the increase in the number of properties brought about more competition. Nevertheless, they felt that there was still a serious issue that needed to be dealt with as soon as possible.

The letter said that a difficult home life affected health, education, use of drugs and alcohol and that poor housing often led many adults living in one-room accommodation to seek out the social community of the pub, 'where excessive alcohol or the sharing of drugs can be seen as an escape from boredom and lack of home life'.

Among other concerns detailed were the spilling out into the street at night of anti-social, noisy and sometimes aggressive behaviour, the recent spate of redundancies across the Island and the five-year rule that barred certain jobs to newcomers.

The letter concluded: 'It is essential that these issues and concerns be considered and debated in our town and Island, especially by our elected politicians.'

Chapter 20

HOME FROM HOME?

Jersey and its immigrant and migrant workers

FOR centuries the wheels of the Island's economy have been greased by the efforts of migrant workers. Up until the mid-20th Century, these were mainly French people from Normandy and Brittany who came as farm workers and domestic servants. It is because of this French influence on the Island that so many Catholic churches were needed around the Island and so many French clergy were posted to Jersey.

Although many of this French population returned home to France in due course, be it after one or two potato seasons or after having spent years in the Island, others stayed on. The more industrious bought smallholdings, worked them and became assimilated within the Island's farming community.

In more modern times, easier and cheaper transportation attracted workers from further afield. In the years following the Second World War there was an influx from Italy to work in Jersey's burgeoning tourism industry. In the same way as the French workers of previous generations, those who stayed became fully assimilated in Island life, in which many of them have since played a full and distinguished part.

By the 1970s Portuguese workers, many of them from Madeira, were coming to Jersey to work, as improving economic conditions, thanks to EEC funding in France, particularly in the hitherto depressed area of Brittany, meant that fewer French workers were coming to Jersey to work.

The Portuguese element in Jersey society has increased over the years until at the time of writing some 10 per cent of Jersey's population is of Portuguese origin. Most latterly, once again because of improving economic conditions in Portugal, the Island has sought workers from eastern Europe, particularly from Poland and, most lately, Romania. There is also now an element of Kenyan and Filipino Catholics working in the Island.

In 2005, Muslims in Jersey were invited to use the Community Centre at St Thomas for Friday prayers, daily during Ramadan. This continued

191

until, with some assistance from the Catholic Dean, they secured the former Methodist chapel in Aquila Road to be their mosque.

Both Portuguese and Polish Catholics have brought with them their own national religious traditions. A visit to Christmas Midnight Mass at St Thomas' – so much a part of the Portuguese celebrations of Christmas – might give the impression that the church is located in Funchal or Lisbon, so tightly packed is it by the predominantly Portuguese congregation. Classes for children intending to take Holy Communion and Confirmation at St Thomas' are also predominantly filled by young Portuguese.

In May 1979 over 2,000 members of the local Portuguese community paraded through the streets of St Helier behind the Roman Catholic Bishop of Madeira, Bishop Francisco Antunes Santana, when he made his first visit to the Island.

Statue of Our Lady of Fatima brought to St Thomas'
by the Portuguese community

He first blessed a statue to Our Lady of Fatima that had been bought from the £1,000 plus raised by members of the Portuguese community especially for the occasion. The short blessing was performed before the altar at St Mary and St Peter's.

The statue was then carried aloft in a procession to St Thomas' where it was installed before Mass, conducted by the Bishop, accompanied by two Portuguese priests and Mgr Raymond Lawrence, who represented the Portsmouth Diocese. The church was crowded for the Portuguese service.

St Thomas', since its restoration (as recorded elsewhere in this book), has Lady chapels dedicated to Our Lady of Lourdes and to Our Lady of Fatima and a shrine to Our Lady of Czstochowa.

All the various migrant nationalities have been almost always Catholic in their faith. French and French-speaking clergy were easily available for the French immigrants but the same could not be said in more modern times for the Portuguese and for Polish Catholics when they first arrived.

For ten years the Portuguese community in Jersey had its own non-territorial parish: Our Lady of Fatima. On the arrival of Canon Nicholas France, he was informed that the priest of this parish, Fr Philip Doyle CSSP, who had been a missionary priest in Brazil and was fluent in Portuguese, would continue in place so that there would be little for him to do. It was, he joked, a comforting thought, since his own Portuguese did not exist much beyond 'Mateus Rosé'.

However, within weeks of his arrival in Jersey in late 1999, Fr Doyle left Jersey to take up an appointment in Australia, leaving the non-Portuguese-speaking Canon France to minister to the Portuguese population. At this time, the separate Portuguese parish lapsed and was integrated within the other Catholic parishes, now the one Pastoral Area.

In July 2000 he told the Jersey Evening Post: 'We haven't done enough as a Catholic community to integrate the Portuguese in our parishes and to help those who speak very limited English to feel at home here. In many ways, their Catholicism, which is part of their traditional culture in Madeira, hasn't transplanted so well to Jersey. Their faith was part of their own culture and it's not part of their culture here. That has to be damaging for them. It means a personal or social dislocation in their lives and as everywhere where the world of work takes over from the world of faith, ultimately it is dehumanising.'

A quest to find a permanent Portuguese-speaking priest for Jersey has been a constant - and at the time of writing in 2016 - still an unfulfilled quest.

The first attempt was for Bishop Hollis to ask Portuguese Bishops at the European Synod in 2000 if a Portuguese priest could be made available. Canon France also hoped that Portuguese religious sisters might be able to help. But only temporary solutions were available: a priest from Madeira came for a few weeks; a Brazilian student nearing ordination came for another nine months – it seemed there were only stop-gap solutions available.

Dom Januário Torgal Ferreira

In April 2004 Canon France travelled to Portugal to meet the Portuguese Bishop responsible for the country's migrants, Dom Januário Torgal Ferreira, and had discussions with him at the Shrine of Fatima about the pastoral needs of the Portuguese community in Jersey. He also made a request for a Portuguese priest to come to work in Jersey as part of the parish team. It was one of many appeals that ultimately have been unsuccessful. The difficulty, he was told, was the lack of clergy in Portuguese dioceses.

Dom Januario made a reciprocal visit to the Island in December 2004, to discuss with the Portuguese Catholic community how best their pastoral needs could be met and in subsequent years Don Januario has come to Jersey each June to confirm Portuguese children and adults.

During a Mass at St Thomas, he watched 73 children being enrolled in the preparation programme for First Communion; 61 of them were Portuguese.

A visit to Jersey by the Bishop of Funchal in October 2010, António José Cavaco Carrilho for the Festa of Our Lady of Fatima also produced no answer to the question of the lack of a Portuguese priest. He explained that he could only ask for priests to volunteer to come to Jersey he could not order them to come- and no one had responded to his invitation.

In early 2016 there are still only stop-gap solutions available, but at the time of writing at least two Sisters of the Order of Christ of Bethany, arrived from Portugal to help in the Jersey Ministry to Portuguese speakers.

In recent years a fine Filippino choir, comprising professional workers on contract to Jersey companies, has graced the Sunday evening liturgies at St Thomas'.

—ooo000ooo—

Writing in the Jersey Evening Post in March 2008 on the theme of migrant workers in Jersey, Nicholas France wrote: 'We're all Islanders. As a newcomer myself, I have readily identified with my fellow immigrants, especially as most were Catholic. ..

'...While discerning why people want to come here, I also try to understand the mixed feelings of Jersey folk, who fear that those who come may only want to take and not to give in return.

'...Many immigrants are not well educated, struggle with English and are resigned to taking the jobs and working hours that Islanders don't want to accept. They often have to live in poor accommodation. Sometimes that may seem their fault, as they wish to put their money into buying or building a house at home in Madeira or Poland. Others, however, feel impotent in dealing with remote landlords who ignore their complaints about damp walls and ceilings, overcrowded lodging houses and shared bathrooms for children and adults who are strangers. My plea since coming to Jersey is for better regulation of conditions and pricings for those without qualifications. I am told it is far too difficult to regulate. That I find hard to accept.

'Another negative phenomenon associated with poor housing is parents limiting themselves to one child – often over-indulged – in an attempt to compensate for the long, sometimes too long hours the parents work.

Family life in Jersey is often under great strain…..

'…Those who lose or fail to value their own culture and identity are often attracted by the worst aspects of Jersey life and are corrupted by the easy access to drugs, alcohol and casual, uncommitted sex. These may bring about marriage and family break-up or the misuse of drugs and drink, often leading to a spell in La Moye prison, where I recognise many faces…

'…For me, our immigrants are the poor of Jersey… Many are poor in terms of education, parenting skills and isolated from family support and faith traditions. You can be materially rich but spiritually poor. As a body needs a heart, so this Island needs a soul. In vain will be Jersey's continued growth in material prosperity, unless we build up its soul in family, social and spiritual values. This is a societal duty. We must all accept responsibility for it.

'Pope John Paul II said that the measure of a society is how it treats its weakest members. I am in no doubt that pre-eminent among those who fulfil that description are the unskilled, residentially unqualified immigrants with poor English, who continue to flock to our Island to do the jobs that we don't want to do ourselves.'

—ooo000ooo—

It was to help Portuguese-speakers – and other nationalities - whose English-speaking skills were negligible that the Welcome Centre was created beside St Thomas', as is detailed elsewhere in this book.

'I was not sure it would all work out,' Nicholas France said, 'but actually it worked out very well'. The principal of Highlands College, Professor Dr Ed Sallis, was very pleased to use this as a base from which people could learn English.'

The Welcome Centre was praised by the then Conservative cabinet minister and party co-chairman, Sayeeda Baroness Warsi, in a speech made to the Catholic Bishops ' Social Action Conference in April 2011. She gave the project as one of three examples of what the Church was doing at a local level to improve people's lives around the world. The two other examples she gave were in New York and Vienna, places rather different from Jersey.

—ooo000ooo—

Apart from Polish soldiers who stayed in Jersey for a few years after the Occupation to help with a new fight for them - the repulsion of the Colorado beetle from the Island's early potato crop - the first Polish workers in modern times to come to work in Jersey were sourced by the Jersey Farmers Union. A JFU delegation visited Poland late in 1999 and early in 2000 the first party of workers arrived in Jersey in the cold darkness of a January morning. Soon, more and more Poles arrived in Jersey, their presence encouraged by a liberalisation of laws regarding entitlement to work in Jersey.

The pastoral needs of Polish immigrants have been easier to meet. The first Polish priest in Jersey was Fr Piotr ('Peter') Glas, who came to Jersey in late 2002 as assistant priest to Nicholas France and subsequently became the priest for the west of the Island.

He grew up near Krakow in southern Poland and after ordination was one of the country's first military chaplains after Poland threw off Communism. He was later sent to the UK to help the large Polish communities who had settled there, working in Manchester and Southampton for ten years before joining the Diocese of Portsmouth and being sent to Jersey by Bishop Hollis.

Soon after his arrival, Polish Masses began in the Island, with special Easter and Christmas services filling St Thomas' to overflowing. There were then some 1,600 Polish workers in the Island; by the following year the number had increased to 2,500 and it continued to rise.

The death of Pope John-Paul II 2005 was perhaps felt most keenly by his Polish compatriots. He died on a Saturday evening; the following morning services of all denominations paused to pay tribute to the deceased Pontiff.

The Island's Polish community mourned the loss of their 'greatest Pole'; a special Polish Mass was held a week later; meanwhile a service of remembrance was held at St Matthieu's on the day following his death. A Book of Remembrance was opened at St Thomas'.

The church was opened until 1am on the day of his death as a steady stream of people descended on the church to pray and mourn the loss of the Pope. Flags around the Island were ordered to be flown at half-mast. At Mass at St Thomas' the following morning, two female police officers who issued nine parking tickets to cars parked improperly at the curb of Val Plaisant were chased off by angry mourners, who vented their frustration by shouting at the officers and thumping the patrol car as they fled.

Nicholas France had been presented to the Pope on one occasion when he had been the chaplain (personal secretary) to Bishop Derek Worlock and the Pope was the Archbishop of Krakow, Cardinal Karol Wojtila. He had attended over five years the 'Council of Laity' in Rome at which the English Bishop and Polish Archbishop were both 'consultors'.

When the Pope made his state visit to Britain in 1982, Nicholas France was the assistant master of ceremonies at the Mass held at Wembley Stadium.

He said at the time of his death that the Pontiff had 'shown us how to live and how to die'.

In 2006 a second Polish priest came to Jersey on a two-year secondment from his home Archdiocese of Krakow, Fr Marcin Drabik. He was an acquaintance of Fr Glas and in fact stayed for nearly four years, not only overseeing the Polish community but also the Catholic Church in the East of the Island. Some 200 people attended a concert held at St Patrick's to say goodbye to him. He was succeeded in 2010 by Fr Jan Swiatek, the first priest sent to the Island from the Polish Catholic Mission.

By now, regular Polish Masses at both St Thomas' and St Mary and St Peter's were attracting congregations of around 400 and it was supposed that the number would have been ever greater if many would-be churchgoers had not been prevented from attending by their working hours. At Easter time hundreds of young Polish worshippers have come to church to enact the ancient Polish tradition of *wi conka* – the blessing of baskets of special Easter food - one of the many traditional Polish Catholic customs that Jersey's Polish priests have introduced for their nationals in the Island.

Speaking at the time of his visit to Jersey to rededicate St Thomas', Cardinal Cormac Murphy O'Connor said that he believed Jersey could be an example to other places in the way that it had assimilated its migrant workers.

This might have been demonstrated by a Requiem Mass held at St Thomas' in April 2010 to mourn the death in an air crash of Poland's president, Lech Kaczynski and his wife, as well as the plane's passengers: high-ranking officials, public figures and aircrew. The Polish community in Jersey gathered in its hundreds for the service.

Nicholas France commented afterwards that it was very interesting to see how, in ten years, a new community could be born in Jersey with such a powerful identity as the Jersey-Polish community.

Unfortunately, the peaceful nature of life in Jersey was horribly marred by a knife attack on a Sunday afternoon in August 2011 that killed six people of Polish origin. Three of the murder victims were children; all of them were under six; one of them was 18 months old. The accused was a 30-year-old Polish man, who killed his wife, two children, father in law, a women friend of his wife and the friend's own child.

Afterwards he attempted but failed to knife himself, but was taken under police guard to hospital. He was named as Damian Rzeszowski, who had lived in Jersey for ten years. Friends described him as having been suicidal in recent weeks.

The killer worked as a block layer on building sites and was said by workmates to be a clean-living man, not into drink or drugs, who did everything for his family; a reliable person, and often seen shopping with his children in the supermarket.

The attack happened, incongruously, as St Helier was celebrating its first Polish festival and as news of the attack spread, a book of condolence was opened at the Town Hall; it was moved to St Thomas' four days later.

This tragic event attracted media attention from all over the world, and as Catholic Dean and parish priest, Monsignor France was asked to comment. He always gave the same response on behalf of the Catholic community in Jersey: that this was not only a tragedy for a particular family and for the Island's Polish community, but also a wound felt by the whole Island.

A special Requiem Mass for those who had lost their lives, for the bereaved and for peace and harmony in the Island was celebrated by him and by the Island's acting Polish priest, Fr Stanislaw Adamiak the following Thursday at St Thomas' and attended by the Bailiff, Michael Birt, the Island's Chief Minister, Senator Terry Le Sueur, the Anglican Dean of Jersey, the Very Rev Bob Key among other Island officials. Some 1,000 people crowded into the church; every seat, aisle and doorway was occupied.

In his homily, Nicholas France said: 'We can learn what we may have taken so often for granted – namely, the relative harmony in Jersey between people of different language groups and faith. From this week, let us recommit ourselves to valuing the gift of human life and the respect that we should always show one another, whether we are Jersey-born or come from other countries.'

Chapter 21

THE CHURCH AND YOUNG PEOPLE

TO ignore or downplay the distasteful subject of child abuse or to evade giving this subject - currently the stuff, tragically, of so many headlines - its proper prominence would be wrong. Once upon a time, a Catholic priest would have been seen by most people – Catholic or otherwise - as an ideal guardian or instructor of a child; sadly, even though the abuse has been committed by half of one per cent of Catholic clergy, that confidence no longer exists as cleric after cleric in country after country makes news and besmirches the Church by his actions.

In November 2000 an apology on behalf of the Roman Catholic Church was made by Bishop Hollis in relation to victims of child abuse in a pastoral letter to the diocese, which was read out in churches.

Referring to publicity attracted by the Diocese of Cardiff and in a Panorama television programme, he said: 'There is a perception, largely outside the community of the Church, that we do not provide a safe environment for children. We know that it is not true, but the perception is there because of the evil and highly publicised actions of a few, among who are to be found priests, religious and lay people. Their actions have been a tragedy for us and for their victims and they shame us deeply. ..

'We cannot undo the past, but we can make absolutely sure that we do our best to help restore lives that have been shattered in this way. Most importantly, we have to do everything we can to make sure that these things do not happen again and cannot happen in our community.'

In Jersey, there has been no incidence of clerical child abuse and at the time of writing, when new cases of child abuse or historical child abuse in the UK seem to be reported on every news broadcast, it is at the forefront of Island clergy's minds to ensure that any such case does not happen in the Island.

The manager of Catholic Pastoral Services, Delia Hardiman, said: 'We know we have a duty to value all people and therefore to support them and protect them from harm. Over the years we have been fortunate to have large numbers of dedicated volunteers, enabling us to provide carefully planned activities for children, young people and adults; we support families under stress.

'We know that all clergy and lay people working within all these varied ministries need to provide a safe environment for all, one that promotes and supports their well-being. This now includes carefully selecting and appointing those who work with children, young people or vulnerable adults and responding robustly where concerns arise.'

'In Jersey we appoint a safeguarding representative for each church and have an overall Island Safeguarding Officer. We also employ an administrator to collate and action all paperwork, providing support to representatives. She has responsibility for promoting good and safe practice in all activities involving children, young people and vulnerable adults within the parish.'

'All churches and faith communities are now expected to have in place arrangements that enable safe recruitment procedures, protecting all – the young, the vulnerable, the elderly, as well as priests, deacons and religious.'

'Jersey follows rigorously the Safeguarding policy of the Catholic Diocese of Portsmouth.'

Over ten years from 2003 Mary Cahill was 'Youth Ministry Co-Ordinator' for the Catholic Church in Jersey, a title chosen to emphasise the fact that 'youth work' is 'youth ministry' work. She said: 'In my years of working in the Church I have seen many major changes and initiatives to improve safeguarding the young and vulnerable.

'A very different approach is apparent: there are many more professional guidelines in place. I am one of a team of trained facilitators for training all our volunteers to be aware of safe practice as well as how to recognise abuse or cope with disclosures in a clear and unwavering manner.'

'There is a dedicated employed person employed at Diocesan level as well as many dedicated and trained volunteers in each worshiping community to be vigilant and present in ensuring safeguarding guidelines are adhered to and followed through. There are very clearly defined routes of enquiry and systems in place to protect both our clergy, volunteers and of course the young and vulnerable members of our church family. All in our communities are called to a high level of good practice and care.'

—ooo000ooo—

TURNING to the subject of Catholic Youth Formation in the Island, the first mention, apart from the founding of Le Cercle St Thomas in the 1870s (see page 274 - 275) was the Catholic Boys Brigade in 1905. Catholic Scout troops and Cub packs were formed in the three main parishes after the First World War as well as a joint company for girls from both St Thomas' and St Mary and St Peter.

St Thomas' Sports Club was started in 1946 Père Pierre Jort, who had then just taken over from Père Maré as Rector, with the help of Mr Robert and Mr Aubert. The club rooms were at St Mary House, Roussel Street and the club had a large following, coming to an end only in the 1960s. Its treasurer, then president, was the late Bernard Holley, who recalled the annual summer fête that took place on the last Thursday of August each year in the grounds at Summerland. It was organised by John Etienne for nearly 30 years and generally included a spectacular gymnastics display.

The Church Scout Troop at St Thomas was re-started after the war. The 3rd Jersey- St. Thomas Troop was a land Troop which lasted until the mid-1960s. In the early to mid-1970s the Jersey Scout Association decided to resurrect the Troop again but this time as a Sea Scout Unit. It was very successful, so much so, that it was over-subscribed on the opening nights and this put pressure on the existing Leaders to find extra adult helpers for the Troop, Unfortunately their efforts were unsuccessful and although they struggled on for a while it was a difficult and unsustainable situation and eventually the Troop closed down. In the early 1970s, Canon Arthur Olney was given diocesan funding for a Youth Officer and in the same era, the curate at St Mary and St Peter's at the time, Fr Francis Isherwood, initiated the 'Revolution Club' (or 'the Rev' as it was familiarly called).

A Catholic Youth Group was initiated in the mid-1970s by a group of young people including Marta Pugsley, Joanna Little and Gio Pollano among them. Fr Colin Ward of St Patrick's Parish was very supportive of the group. They formed a music group – guitarists and singers – who would visit churches on Sundays to sing at Masses – something that was considered to be quite novel at the time - and produced a bulletin for young people, titled 'Reach Out', written mainly by Karen Blampied.

They also organised a youth pilgrimage every year from town to the chapel on top of La Hougue Bie, Notre Dame de la Clarté, where a Mass was celebrated. The 'Pilgrimage of Light' took place on or near to

8 September, the Feast of Our Lady and it was held for some six years before the group ceased its regular activities.

Over the years there were various other initiatives: there was an active youth group at St Matthieu during the 1980s and there were not too successful attempts to form a parish youth assembly in the early years of the present Century.

In August 2005 a group of 22 young Islanders all aged between 16 and 25 attended a Mass by Pope Benedict XVI in Cologne as part of the 20th World Youth Day. They were accompanied by Nicholas France and four Jersey lay helpers.

The leader was Mary Cahill. They took part in a three-day festival of music, discussion and worship.

Nicholas France said afterwards: 'It was a challenge for me at the age of 62 to sleep on a gym floor during the week in our host village, before enduring a cold night under the stars with 800,000 others on sleeping bags, side by side in the festival field, in preparation for the Papal Mass on the Sunday, where we saw Pope Benedict.'

On their return to Jersey, Mary Cahill took over the role of 'Youth Ministry Co-Ordinator' and has since received a national award for her work.

This trip was the genesis of what has become the Jersey Association of Catholic Youth (JACY). The young people who returned to Jersey were responding to Pope Benedict, who wanted to 'share what they had received'. Aged 15 to 30 they wanted to deepen faith and share prayer as well as to socialise and reach out to others. Since then the association has spread out as an umbrella to develop many opportunities for children, young people and young adults.

The following year, in April 2006, Fr Piotr (Peter) Glas led a pilgrimage of young people aged between 15 and 29 to Taizé. JACY went on to send pilgrims to Taizé again in 2007 and 2009 as well as a group of 42 to World Youth Day in Sydney, Australia, in 2008. They also attended WYD Madrid in 2011 and are currently preparing for WYD Krakow 2016. Young Catholics travelled to London in 2010 to see the Pope, chaperoned by the then Catholic Pastoral Services administrator, Maureen Corrigan and led by Mary Cahill and Joe Richardson (a JACY young leader). Beaulieu School had three students at St Mary's College for the 'Big Assembly' gathering and Jersey sent eight young people to attend the Mass at

Westminster Cathedral and then to the event at Hyde Park that was termed 'Glastonbury with God' by the media. Christopher Anderson, then aged 16, was selected to be in a group of youngsters on the steps of the cathedral and was pictured in the group that met the Pope.

In 2010 twice as many young people as in 2009 registered for Confirmation classes – more than 140.

JACY's base is the 'Youth Room' at St Thomas' Hall, known as 'the Upper Room'. Monthly groups for young people have been created, and have helped to draw in more young people, who meet and work in their local worshipping communities.

JACY offers opportunities under its umbrella for young people to be part of the Youth St Vincent de Paul Association, a national organisation that helps young people put faith and concern into action for people in need. The Jersey members visit the elderly residents at Jeanne Jugan House, they collect food for the needy, run a children's church faith sharing group, and do such projects as collecting shopping vouchers for families in need. So much interest was generated that two more YVSP groups were formed at Beaulieu and De La Salle Schools.

A Youth 2000 group celebrates a monthly 'Sleepover with God' at the Oasis of Peace: they share faith, relax for supper and keep an all-night prayer vigil as well as meeting weekly for the 15-30 age group.

In short, JACY has stood for 'sharing, faith, friendship, food and fun'.

Following the appointment of Mary Cahill to undertake a new ministry for marriage and family life in the Island, Sarah Wakeling was appointed as the next co-ordinator for youth ministry. Sarah was one of the original young people attending world youth days in Cologne in 2005. A mass of dedication took place for Mary and Sarah in their new roles in St Thomas in September 2015.

Jersey Catholics queuing for the Public Gallery of the States Chamber to listen to a States debate on funding for Catholic education. Pictured ninth from the right is the is the young Francis Hamon, later to be Deputy Bailiff.

Chapter 22

A CATHOLIC EDUCATION

There have always been continuing problems with providing an affordable Catholic education in Jersey

THE education of young people has been a major concern of the Church since the a very early period of its ministry, especially when Christian priests and other Religious tended to be the only literate people in an illiterate society. The Channel Islands' first schools were established, for example, in the 6th Century.

Making a small jump from then to Victorian time, the Belgian priest, Père Jean-François Volkeryk, brought the *Dames de St André* from Bruges in 1860 to provide free education for poor girls.

In 1864, St Mary and St Peter's was the only real Catholic school in the Island, but between that date and the Education Act of 1899, the *Dames de St André*, with the cooperation of the Rector of St Thomas', built nine primary schools for the French-speaking children of Jersey. These schools cost their builders some £60,000.

French Jesuits flocked to Jersey to escape the anti-clerical laws of the secular French state. As detailed in this book in the chapter on the Jesuits in Jersey, they turned what is now the Hotel de France and Highlands College into training colleges and functioned successfully in the Island until the post-war decades, although these establishments were not for local school-children.

French De La Salle Brothers came to the Island in 1866. They departed again after a spat with the Oblates in 1896, but returned in 1917 and a year later the school that would evolve into De La Salle College came into existence.

After the passing of the New Act in 1899, a UK Schools Inspector visited all the Catholic schools. He passed St Mary and St Peter's as efficient, and eligible for a grant. The French schools were given only a month's notice of their examination under the English Code, but two girls' schools were declared 'efficient'. The rest were told to re-staff with English-certificated teachers, which they did, and were then passed as 'efficient'. But none of the former French schools were made eligible for a grant.

A large amount of opposition seems to have been stirred against them at this time because of the then prevalent anti-French feeling. When they did apply for a grant, a new *Projet du Loi* was passed to the States on 13 February 1900 limiting the grant to those schools only which had been receiving it at the end of September 1899, and stating that in any school eligible for a grant, religious instruction should be limited to the reading and explanation of the Bible.

It was against this harsh discriminatory measure that the Catholic clergy and the *Dames de St André* made their first Petition to the Privy Council, to prevent the Royal Assent being given to the States *Projet*. The Petition failed, however, for the law was confirmed on 28 December 1901.

The year 1906 was a controversial moment for Catholic education in the Island and a year of upheaval for Catholic schools. The relationship between the Catholic Church and the States worsened further as the States passed a measure taking control of all primary schools. All tuition had to be in English with French as a secondary language and the teachers were required to have the English Teaching Certificate.

In addition, fines would be imposed on parents who sent their children to Catholic schools that did not meet these guidelines.

In 1909, a new Education Act was mooted, the scope of which was to put the Education Committee in complete control of all the elementary schools in the Island, especially as to the nomination of teachers, and at the same time raising the school-leaving age to 14. Schools that did not come into the scheme were to be deprived of all grants and could be closed more or less arbitrarily. A great storm arose in the media of the day over the centralising of control, and especially over the clause concerning the teaching of religion in the schools. This, if given by the teachers, must only consist of the reading and explanation of the Bible, with no Catechism or religious instruction pertaining to any denomination, though ministers of religion were to be given the right of entry for this purpose.

In 1912, the 'Law on Public Instruction' was passed, despite petitions to the Privy Council and delegations to it by Bishop Cotter and the Bailiff, Sir William Venables Vernon.

On 23 December the States announced that the country Catholic primary schools would close that day and not be re-opened. The new law allowed for a Priest to teach Catechism classes to Catholic children in the schools, but only between 9.15 and 9.45am.

Thus, at one stroke, the Catholic schools that had been built and run for a number of years ceased to exist as such and were eventually closed completely, with the exception of two of the Town schools, which remained open and working, but on definitely non-denominational lines, as laid down in the Law.

There were further petitions and further acrimony between the Church and the States. Then the First World War started, altering people's sense of priorities. With the advent of peace, a further petition lodged au Greffe on 17 February 1920, was signed by Canon John Hourigan on behalf of Bishop Cotter, protesting against the new law, but that likewise had no effect.

Since that time, the provision of a free Catholic education in the Island has always been something of a problem - Jersey was to become the only place in the British Isles where a free Catholic education was unavailable.

The States decision to take control of primary education mirrored a parallel contention in the mainland UK. There, the Methodist lobby declared: 'We don't want Rome on the rates and we should do away with all religious schools.' However, in the UK the Anglicans and Catholics fought and won that battle, while in Jersey, it was the Methodist lobby that won.

A more positive development was the arrival in Jersey in 1911 of the Sisters of the Faithful Companions of Jesus. Their teaching nuns had the right English certificates and they took over the two Jersey schools at St Matthieu and David Place from the *Dames de St André* as well as opening a boarding school at 'Bagatelle'.

Beaulieu Convent, then occupied by 'the Helpers of the Holy Souls' was also available for supplementary classes and tuition and in 1952 it was re-opened by Sisters of the Order of the Immaculate Conception of St Méen Le Grand.

Thus, although Catholic primary schools were secularised, the Religious Orders helped out by providing what they could.

Education was both fee-paying and non-fee paying. At the FCJ Convent in David Place, there were effectively two schools: an 'upstairs' fee-paying school, where the girls wore white gloves and straw hats in summer – and a 'downstairs' school for girls whose parents could not afford to pay fees. One might say that the rich were robbed to pay the poor. Similar arrangements happened at De La Salle College.

The system was possible because sisters and brothers did all the teaching; they didn't have any salary and thus everything could be ploughed back into the school.

After the Occupation and in the 1950s there were many protests by parents about the difficulty in securing an affordable Catholic education for their children. In 1953 the newly-formed Jersey Catholic Association felt that the field of Catholic education should be the place for a concentrated effort on its part.

Under the chairmanship of Leonard Du Feu, the central committee of the Jersey Catholic Association researched the history of Catholic schools in Jersey and ways in which the situation could be improved.

In a manner that seem familiar to other, more recent areas of public debate and discussion, there then ensued a period of a few years in which took place Special General meetings, an inter-denominational conference, a formal interview with the Public Instruction Committee, memoranda, a falling out between Catholics and Free Churches, the setting up of a Joint Standing Committee... much sound and fury, but little or nothing achieved in the way of progress.

A petition for help for States help for Catholic independent schools was collected in 1956 with over 2,700 signatures (who were limited to parents of children of or under school age). It was presented to the States on 1 June by the Catholic States' Member, Deputy George Troy, and referred to the Education Committee.

It had two main points:

(1) To re-group certain of the Infant and Junior children attending the States primary schools in St Helier and St Saviour so that the school buildings owned by the Catholic Church in St Helier (and used since 1912 by the Education Committee without payment or compensation to the owners) should become denominational schools for Catholic children;

(2) Parents of Catholic children over the age of 11 be given the option of sending their children to one of the existing Catholic Private Schools, with the cost and conditions of doing this to be the subject of negotiation between the States and Governing Bodies of the schools concerned.

The following year (1957) Canon Arthur Olney, writing in the June edition of the JCR, introduced a new scheme: 'As many people as possible should lend a little money to the JCA Educational Fund, free of interest. They would be able to get back their money whenever they wished, but the Fund, not themselves, would get the bank interest on it. We say "a little money", although "a little" in the case of a rich man would amount to a good sum. But so would a pound or two each from a thousand people; and some could afford to lend £5 or £10 or £20.

'Not that *gifts* would be ruled out. And the advantage of giving is that you can give less than £1 and can give more than once. Nothing would be refused in the way of a gift – even coppers – although, to save labour in accountancy, loans must be at least £1.

'So much for raising the money. On what would it be spent? The spending would be done by the Central Committee of the JCA, but the most likely object at the beginning would be to make grants to existing Catholic schools – The Beeches, the two Convents, the Sacred Heart School – to help them with the building of new classrooms, the equipment of labs, furnishing, the salaries of lay teachers etc. This sounds ambitious, but we must remember that in many parts of the world not only all these things, but the whole cost of school buildings in the first place has been raised by the efforts of the faithful... and Jersey is a prosperous Island.'

Within four weeks a total of £1,657 was donated to the new fund after which the total continued to climb, although slowly. Six months later, £5,121 had been collected and a further £2,378 in interest-free loans.

The States debated the first section of the Catholic petition in February 1958 but did not vote on it, although it gave the Catholic community grounds for optimism. This was followed by further meetings between the Catholic delegation to the States (Senators Troy and Rumfitt, Canon Olney, Brother Elwin from De La Salle and the president of the Jersey Catholic Association, C J Dupré) and the Education Committee.

A second debate was held in March 1959. The result came as something of 'a rude shock', according to the following month's article in the *Jersey Catholic Record*: 'We were under the impression that what we had pressed for was two Catholic primary schools. After the Debate in February 1958, and once the Education Committee recommended it, we thought it would go through.'

The second part of the petition (for grants to parents towards school fees) was also debated – and voted upon – and defeated by 29 votes to 20. It was noted that the Constables voted practically en bloc against the motion, but not one them contributed to the debate.

'Most evidently, Heaven must have other plans for us,' mourned the *Jersey Catholic Record*.

A proud moment for Sister Loretta the headmistress.

It was in 1964 that a law to provide some financial help for independent schools was finally passed.

In 1971, the new FCJ Convent School at Grainville was inaugurated by Cardinal Heenan, Archbishop of Westminster. In his speech, he asked for more States support for the Jersey Catholic schools: FCJ, Beaulieu and De La Salle – something that happened only gradually over the years.

Catholic education remained a big preoccupation for Canon David Mahy. In May 1978 Catholic parents were handed a questionnaire in church, asking if they wanted a Catholic primary education for their children. It was the same story as ever: it was stated by Canon Mahy that States aid to the schools should be increased.

In July 1984 he wrote to Bishop Emery asking for money in the form of a Diocesan Levy to keep the Jersey Catholic schools going, but only received an equally hard-luck letter back saying how difficult it was in England:

'In our Diocese we have more Independent Schools than in any other Dioceses in England and Wales…. This means that a very large number of parents are paying full fees for their children's education, and in the case of Secondary Schools, a majority. In some cases, but not all, the parents do not have a choice of a Maintained School. They would be delighted to have the Jersey system of a 50 per cent or 25 per cent subsidy on fees. There are many parishes without a Catholic Voluntary Primary School and they get no grant from the Diocese or elsewhere towards the fees at Catholic Independent Schools.

'Another important factor is that Jersey Deanery will be receiving proportionately a greater benefit from the Levy by way of interest-free loans than most other Deaneries in the diocese. Indeed, Jersey will be receiving a much greater amount than it is contributing to the Fund. '

He added what he said was a comment 'tongue in cheek': 'The Diocese would be much better off if Jersey paid no levy and became self-financing.'

Cardinal Basil Hume visited the Island in 1988 and celebrated Mass in the grounds of Beaulieu School and presided at evening prayer in the grounds of FCJ, just yards from where Cardinal Heenan had laid the foundation school of what would be the new FCJ Convent School. The evening prayer, followed by Benediction, was attended by clergy and laity from many Island churches.

The 1994 Jersey Catholic Pastoral Review summarised the position of Catholic education in Jersey:

'There are no Voluntary Aided Schools in Jersey, so the majority of Catholic children are educated in the States schools. The Roman Catholic Church has a right to go into States Primary Schools to provide catechesis for Catholic children....

Head teachers are very aware of the divisive nature of Independent education and make every effort to accommodate the needs of the local community. They are conscious of the large percentage of children who have to attend the State Schools. The number of Catholic children in each school reflects the commitment and sacrifices parents are prepared to make for a Catholic education. Many others would like to do the same but simply cannot afford it. Many parents from other Christian traditions apply for places at the Catholic schools where they hope to find support for sound Christian values.'

The report also mentioned the assisted Places Scheme that had been established with the support of Bishop Emery during the 1980s to give financial assistance to practising Catholic families who were anxious for their children to be educated at a Catholic school.

Quoting from the report: *'It aims to concentrate funds on primary education in order to educate as many children as possible within a Catholic environment. Usually an agreed contribution is made by the parents. The schools meet one half of authorised grants and the rest is paid by the Scheme. The Scheme's income is from termly collections and agreed contributions from each parish, a grant from the Jersey Catholic Education Fund and private donations. Personal contact is essential to maintain lay involvement and support.*

'A panel of 4 people deals in confidence with applications. A financial statement is required. Priority is based on need and families are interviewed as and when required.'

The Assisted Places Scheme still existed at the beginning of the 21st Century. The Catholic Dean, Canon France, was not particularly comfortable with its existence. He said: 'Gradually people seemed to stop applying for places. Then FCJ felt that the Scheme should be administered by the school itself and not by the Church. We said that it would be improper to collect the money and then hand it to the school to administer. I was not very comfortable with the whole system – and much preferred to put available money into catechetics. In the end, we pulled the plug on the scheme, especially as no parents were now applying for it. It also appeared invidious to be taking this Collection in churches like St Thomas' where hardly any children benefitted from the income.

'I suppose I was influenced by the fact that 80 per cent of our confirmation candidates don't go to Catholic schools, anyway and perhaps 90 per cent of Catholic children don't go to Catholic schools.'

All three Catholic private schools – FCJ, Beaulieu and De La Salle – have now established their own bursary schemes.

De La Salle headmaster John Sankey, on his retirement as Head in August 2000, said: 'In 1960, church schools were regarded as, at best, an irrelevance; now we are welcomed and valued as part of the Jersey family of schools.'

But at the time of writing in 2016, there still remains no free Catholic education in the Island – although Mgr France still lobbies for this with States of Jersey Education Ministers.

X. THE PAST, PRESENT AND FUTURE

Canon David Mahy, Catholic Dean Emeritus of Jersey

Chapter 23

CLOSING THE SECOND MILLENIUM

By Canon David Mahy, Catholic Dean Emeritus of Jersey

THE year was 1960. The day was 15 July, the Feast of St Swithun, Bishop of Winchester - an annual celebration day in the parish where I arrived as the newly ordained junior assistant priest.

It was an exciting time in the Church. A new Pope had been elected and for me there was plenty of pastoral work in the parish:: two churches, three hospitals, several nursing homes, the prison, a young people's remand centre, the parish school, three military garrisons, two convents a never-ending lists of homes to visit.

Then, in 1962, Pope (now Saint) John XXIII opened a General Council of the Church, gathering all the Catholic bishops of the world. There were eventually four sessions of the Council in Rome, which Pope John saw as having being inspired by the Holy Spirit.

Our bishop, John Henry King, lived with four of us priests in the presbytery where he had at one time been parish priest. With his great sense of history, he welcomed Pope John's call for the renewal of the Church, which he too saw as inspired by the Holy Spirit.

Archbishop John Henry King, 4th Bishop of Portsmouth

When, in 1962, the Bishops gathered in Rome, he was not physically up to attending the Council, so we all crowded into the housekeeper's flat in front of her black and white television and he watched the proceedings with much delight.

John Henry King died peacefully in 1965. The Vatican Council was still in progress.

Monsignor Derek Worlock had been priest secretary to three successive Cardinal Archbishops of Westminster. Cardinal Heenan appointed him to a parish in the Archdiocese as parish priest. He was also appointed to accompany the English and

Welsh bishops to the Council sessions in Rome as a '*peritus*' or ecclesiastical expert. At the end of 1965 and of the session of the Council, Derek Worlock was ordained in St John's Cathedral as the fifth Bishop of Portsmouth.

He encouraged the clergy to recognise the vital role of the laity in proclaiming the gospel to the world, in word and action. He saw the Council as a major event in the story of the Church. Through the revision of the Liturgy, spoken and sung in our own language, the Church was opening up the scriptures anew. In Winchester we were encouraged to reach out to our fellow Christians. I know this was happening in Jersey too. Throughout the Diocese, Catholics joined in shared prayer with other churches. With our Anglican colleagues from Winchester Cathedral we inaugurated a joint chaplaincy in the County Hospital.

Towards the end of my time in Winchester we were joined by a young deacon who was in the final stage of his preparation for priesthood. His name was Francis Isherwood and in due course, at the Cathedral in Portsmouth, I would arrange his ordination as a priest, prior to his first posting in Southampton, after which he was appointed to Jersey, where eventually he would be waiting to settle me in on my own arrival as Dean and parish priest of St Mary & St Peter's. Francis's next move, after Jersey, was to be a priest in our newly twinned diocese of Bamenda, West Africa.

—ooo000ooo—

IN March 1967 the Bishop called me to say that he wanted me to move to the Cathedral. A few months later I was appointed Administrator (that is to say, the Parish Priest) of the Cathedral. The Bishop's chaplain at that time was Father Cormac Murphy O'Connor, who later was Rector of the English College in Rome, then Bishop of Arundel and Brighton and then Archbishop of Westminster (and Cardinal), His replacement was Father Nicholas France, who had been ordained in the Cathedral in 1968 and who would return to Portsmouth a couple of years later as Chaplain to Bishop Worlock and therefore would visit Jersey periodically with the Bishop.

Father Nicholas, some years later, would be among the priests present at the opening of the new Church of St Mary & St Peter when Bishop

Anthony Emery announced that we were both to be appointed Canons of the Cathedral Chapter.

For both Nicholas and me the years when we were in the household of Bishop Derek must have been truly formative. The Bishop, when appointed to Portsmouth, had hit the ground running. He was completely dedicated to implementing in our Diocese the decrees and the spirit of the Second Vatican Council, and, above all, the Gospel. Nicholas in particular had the job of keeping up with him.

One of my own tasks was to oversee the re-ordering of the Cathedral's interior to accommodate the reformed liturgy. In years to come, in Jersey, I was to stand within the crumbling shell of the old St Mary and St Peter's, remembering the demolished 19th century sanctuary of St John's Cathedral with a sense of *déjà vu*.

Although born in Portsmouth, I am a Guernseyman. The names of my ancestors are written in the pre-Reformation baptism records of Guernsey. Considering my 'foreign' origin, the people of Jersey gave me a very friendly welcome when I arrived in September 1975. I was following a much-loved priest, Canon Arthur Olney, who had been in the Island for 27 years. Despite the fact that on a clear day the coast of Jersey is visible on the horizon from Guernsey, and the fact that my maternal grandmother had been born into the French community in Jersey, like many I had never been to what would now become my home.

As Administrator of the Cathedral, I already knew Canon Olney. He was a member of the Chapter of Canons, and my duties included ensuring that all was ready for the Canons' Chapter Mass in the Cathedral and laying on lunch for them in Bishop's House afterwards. Canon Olney always went out of his way to spend time with me, still a very junior priest, and he impressed me as a kind and gentle man. On my arrival in Jersey I soon learned what a good and devoted pastor he always was.

—ooo000ooo—

Early in the summer of 1975 Bishop Derek took me aside and asked me to accept a new mission. Canon Arthur Olney would be leaving Jersey after 27 years as Parish Priest of St Mary and St Peter's and as Catholic

Dean in Jersey. I felt I would be hard put to it to follow the footsteps of a so much loved pastoral priest. Moreover, I was a Guernseyman.

But as Bishop Derek reminded me, Canon Richard Arscott, also a Guernseyman, had survived the Occupation! Arriving in Jersey I was enormously impressed at how the congregations were responding to the message of the Vatican Council.

In 1975 we were just two priests living in the Vauxhall presbytery. My assistant priest was Father Francis Isherwood. There were at that time a dozen priests in the Island but there was also much lay activity and initiative in the churches and schools, and we valued the devotion and commitment of the religious orders of men and women.

By that time the French and the Irish who had brought their faith to the Island over the past century and a half, were joined first by Italians and then by nationals from other Catholic countries in Europe, especially Madeira. At one stage a couple of us clergy were saying parts of the Mass in Portuguese (after phonetic coaching and causing some amusement to the congregation!).

In September 1975 Bishop Worlock, accompanied by Father Nicholas France, his chaplain (and partial instigator of my appointment!), came to Jersey to induct me as Parish Priest of St Mary & St Peter's Church and Catholic Dean. The splendour of the occasion surpassed anything we were accustomed to in Winchester or Portsmouth. The Lieutenant Governor and the Bailiff, church leaders, States Members and all the great and good of the Island, were there, with the French and Irish Oblate clergy and friends from all the churches.

Within a few months of my move to Jersey Bishop Derek Worlock was named as Archbishop of Liverpool. His successor was Bishop Anthony Emery. What we used to call the "lay apostolate" was flourishing in Jersey. Particularly impressive was the St Vincent de Paul Society which reached out to the poor in so many practical ways.

Jersey was then, and still is, widely thought of as a prosperous society. There was however at that time much cause for concern at the situation of many immigrant workers, an issue which Bishop Anthony raised on our visit to the Bailiff who acknowledged the problem sympathetically.

Relations with my "opposite numbers" in the other Christian churches were always good, and I imagine that had been the case ever since the

Occupation years. Indeed I can say the same of all the church leaders and their congregations during my years in Jersey.

On arrival in Jersey I had to learn the history of educational provision for the children of the Island. The schools run by religious orders were necessarily fee-paying, although individuals were helped by the schools themselves where funds were available. I appreciated very much the easy approachability of our legislators, the States members and Crown officers, when we had cause to raise sensitive issues affecting our Catholic and Christian faith.

A major change for the congregation of St Mary & St Peter was the move from Vauxhall in St Helier to a new site in Wellington Road (although still sited in the parish of St Helier). On 27 September 1985, in the presence of Archbishop Derek Worlock of Liverpool, the new church was opened and consecrated by Bishop Anthony Emery. Although it was a new building, it was built on the living stones of the continuing congregation.

During the 1990s the Island church welcomed its first deacons. They were married men with families and as their diaconate was not a stage to the priesthood as it had been for me and other priests, the new deacons were ordained to the permanent diaconate. Their ministry was blessing in the way they were able to not only assist priests but act in their own right in celebrating baptisms, weddings and funerals. Deacons are in some way a bridge between the priest and the people and are therefore trained and ordained after years of experience in the lay apostolate. Our first deacon, ordained for the Island but specifically for St Mary and St Peter's Church, was Deacon Iain MacFirbhisigh ordained on 26 June 1993. A few years later, Tony Ward was ordained a deacon with particular responsibility for Our Lady, St Martin. He was ordained on 22 June 1996.

Bishop Emery died in 1988. In the summer of that year, while the Diocese was waiting for the appointment of a new bishop, the Archbishop of Westminster, Cardinal Basil Hume came to the Channel Islands to make a pastoral visit which had already been arranged between him and Bishop Anthony before the bishop died. The cardinal received a great welcome from the Catholic Community and indeed from the whole Island.

Shortly before the start of the Mass for the installation of Bishop Crispian Hollis in January 1989 I was standing in the Cathedral in Portsmouth when the new bishop came up to me and asked which parish I was in. When I told him it was in Jersey, he asked how long I had been there.

"Twelve years" was my answer". He said (but in a friendly way) "You can't stay there much longer"! I had every expectation that I would be moving on from Jersey, but my mother, living in Guernsey with my sister Jeanette and her husband Graham, was now in poor health and was accepted in the Jeanne Jugan Residence by the Little Sisters of the Poor. Bishop Crispian, with great kindness, deferred my move. Although my mother died in 1992, as it turned out I was only half way through my sojourn in Jersey. It was time to review the situation.

—oooO0Oooo—

The 1994 Jersey Pastoral Review examined how we were fulfilling our mission to spread the Gospel and it proposed ways forward into a future when we would have fewer priests. We were blessed to have many priests in Jersey for most of my time in the Island. Fr Ron Lobb, a retired headmaster gave the last ten years of his life to serve as a priest, and Brian Sandeman has served well beyond retirement age, but the religious order priests, who ministered to Island Catholics for over a century, could not expect to provide priests for much longer in the Island, and the Diocesan clergy were fully stretched. The deacons, since the first was ordained in 1993, have been a true blessing for the Church in the Island, in ministry and in pastoral care. And so have innumerable members of the Island's congregations, not simply supporting the clergy, but fulfilling their own God-given mission to carry the gospel message, in word and deed, to whomever they can reach.

If you read the Jersey Pastoral Review report (Appendix C) you can get some idea of how much was done and how much left undone, since the report was written. But if you are involved in the life of the Jersey Catholic community today, you will also realise, as this book tells, how much more that is good has been done, beyond what we could have foreseen, by so many faithful people, by the grace of God.

Monsignor Nicholas France MBE
Catholic Dean in Jersey
Photographed by Stuart McAlister, Photographer, LMPA LBLPP ©

CHAPTER 24

THE NEW MILLENNIUM

The first 15 years - by Monsignor Nicholas France MBE

THERE is continuity in the on-going story of the Catholic people of Jersey who are constantly joined by others who seek to make their home and workplace in this island. This is not so in the case of the clergy, none of whom in recent times have been native Islanders, yet have been sent here by either their Religious Superiors or by the Bishop of Portsmouth. Some have died in office.

However, recent Catholic Deans have even gone on to other responsibilities, first, Canon Olney who took on a small parish in southern Oxfordshire and secondly, Canon Mahy, who became parish priest of Aldershot from 2000 until 2013.

A priest's appointment is made after consultation by his superiors and not by himself. So his life and ministry could never be seen as a career. At the more profound level, a diocesan priest sees his obedience to his Bishop as obedience to Christ, who 'came not to be served, but to serve and to give his life as a ransom for many'. This is the motive behind all pastoral responsibility that is undertaken.

It was this thinking that underpinned my response when asked by Bishop Crispian Hollis in the summer of 1999 to move from the city centre parish of Southampton, where I was Dean of that city, to become Catholic Dean in Jersey. I was happily preparing for the religious celebrations of the Millennium in Southampton, when the Bishop asked to come to see me to talk about the future.

I didn't want to leave my post and certainly didn't want to move to the Channel Islands, but I had a hunch that this might be in the Bishop's mind. When I awoke on the morning that he was to come and see me I reached for my Bible next to my bed to seek inspiration. It fell open at Isaiah chapter 49, a page that happened to be marked by a memorial card of my first Bishop, Derek Worlock, later Archbishop of Liverpool. It was to him and his successors that I had I promised respect and obedience on the day of my ordination. His photo on this card faced the words: 'Islands, listen to me, pay attention, remotest peoples. The Lord called me before I was born; from my mother's womb he pronounced my name… He said to me, you are my servant in whom I shall be glorified….'

When Bishop Crispian arrived that morning, he asked me to move to Jersey to be Dean and Parish Priest of St Helier. Without hesitation I replied, 'yes, certainly'. Through the words of Isaiah, the Lord's intention for me seemed very clear and beyond argument.

I began my ministry in the Island on 8 September 1999, the feast of the Birthday of the Blessed Virgin Mary. I arrived in time to celebrate Mass in St Thomas' that evening, seeking Our Lady's patronage.

I had been led to believe that my first priority was to unite the congregation of St Mary and St Peter's church with that of St Thomas' church. The first was an Anglo Irish foundation and the second French. These two communities had been separate for 200 years, with different cultural traditions. While St Mary and St Peter's church had always been served by diocesan priests, St Thomas' was under the pastoral care of priests from the French Province of the Oblates of Mary Immaculate. Within a fortnight of my arrival, I heard that a Holy Ghost Father, Father Philip Doyle, who had had the care of the Portuguese Catholic community in the Island and had been based at St Thomas' for the previous 10 years, would be leaving almost immediately for a new post in Australia.

By the time I was installed as Catholic Dean in St Thomas' church on 28 September, the Vigil of the feast of Saints Michael, Gabriel and Raphael, a ceremony attended by civic and ecumenical guests, I was aware that I had taken over an additional responsibility in the pastoral care of the Portuguese Catholic community. David Mahy helped the smooth handover by remaining until Christmas.

I was glad to be his successor and that of his predecessor, Arthur Olney, as I had known them both from the time of my ordination and held them in great respect. I felt a sense of continuity and even familiarity.

With the opening of the New Year and Millennium in 2000, I began in earnest to see how I would need to re-shape the pastoral structure of the town parish to meet the new situation, particularly recognising that I was the sole priest, having replaced three others. Determined to keep on the Sunday mass in Portuguese until a new Portuguese-speaking priest could be appointed, I maintained the 3.30pm Portuguese Mass together with one Sunday mass at St Mary and St Peter's church with two at St Thomas' and a vigil mass at St Thomas' on Saturday evenings. This meant that for my first years in Jersey I celebrated five Sunday masses every weekend. The last French priest at St Thomas had ceased to celebrate Mass in French two years before he returned to France.

Although I had no other priest assistant, I was well supported by Deacon Iain MacFirbishigh at St Mary and St Peter's church and by Louis Omer, a French parishioner at St Thomas' church, who was ordained to the permanent diaconate in May 2000. Sadly, Deacon Louis' active ministry as a Deacon only lasted a few years, before he was downed by a stroke, dying some years later.

The experience that I had had in running large parishes in Aldershot and Winchester and in the uniting of two parishes in central Southampton before coming to Jersey was to my advantage in reconciling the two church communities in St Helier. There was little opposition, although on both sides there were those who found it emotionally difficult while accepting that was no other option. Within some years the different congregations came to accept one another and even assimilate.

Canon, later Mgr Nicholas France at his induction with Canon David Mahy and Bishop Crispian Hollis.

I expressed my understanding of how people felt when I said: 'Sometimes when your head says something is the right thing to do, your heart is slower to accept this.'

While undertaking the usual civic responsibilities expected of me as Catholic Dean, I was more concerned with, first, the reorganisation of St Helier and secondly, the implementation of the recommendations of the 1994 Pastoral Review, which recommended not only one parish in the town but that the two parishes in the East and in the West also become one in both areas. So early in the year 200 I set up a local pastoral review group to look at all the 1994 proposals in the light of the new situation. Clearly the reduction in the number of priests had forced this pastoral reorganisation to come about.

All aspects of Island life were reconsidered, including the role of the Catholic Pastoral Centre, which needed to be better integrated into the life and mission of the Church, especially because this would be more possible due to a change of clergy at St Thomas'. However, consequent tensions within the personnel at the Centre, due to the appointment of two Religious Sisters, who were not able to integrate with the original team, meant that three of the original members resigned. With this implosion the review team sought to redirect the purpose and vision of the Centre, which over the next few years changed its name to Catholic Pastoral Services so as to denote its outward looking purpose.

During the next few years strenuous efforts were made to make better provision for the Portuguese Catholic community, not only those attending the Portuguese mass but the huge numbers of families seeking the sacraments of baptism, Holy Communion and confirmation. The pastoral challenge was immense. I was greatly encouraged when in the summer of 2000 I secured the pastoral help of Father Bernardino Trindade, a member of the Sacred Heart Order, based in Madeira, who spent June and July assessing the situation and offering advice. He promised to come and celebrate yearly the Festa in honour of Our Lady of Fatima in May and October. Earlier that same year, I was fortunate to secure Manuela Santos as my house manager, who, in addition to her other work, became my liaison with the Portuguese community and registrar for any of the paperwork required for sacraments etc. She has always enjoyed the backup support of Father Bernardino.

Attempts were made in these early years to bring together St Mary and St Peter's with St Thomas' through having a joint Parish Pastoral Council. This proved hard to achieve as the interests and concerns of the different churches were so different. Subsequently, practising subsidiarity, it was easier to establish a church committee for St Mary and St Peter's alone, consulting with parishioners at St Thomas's in a different way.

During the year 2000 the unification of the churches in the East of the Island as one parish was achieved, due to the death in December 1999 of the parish priest to St Martin's, Father Brian Cousins, and retirement from St Patrick's on health grounds of Father Colin Ward in the summer of 2000. By the end of that year, Father Robin Elwood had become the parish priest of the East of Jersey Catholic Parish, working hard to establish a sense of shared parish between those two distinct communities.

Gradually the Catholic people in Jersey were coming to accept that change was not only necessary, but even healthy in achieving a greater unity of purpose, which had sometimes been lacking when there were six parishes in this small Island. The west of Jersey was also united as one parish following the departure, and death soon after, of Father Tom Friery of St Matthieu's and the appointment to a parish in England of Father James Carling of the Sacred Heart Parish. These two were united in 2004 with Father 'Peter' Glas as the first parish priest. The creation of this new parish under one priest led immediately to the need to rationalise the use of the five churches in this new western parish. It was decided to close, as chapels of ease, the church of Our Lady of the Universe at Millbrook and the church of St John and St Anthony at Ville à L'Evêque. Later these sites were disposed of and the money raised was used for the repairs and refurbishment of other churches. In 2008 Father Glas was succeeded by Father Kevin Hoiles, who in the following years has provided stability and unity within this area of the Island parish.

These administrative changes still left a certain inequality between the various personnel and finances of the three new parishes, as has been recorded elsewhere. As this situation was also happening across the rest of the diocese, Bishop Crispian proposed that there should be a Diocesan Pastoral Congress to renew and refashion the Church in our diocese to meet the pastoral realities of the remainder of the century and on into the new millennium. During 2004 consultations were made in all the parishes of the diocese to ensure that ordinary parishioners were fully involved in order to avoid top-down decisions, which would prove less acceptable in implementation.

In August 2005 a sizeable contingent from Jersey attended the Pastoral Congress in Reading. Among the recommendations, as published in Bishop Hollis' vision document, *Go out and bear fruit*, was the creation of what were initially called Greater Pastoral Areas, linking parishes together more closely and in smaller number than in the previous deanery system to enable them to share better both personnel and resources. This seemed to be an obvious development to enact in our Island. This diocesan policy was also intended to lead to Pastoral Areas becoming a new kind of greater parish, with a parish priest as coordinating pastor with a number of associate pastors. By the year 2007 I had sought from the Bishop and his Council of Priests permission to take Jersey forward into becoming this new kind of parish. Unfortunately, most of the other pastoral areas of the diocese didn't follow suit. However, the natural boundaries of an island made it much easier to achieve this new way of being a united local church in Jersey.

One of the principles in the keeping or closing of places of worship was that a church should have either a Presbytery or Hall attached where people could meet and where catechetical formation could take place. In St Thomas's, in addition to facilities in the church hall, I felt that better provision should be made for Catholic Pastoral Services and its five staff members and for a meeting place for the Portuguese Catholic community, a Welcome Centre, which they could call their own. The building chosen was the one time Val Plaisant school, later a social club, on the north side of St Thomas' church. It was redundant. With fundraising led by former Senator Dick Shenton and a very sizeable bequest, the building was converted at the cost of over £400,000. The Welcome Centre was opened by Sir John Cheshire, the Lieutenant Governor, who, as a member of an Island trust, has secured a large grant towards this project. The other end of the building, Catholic Pastoral Services, was blessed and dedicated (in the absence of Bishop Hollis on sabbatical) by Monsignor John Nelson, Vicar General with particular responsibility for the Channel Islands.

Catholic Pastoral Services fully began to develop in 2005 with the appointment of an administrator and pastoral assistants responsible for Youth Ministry, Spiritual Development, Safeguarding and States' Schools Catechists, General Catechesis. The only post which became full-time was that of the Coordinator for Youth Ministry. Mary Cahill had been appointed to this post following a week in which she had successfully led, with me, a group of 25 young people and adults from Jersey to the World Youth Days in Cologne that year. Mary was to hold this role and greatly develop this work during her ten years in the post.

The Welcome Centre quickly developed with its café into the social gathering place for many people, especially Portuguese Catholics. In its first years there was a gallery to be used by anyone who wished to exhibit their paintings. This project helped to bridge linguistic cultural divides. The building also provided rooms that could be used as classrooms, when, in partnership with Highlands College of Further Education, English classes were offered on many weekday evenings and Saturday afternoons. Over ten years many thousands have taken the opportunity of empowering themselves with the ability to speak and read English, to their benefit and that of the local economy.

Polish migrants were the first to enrol in these classes, followed by the Portuguese, many of whom had been here many years but had yet to develop their skills of writing and reading. Most students coming to the Welcome Centre choose to do so in preference to attending a large college.

The middle section of the building became the centre of operations for the Society of St Vincent de Paul. It was used for that purpose until, because of the development of its social work, a transfer was made in 2015 to new rooms in St Thomas' Hall.

Before disposing of redundant buildings belonging to the Church in the Island, discernment was sought about alternative uses. Rather than being sold, some were hired out to support Church income. In the case of the Presbytery at St Matthieu, the building was adapted to meet a long held vision of providing a spiritual centre and a house of prayer for Catholics and others in the Island. 'Peter' Glass and I developed this idea and launched The Oasis of Peace in the autumn of 2007, inviting Cardinal Cormac Murphy O'Connor, the Archbishop of Westminster, to dedicate this project when he came for the re-dedication of St Thomas' church. With David Cahill as its first director, the Oasis has fulfilled its original purpose and developed it, including a social dimension in offering hospitality to prisoners' families, as an extension of David Cahill's work as prison chaplain at La Moye.

I always felt challenged by the commitment made to those on the peripheries by recent Popes in their 'option for the poor'. In Jersey, I identified this as being particularly relevant to immigrant families, who were poor in opportunity, security of accommodation, use of the English language, home life and stable relationships. In particular, I identified this with the Portuguese community, providing as best I could for their spiritual and social support, while seeking a Portuguese-speaking priest and Religious Sisters together with better outreach through the development of The Society of St Vincent de Paul and other groups.

In 2014 I was glad to welcome two sisters from the Community of Christ at Bethany, a new Portuguese expression of Religious life. Their particular charism is to imitate Jesus' special friends who lived in Bethany: Martha, in their pastoral work, Mary, in their contemplative life and Lazarus, in their works of compassion.

I was honoured that my concern for the migrant communities was recognised in the summer of 2014 when I was awarded an MBE in the Queen's birthday honours. During the previous year I had established a parish branch of Caritas Internationalis to coordinate social justice work within the Jersey Catholic Parish, to gather a group of informed Catholics as a 'Think Tank' to provide a response from the Church to consultation documents from the States' government, together promoting opportunities to develop a better understanding of Catholic Social Teaching. Caritas Jersey was the first such parish branch in Britain to be established.

Since St Mary and St Peter's Church moved to Wellington Road, St Thomas' church has become a more visible centre of Catholicism in St Helier. Its height and size lead its early French congregations to call it 'La Cathédrale'. In a radical restoration in 1984, during which the fabric was restored, much of the original decoration and devotional artefacts were cleared away and the church came to be seen as austere and oversimplified. Recognising, as I have always believed, that God can be found in beauty, I sought to renew and beautify the building as a place which St Helier's Catholics and others would recognise as their spiritual home and principle church. Over a period of nine months, as explained elsewhere in this book, this restoration took place. It received the appreciation of everyone. The Cardinal Archbishop of Westminster, Cormac Murphy-O'Connor, rededicated the Church, assisted by the Bishop Crispian Hollis in October 2007.

After 16 years as Catholic Dean it is important, as I learned during my sabbatical in California in 2009, that my fellow clergy and I remain open to new ideas, new initiatives and the gifts that new clergy and laity bring with them from other places, as well as local people awakening to their potential and their charisms.

Whatever the future may bring, we need to be aware that the Spirit blows were he wills, that it is not for us to discern God's purposes or predict the next stages of development within the Church in this Island. It will probably be the responsibility of my successor.

In the meantime, I am reminded of the Lord's parable about the servant who was put to work waiting on his master at table after a day of labour in the fields. Jesus teaches us from this that in the end "we are but servants".

Chapter 25

POSTSCRIPT: THE WAY AHEAD

By Monsignor Nicholas France

SEVENTY years from the end of World War II has provided this book with an opportunity to reflect on the change and development of the Catholic Church in this Island in response to pastoral needs and the severe reduction, since 1945, in the number of Clergy, Religious Sisters and Brothers.

Leading up to 2015, bishops, priests, deacons and committed lay people - both here and in other parts of our diocese - have worked hard to renew and restructure the Church's on-going mission and ministry, rather than merely managing decline.

Much of the reorganisation in Jersey has strengthened and consolidated our Catholic communities, which are now centred on well-maintained and well-used seven churches, reminding us of the Seven Churches of the Book of Revelation (The Apocalypse). However, if we use this analogy with those early Christian churches, we should be prepared for the challenging appraisal and criticism they experienced in God's judgement on their fidelity to Christ and the people entrusted to their pastoral care.

In 2013 the Sion Community in England was invited to carry out a three-week Parish Mission in Jersey. In preparation, church records of the names and addresses of parishioners were updated, so that local people could accompany the missioners in visiting as many homes as possible to invite participation in the Mission Services, talks and events. There were three memorable celebrations of faith in the public sphere. There was a Night of Lights in the Sacred Heart church, where passers-by were welcomed to come in through the open doors and participate in silent worship. One Saturday in Millennium Park in town there was a day of fun and games, free food and drink, with Catholic organisations on display, which culminated in the Blessed Sacrament, present in a prayer tent throughout that day, being brought in solemn procession to St Thomas' church for Benediction. On the final Sunday nearly all masses in the Island were cancelled to ensure the presence of over 2,000 people in the Gloucester Hall at Fort Regent for the celebration of Mass together, at the end of which Caritas Jersey was launched and dedicated.

This event was followed by a free lunch!

The purpose of the mission was to renew in the Spirit the face of the Church in this Island. It led not only to a greater commitment to social justice in many different ways, through the encouragement and inspiration of Caritas Jersey, and spiritual renewal through the adoption of the 'Call and Gifted' programme of the Diocese, which encourages people, firstly, to recognise that they are called in baptism to be a disciple of Christ in the world in which they live and work. Secondly, that through the gifts the Holy Spirit they received at their confirmation and in the use of their natural abilities, they can actively share in the New Evangelisation in which everyone is called to participate. Another spiritual development flowing from the mission can be seen in the creation of The Wellspring Prayer Group, which has provided a spiritual outlet for those wishing to express their faith through charismatic prayer and healing.

Inspired by the example of the Society of St Vincent de Paul, in their visiting of those in disadvantaged situations, it is planned to develop a greater Ministry of Pastoral Visiting in all parts of the parish, reaching out to those who are no longer practising or are housebound or on the margins of community life to offer them the hand of Christian compassion, invitation and respect.

And what of the future? Under Pope Benedict it appeared that we were being led to develop a Church that, although smaller in numbers, would be more faithful to Catholic doctrine, moral teaching and formal worship. While being faithful to Catholic Tradition, Pope Francis has challenged us to stop looking inward, where there are ideological differences between Catholics, but to look outward. Before the conclave at which he was elected Pope, he said: 'The Church is called to come out from itself and go to people on the periphery of society where there is sin, pain, misery and injustice and to bring them the good news of the gospel of Jesus Christ.'

He also said on the same occasion that the next Pope 'must be a man who from the contemplation and adoration of Jesus Christ helps the Church to go out to the existential peripheries, that helps her to be the fruitful mother who gains life from the sweet and comforting joy of evangelising.' Since elected, he has sought to implement that vision of a Church not only for the poor, but to be a Church of the poor. As Cardinal Murphy O'Connor has commented: 'Those on the edges of the Church, even those outside it, understand that Pope Francis has a word for them as well, a word of conversion, a word of looking for what is good and what is true in their lives, however broken or far from God they might imagine themselves to be.'

Looking to the future, it is hard to discern which way internationally the Church will develop – perhaps by following the vision of both Benedict and Francis.

While in Africa, Latin America and Asia the Church may grow stronger and larger, more confident and more evangelistic, and capable of providing leadership for the universal Church with successive Bishops of Rome.

While treating our small Muslim community members in Jersey with friendship and respect, it would be naive not to recognise the evangelistic nature of Islam and its desire to convert and reform the countries of Europe in which it is now so embedded. In some European countries the demographic changes brought about by the greater number births of Muslim children compared with those of others, will radically challenge not only the secularism of society and its democratic institutions but also the Christian foundations of these countries.

In Jersey, however, the relative lack of success of the Church in maintaining and sustaining the faith of many immigrants from Catholic cultures in Ireland, Scotland, Madeira and Poland, together with the secularisation and tenuous commitment to the practice of their faith within our local Catholic communities, will lead to a diminishing in the numbers of those we will be able to call active, practising Catholics.

If we were to follow the inspiration of Pope Benedict, we might work in this Island to become a more strictly attentive, even somewhat exclusive, Catholic community, faithful to traditional doctrine and morals that taught and preached with greater clarity and honesty than at present. If we follow Pope Francis we need to become more open, humble and conscious of the way in which Christ dealt with those on the peripheries, sharing with them an experience of God's mercy, which Jesus personalised in his own life and ministry. Perhaps there is a need for a synthesis of both these approaches with the Church being both more faithful and more evangelising, in imitation of Jesus Christ.

Will we survive in our present form? It is a question sometimes asked. The answer in Jersey will be similar to that in other parts of Europe.

Looking into the future of the Church in Europe, Cardinal Basil Hume once wrote that he foresaw the day when, rather like in the days of the Dark Ages, the Church would exist in small pockets such as a few traditional monasteries or in simple new style religious communities, and in some cathedrals and some larger parishes which had remained active and alive. This would translate in Jersey into a small community of priests based at St Thomas', perhaps going out to serve groups of Catholics, perhaps in their current churches, on a weekly or monthly basis. Ironically, this would be a return to what happened very similarly in the 19th century in the work of the Oblates of Mary Immaculate.

There is no certainty that the Catholic faith will survive in Europe any more than it exists in North Africa, where it once flourished in the early centuries of Christianity. But unless it is forced underground or actively persecuted, the light of Christ is likely to endure if it is passed on in small gatherings of the faithful, both Catholic and non-Catholic, as other Christians, who are faithful to doctrinal basics, will suffer the same as Catholics from the withdrawal from active worship by many of their adherents. Perhaps there will be martyrs, as already Christians have had to suffer discrimination and legal action from the intolerance of the tolerated and political correctness, particularly through upholding traditional values about marriage, parenthood and the sacredness of the beginning and end of human life.

Many of the other cultural wars have been lost already.

One of the most chilling questions that Jesus poses in the gospel is: 'When the Son of Man comes, will he find faith on earth?' As we look back on the past 70 years of Catholicism in this Island, we give thanks for the fidelity and sacrifices of those whose patronage we enjoy in the beautiful buildings in which we worship, while praying that we may be faithful to the Eucharist for which these churches were built, in order to ensure that those who come after us will use them for the same purpose: to find Christ and to hear anew his gospel compelling them to go out with the Holy Spirit to guide them as they seek to renew the face of the earth.

APPENDICES

Appendix A: *The Religious Orders*

(1)   Holy Ghost Fathers

(2)   The Religious Sisters at Beaulieu

(3)   De La Salle

(4)   The Jesuits

(5)   FCJ (and their antecedents, Les *Dames de St André*)

(6)   Le Sacré Coeur

(7)   Little Sisters of the Poor

(8)   The Limes

Appendix B: *Catholic Clergy – A Roll of names*

Appendix C: *The 1994 Catholic Pastoral Review: recommendations of the Report*

Appendix D: *'Home grown' – Priests with a Jersey connection*

Appendix E: *Catholic Lay Societies in Jersey*

APPENDIX A

THE RELIGIOUS ORDERS

(1) *The Holy Ghost Fathers*

THE full title of the Holy Ghost Fathers (or Spiritans) as they are officially called) is the Congregation of the Holy Spirit under the protection of the Immaculate Heart of Mary, or in Latin, *Congregatio Sancti Spiritus sub tutela Immaculati Cordis Beatissimae Virginis Mariae,* and thus abbreviated C.S.Sp. It is a Roman Catholic congregation of priests, lay brothers, and since Vatican II, lay associates.

Founded by the son of a wealthy bourgeois merchant and member of the Breton Parlement in Rennes, the founder, Claude Pouillart des Places trained as a priest and then founded a society in 1703 to help poor students with a vocation for priesthood but insufficient money to afford to do so.

Since then, despite a major setback at the time of the French Revolution, it has become a major missionary order, especially in Africa, but operating in at least 57 countries; it has been established in the UK since the early 20th Century.

The Order agreed to take on the Jersey parishes of St Matthieu and Sacred Heart in 1988, following the decision by the Anglo-Irish Oblates to relinquish these parishes.

In that year there had been considerable discussion about the possibility of providing a Portuguese-speaking priest to serve the thousands of Portuguese-speaking workers in the Island. The Holy Ghost Fathers were also asked if they could provide a priest to fulfil this mission. As it is the custom of the Holy Ghost Fathers to live in community in a Spiritan House, agreement was ultimately reached between the Order's Provincial Superior, Fr Vincent O'Toole and the Bishop of Portsmouth for the Order to provide a Parish Priest and an assistant priest to take responsibility for St Matthieu's parish and a further priest to serve the Portuguese community.

In May 1989 Fr Tom Friery CSSp was appointed as the new parish priest with Fr Jim Taylor as his assistant. The Presbytery became a Spiritan House and Fr Doyle, who at the time was working in the Trans Canadian

Province, took up residence in the House that September to be in charge of the 'Personal Parish' of Our Lady of Fatima. Fr Taylor died in residence in 1991.

Fr Friery was born in Liverpool in 1933 - although all four grandparents were Irish - he served as a Holy Ghost Missionary in Nigeria during the Biafra War: life became especially difficult when his parishioners were confused between the words 'missionary' and 'mercenary'.

He was so adept at raising money for clinics that he was sent to the USA, where he lived both in Washington and Beverley Hills to be near the source of gift funding. Through his efforts he raised funding for three hospitals, six maternity clinics and for schemes to fight disease. Before coming to Jersey, he set up charity projects all round the world, from Nigeria to Las Vegas.

After six years he returned to the UK to become Provincial of his Order. He once joked: 'The Holy Fathers are like the SAS of the Church. The training is very hard, and we are asked to take on jobs that are very difficult and don't attract volunteers – but that is no reflection on Jersey!'

In Jersey he continued his successful fund-raising career on a local scale, successfully funding improvements to the church, including 'Uncle Tom's Cabin', a charity shop in former outhouses behind the presbytery, and found £60,000 to replace the leaky and unstable bell tower: and coffee room in 2002.

He retired in the spring of 2003, after a long period of ill health. He was the last parish priest of St Matthieu, which was then absorbed into the Sacred Heart parish.

Father James Carling was the first Spiritan Rector of Sacred Heart parish. He spent two years as a student priest in Sierra Leone and was ordained in 1982; afterwards returning to Sierra Leone where he spent a further 11 years before being posted back to England in 1994.

'One of the first things that struck me [on my return] was the lack of young people in church,' he told the JEP in 2000. 'It was certainly a change from the 600 children and teenagers who were always on time for church in Sierra Leone.'

Fr Carling came to Jersey in 1995 and stayed until September 2003 to become the parish priest of Thatcham in Berkshire. With him went the other Holy Ghost Father left in Jersey, Father Ken Martin, who was retiring as a priest after 43 years.

Fr Doyle left Jersey for a new appointment in Australia late in 1999. With the withdrawal of the Holy Ghost Fathers in 2003, all the parishes became served by diocesan priests.

(2) *The Sisters at Beaulieu*

An order of Religious Sisters came to Jersey in 1880 in the form of three Sisters who had travelled from Paris: *La Société des Auxiliatrices des Amis des Ames du Purgatoire* (in English, 'the Helpers of the Holy Souls'). The Order was inspired by the teachings of St Ignatius of Loyola. They purchased a house at Wellington Hill, known as Beaulieu and began their work of visiting the sick and teaching, complementing the work of the *Dames de St André*. The foundation stone of a new chapel was laid in 1895 and in 1906, the statue of Christ that still stands in the grounds of Beaulieu School, was commissioned to celebrate the 50th anniversary of the foundation of the Order.

The Order stayed at Beaulieu throughout the Occupation, but in the years following Liberation they realised that not only had their work suffered during the Occupation years so that it would be difficult for them to continue to live at such a high-cost location, but also that their services could be put to better use elsewhere. In 1950 they left the Island and their convent was sold to another Order, *Les Soeurs de l'Immaculée de Saint-Méen-Le-Grand*, who had been occupying the convent building at St Matthieu.

—ooo000ooo—

The new occupants of Beaulieu had been in the Island since 1924. In that year, the FCJ Sisters – who had been occupying the convent next to St Matthieu's Church since 1911 - sold that building.

Relations between the vendors, the FCJ Sisters, and the Oblates had gone from bad to worse in the previous years, not least because the FCJ wished to sell the building to Protestants – more specifically, to the States for the creation of a home for boys. The Oblate Rector of St Matthieu, Père Pitard, was incandescent at the prospect, and the head of the Oblate Mission in Jersey, Père Mao, went as far as to write to the Pope asking him to block the sale. It appears that this appeal was successful because permission to sell the St Matthieu convent building was denied, and the contract of sale with the States had to be broken.

Instead, it was acquired by Bishop Cotter on behalf of Les Soeurs de l'Immaculée de Saint-Méen-Le-Grand, a French religious order from Brittany.

The convent had been empty for a year before the new occupants arrived to take up residence there.

The Sisters were not allowed to open a school, but helped the Oblates with catechism classes and the Jesuits at Maison Saint Louis. They also helped out local pupils by giving them extra lessons. In 1937, a local resident, Mrs Olympe Rose du Feu, who was having her ailing 14-year-old son educated at home, decided to help other children who needed home tuition. She did not have the space at home to do this, but contacted the priests at St Matthieu, who suggested using a room at the convent. By 1938 these two groups were united as a small school under one roof. However, during the Occupation, German soldiers were billeted in the Convent and alternative accommodation for the Sisters and for Mrs Olympe du Feu was found at Glenside Lodge, Bel Royal by the Constable of St Mary. There they resumed their teaching for the duration of the Occupation and afterwards moved back to the Convent.

However, as it was their wish to develop a productive school in Jersey, it was obvious that St Matthieu was not an ideal location to do so. A building in town would be much better for their needs than such an out-of-the-way location 'out west'.

Relations with the Oblates at St Matthieu were far better than had been the case between the FCJ Sisters and the Oblates. Also, the war had changed many things – and there was no dispute about the need to move away from St Matthieu and to sell the old convent building. Indeed, the Rector, Père Le Bas quite agreed with the Sisters about the necessity of moving to town and establishing a flourishing school there.

So the Saint-Méen Sisters purchased the Beaulieu Convent and moved there, along with Mrs du Feu, on 2 October 1950.

The Beaulieu building needed a lot of work doing to it to make it fit for its purpose – the outgoing owners had had little funding in their final years there and the place was gloomy and dank. That winter, everything possible was done to clean and brighten it up and by January 1951 the first pupils arrived: 16 girls and 18 boys of infant school age. Numbers rose quickly: by 1958 there were already over 200 pupils. For some years In addition, the 'Beaulieu Sisters' also ran a small school on Mont Les Vaux.

Very soon, Beaulieu was a first-class Catholic school. Sister Marie-Louise Serveau oversaw much of the post-war history of the school, arriving in 1958 and retiring in 1989. She was succeeded by Mrs Rosemarie Hill, who was the first lay headmistress; Christopher Beirne became Head in 2006.

At present in early 2016 there are over 700 girl pupils from the ages of 4 to 18; 210 in the primary School and 530 in the Secondary school.

In 2000 the School became a charitable trust and the Order relinquished all assets and control, although the Sisters are still represented on the Board of Trustees.

(3) De La Salle

THE Order of the Institut des Frères des Ecoles Chrètiennes (Brothers of Christian Schools or De La Salle Brothers) was founded in 1680 by Jean Baptiste de la Salle, a French priest and educational reformer. In 40 years, Jean Baptiste de la Salle and his Brothers succeeded in creating a network of schools throughout France to help less fortunate children. He was canonised in 1900 and named the Patron Saint of Teachers in 1950.

Although two Lasallian Brothers were in Jersey at the time of the French Revolution – one of them opened a small school – their presence in the Island was only temporary. The Order came to the Island in 1866 and opened a school in Berri House, next to St Thomas's Church. The school was immediately successful, thanks to the outstanding qualities of the first two Lasallian Brothers, who had come from London: Brother Thomas and Brother Alban.

However, after 30 years, as a result of disagreements between the Lasallians and the Oblates, the Brothers left Jersey and did not return until 1917. This time there was no clash of personalities and with both

Oblates and Lasallians working together, and also with the financial help of Jersey Catholic Louis Sangan, the French Brothers were given permission by the States to reside and teach in Jersey. The condition was that the school had to abide by the British educational system and to possess the required English teaching qualifications.

While a property for use as a school was being sought, the Brothers used Berri House once again, with 12 pupils in the opening intake. A school and a suitable building was found on Wellington Hill, in the milieu of the "Holy Hill" and its many Catholic organisations located there, between Beaulieu Convent and the house in Westbourne Terrace that was being used by Carmelite nuns. It was called 'The Beeches' - a large house with extensive grounds and ideal for a school and the De La Salle Brothers opened a school there the following year. By 1923 it had a total of 164 pupils, by 1934, 221 pupils.

'The Beeches' still used as an alternative name for De La Salle

By 1938, the College was able to celebrate its 21st birthday and had already made a name for itself as an excellent scholastic institution. The school endured the Occupation as best it could; the number of pupils declined sharply; there was a lack of teaching staff and the

244

Occupation conditions caused a decline in health among both teachers and pupils.

The College was transferred in 1948 from the French Province of Quimper to the Province of London, although the same members of staff were kept on at the college in order to maintain continuity. There was a big increase in the number of pupils and the school was expanded.

Brother Edward, who had been the College's headmaster for almost 33 years, retired in 1949-50. He returned to Quimper, but so great had been his influence and popularity that when he died in 1960 the Old Boys made arrangements for his body to be brought back to Jersey; he was buried in St Martin's Catholic Cemetery.

A great post-war Headmaster was Brother Lawrence Anthony, who transformed de la Salle School between 1963 and 1970. A man of considerable energy and vision, he was a dynamic and innovative head of school. During his period the church schools received the first States grant for running costs and a building fund was established. A large team of fund raisers, led by the future States Member and Senator, Dick Shenton, raised £100,000 in the years 1966 and 1967 and the upgrading of the school buildings began. New sports were introduced and exam results steadily improved. He died in February 2001, aged 85.

The community of Brothers left the school in August 1995, and Mr John Sankey became the first lay Headmaster in September, retiring five years later - after a career spanning 40 years to become foundation governor. The headmaster at the time of writing is Mr Jason Turner.

The College remains the property of the De La Salle Brothers and is under their trusteeship; one of the Brothers is on the Board of Governors.

(4) *The Jesuits and the Brothers of Christian Instruction at Maison Saint-Louis and Bon Secours* - *the Catholic presence over 92 years in what is now the Hotel de France and Highlands College*

IN 1880 a French Jesuit priest called Père Chambellan arrived in Jersey from Paris, commissioned to purchase a large property from which his Order could operate more freely than was possible in the anti-clerical atmosphere of Republican France. A number of attempts to do the same thing had been made throughout the previous 50 years, but all had been unsuccessful.

More specifically, knowing that their Order was likely to be forced to leave France, they wished to transfer a Jesuit seminary from Laval, south of Normandy, and saw the potential of using Jersey as a new base for it.

Imperial Hotel (Maison Saint-Louis) photographed by Ernest Baudoux

The large 'Imperial Hotel' on St Saviour's Road was purchased on 8 June 1880; on 28 June the Jesuits were expelled from their seminary in Laval; by 1 September the first students and teachers were moving into the former hotel, now called by them 'Maison Saint Louis'. The Jesuits overcame initial anti-French and anti-Catholic prejudice and the Maison Saint Louis became a distinguished centre of higher education with a library of 200,000 books.

The following year, in 1881, another Jesuit establishment was opened: this time it was a French self-governing naval preparatory school, the Ecole de Notre Dame de Bon Secours. It too was affected by French anti-Catholic legislation and decided to move to Jersey. As no suitable property could be found at the time, they settled into villas at Waverley Terrace, just up the road from the Maison Saint Louis, and the new school soon became renowned for the excellence of its education, sending, between 1880 and 1900, more than a fifth of the cadets to the French Naval College at Brest.

A suitable property was found in 1894: Cardwell House, a large property in the grounds of Highlands that had been used as a school. Suitably, the grounds bordered those of the Maison Saint Louis. A new building was proposed, which was built and ready by the end of 1896. Unfortunately, only a few years later, French resentment against the Jesuits and the 'foreign' education of French naval officers resulted in French legislation that meant the closure of the Bon Secours school in Jersey and by 1900 the school had to be relocated back to France.

In the meantime, a Jesuit staying at the Maison Saint Louis, Père Marc Dechevrens, who had a passion for physics and meteorology, planned and had built an Observatory and weather tower, which were ready by 1894. The weather tower was demolished in 1929; the Observatory has always played a valuable contribution to the science of meteorology in Jersey, particularly under Père Charles Rey.

Père Rey (1897-1981) had been a student at Maison Saint Louis and returned to Jersey in 1934 as director of the Observatory. He worked there for the next 47 years. A seismograph was introduced to the Observatory in 1936 and is believed to be still in use at the time of writing in 2015.

With the departure of the naval cadets, Bon Secours College became a school for the training of Jesuit novices. In 1903 the Jesuits made further use of the college buildings by opening a private boarding school for boys from France, whose parents wished them to have a religious element to their education (which was impossible in the French educational system at that time). The idea proved very welcome to French parents and educational standards were high. One of the most famous students at Bon Secours and Maison St Louis was the young Jesuit, Teilhard de Chardin, later to achieve world-wide fame as a philosopher and scientist. The numbers of pupils grew, especially during the First World War period, when some Jesuit schools in northern France were closed down. The college closed in 1919, partly because of the effects of the war and also of a terrible swimming accident at Portelet in 1915, in which eight pupils lost their lives. More fundamentally, in post-war France anti-clerical laws had become considerably more relaxed.

From then until 1945, the buildings of Bon Secours were used by a French teaching order, Les Frères de l'Instruction Chrétienne de Ploërmel, which had been in the Island since 1896 in a teaching role, mainly at the Oblate schools and the Orphanage. Cardwell House, the main building of Bon Secours, became the international headquarters and study centre for students and teaching staff.

During the Occupation numbers of both staff and students dwindled: first of all, some Jesuit Fathers at Maison Saint-Louis were deported or interned (by 1945 there were only ten left) and then at Bon Secours all the French students were ordered to return to France immediately. Fortunately, having a large kitchen garden ameliorated the worst hardships of strict rationing. In 1941, both Maison Saint Louis and Bon Secours were taken over to house German troops.

The dismal years of Occupation finally came to end and Maison Saint-Louis was taken over by British troops. The day after Liberation Day was Ascension Day – and the remaining Brothers at Bon Secours moved back into those parts of the College that had been appropriated by German troops. It took two years to make all the necessary repairs – including the repair of 200 window panes.

In March 1947 the first group of English and French students arrived at the College; by Easter they had 73 students.

After the War there were only ten Jesuits remaining at Maison Saint-Louis. The years of billeting it had provided first to German troops and then to English troops had not improved the state of the property, making the idea of rehabilitating the building for the return of students ultimately impractical. With no anti-Catholic sentiment or Government sanctions in France, there was every reason to return there rather than remain in Jersey. So their vast library and most of the furniture was shipped back to France and the house was sold. Just as it had been a hotel before the Jesuits arrived in 1880 so it was converted back into a hotel by the purchaser of the Maison Saint-Louis building in 1953: it became the Hotel de France.

Before leaving, the Jesuits donated the high altar from their chapel to St Joseph's Church, Grouville.

The only Jesuit to remain was Père Rey, who stayed on at his beloved Observatory. In 1969 the Observatory became Jersey's official Health resort station. It was bought by the States in 1974, with Père Rey staying on in charge. He remained there for another five years, until an accident in 1979, which is supposed to have indirectly caused his death in 1981.

After his death, the records have continued to be maintained by the Met department of Jersey Airport.

1947 saw the return of the Brothers to Bon Secours College and life continued there much as before for the first 20 years or so, but there were a decreasing number of young men wishing to join the Order. In 1970 the college was put up for sale. It was bought by the States Education Committee in 1972 so as to establish a college of further education as well as a seat for the Committee itself.

During the summer of 1972, although the contract had not yet been signed, the Brothers removed all their belongings out of the property, including a library of 15,000 volumes as well as the mortal remains of the Brothers who had died in Jersey. The exhumation ceremony took place on 7 June 1972 at the foot of the 29 graves. Overnight on 16 - 17 June a large container of coffins was shipped to Saint Malo on the *Commodore Goodwill* and then transported to Ploërmel, where some of the coffins were re-interred and others were buried in Josselin.

By the end of September, all the Brothers and Novices had left the Island.

(5)   FCJ – *Faithful Companions of Jesus* (and les Dames de St André)

IN Jersey in 1863, the Belgian priest, Father Volkeryk, was looking for pastoral help for his parish in the field of education and care for the poor. An enquiry to Les *Dames de St André* – an old-established Belgian Order - met with a very positive response and in July 1863 the first three Nuns from this Order travelled to Jersey from their convent in Bruges.

By October were ready to take in their first pupils. Starting with 56 pupils, the numbers quickly doubled, and they found themselves cramped for space. In 1866 they were given permission to move to bigger, more spacious premises at Albion House, New Street, while plans were made to expand even further: to buy or even construct a convent, school and chapel in St Helier.

A suitable large building was found fronting David Place and Val Plaisant. Although it needed substantial adaption, it was deemed suitable, the conversion was made and the Sisters moved in with 212 pupils in 1874. It was known as Le Couvent Saint-André. The nuns undertook other teaching and charitable work, and the Jersey branch of the order went on from strength to strength. When the Oblates took over the St Matthieu parish in 1882, the *Dames de St André* were asked to reactivate the school that had been established there.

The old convent school in David Place

They moved there and two years later in 1884 a plot of land was purchased opposite the church and, using mostly French labour, built the convent school building that still remains there today. It opened the following year and the Sisters also taught in new Catholic chapel-schools built in St Ouen (St Anne's) and at Hautes Croix in St John. In 1891 after the Oblates had taken over the eastern parish of Our Lady in St Martin, Les *Dames de St André* also built and ran a school there.

The Sisters were very much part of the Island community and performed useful work, but in 1911 they were forced, because of new States education legislation, to leave the Island; their place was taken by the Sisters of the Faithful Companion of Jesus.

—ooo000ooo—

THE FCJ Order was founded in 1820 in France, and had established a community in Guernsey in 1907 after the imposition of anti-clerical laws in France impeded their work and disrupted life in their former home in Brittany.

In Jersey there was still in some official quarters a climate of opposition to Catholicism, and to French Catholic education, and – in total contrast to today - a desire to distance the Island from its historical French heritage and culture.

A series of laws passed by the States in the years before the First World War, aimed principally at the French Catholic clergy in the Island, stated that all children's education had to be in English, and that members of staff had to be fluent in English and have English teaching certificates.

Thus, religious French Catholic teachers were effectively barred from working in the Island. Numbers of pupils in Catholic schools dwindled, and Bishop Cotter decided that the French-speaking *Dames de St André* would have to leave Jersey, and be replaced by English-speaking teachers.

He contacted the Faithful Companions of Jesus in Guernsey, and invited them to come to Jersey. Although the FCJ sisters had come originally from Brittany, most of their members were English or Irish, and therefore had the right teaching qualifications. Thus the replacement of the *Dames de St André* by the FCJ Sisters neatly circumvented the States law.

Bishop Cotter warned the FCJ sisters that if they accepted his invitation, it would be 'an act of heroism' since all the six Catholic elementary schools in the Island's rural parishes would need teachers as well as the town schools and the two convents at St Matthieu and David Place.

The Sisters were not put off by that idea, and they arrived in the Island on 29 July 1911, where they settled into the convent building at St Matthieu sold to them by the *Dames de St André;* the 32 *Dames* left the Island. By May 1912 the number of pupils at the schools had almost doubled.

The FCJ headquarters in Jersey was set up at a house called Bagatelle, which became a boarding school, mainly for French girls, and worked in tandem with the Jesuit boys' school, Bon Secours, located at Highlands.

The first superior, a formidable character called Mother Magdalen Harding, was nicknamed 'General Harding' and 'the Dreadnought' by Islanders who saw her sweep in to the market to sell vegetables from the grounds at Bagatelle.

There were originally three main FCJ establishments in Jersey: Bagatelle, St Matthieu, and the convent in David Place that had been the 'headquarters' of the *Dames de St André,* and now became an English-speaking secondary school, both for boarding and day pupils. St Matthieu and Bagatelle were both sold in the 1920s, and from then on all the FCJ's schooling was centred at the David Place convent.

There the community and its school stayed throughout the Occupation and the post-war decades until the move to Grainville in 1969.

Times were changing: the boarding school part of the David Place convent was closed in 1966 – it was now easy for all pupils to attend as day-girls.

The school was thriving, but unfortunately that is more than could be said for the fabric of the old convent building, much of which was built in the early 1870s as an extension and conversion of an existing lay property. The FCJ faced problems of too many pupils for the available space and facilities, and rampant dry rot in the fabric of the building. It was felt that it could only have a limited life as a school building.

In the 1950s, Midvale House was purchased by the Superior, Mother Eustochium Tyler, on behalf of the Order, to help house the growing number of pupils. Old FCJ Girls will remember the 6ft high statue of the Sacred Heart that was placed in front of the entrance in 1961. However, the acquisition of Midvale House proved to be only a short-term solution as it was too small for all the school activities and classes.

The FCJ Sisters realised that if they were to stay in Jersey, they would have to purchase land and build a new school. Negotiations were put in hand to buy the site of what would eventually be Grainville School – then the old house known as Granville Manor, which was in a very poor state of repair.

Addressing parents at the 1968 Prize giving Day, Bishop Worlock said that he was fully behind the decision.

The purchase went through in 1969. The old buildings were demolished, and in their place arose a modern convent school, capable of housing a preparatory and secondary school as well as outdoor facilities.

In September 1969 the new Primary School was inaugurated, and almost two years later, the new senior school and convent were blessed and officially opened by Cardinal John Heenan, Archbishop of Westminster.

The old David Place convent and Midvale House were sold to the States. Midvale House was demolished in 1970 and States rental accommodation took its place. A year later, in 1971, the former convent was also demolished, along with its 96-year-old chapel. Convent Court high rise flats took its place.

Grainville Manor was demolished, and the destruction of both manor and convent buildings has been frequently criticised since then. In his book: *Jersey's Lost Heritage – 50 Years of Needless Destruction*, the author, André Ferrari said: 'Said to be structurally unsound... we now know that [the convent] could have converted to another use, even housing, and the fact that so much fine craftsmanship should have been bulldozed is almost beyond belief.'

But although it is difficult to find a good word to say about the design of the modern Convent Court block of flats, the new school at Grainville was able to provide a much higher educational standard than the out-dated school buildings in David Place.

In his address at the blessing of the new building, Cardinal Heenan praised the beauty of the new school and expressed his pleasure at hearing that the Catholic schools were finally receiving help from the educational authorities.

The States, which were already providing grants to the Catholic schools, were concerned that the number of secondary pupils on the Island was in decline. The three Catholic schools were asked, therefore, to rationalise their provision at secondary level. The plan was that De La Salle and Beaulieu, because of their proximity, would provide only secondary education and that FCJ would focus on mixed primary education. Plans to phase out FCJ Convent Secondary School were implemented, and the buildings of FCJ Prep School were extended to accommodate the expected increase in pupils, both boys and girls. Although De La Salle and Beaulieu decided to retain their own prep schools, FCJ remained committed to giving wider access to Catholic primary pupils, and was fully supported in this by the Diocese of Portsmouth. To meet continued demand, FCJ Primary School was further extended in 1997.

Lay teachers took over the FCJ teaching posts, and in 2002, the last teaching Sister, head of school Sister Cecilia Connolly, retired, ending 91 years of direct involvement of the Order. A centenary celebration, including a special Mass at St Thomas' celebrated by Bishop Hollis, took place in June 2011.

In autumn 2002, Miss Maureen Doyle became the first lay head of the FCJ School and she was succeeded in 2014 by Ms Donna Lenzi.

The school is currently thriving – with full numbers and a waiting list for most year groups. It is co-educational, and both the FCJ Order and the school in Jersey have every intention of this continuing. The happy, secure and loving atmosphere of the FCJ School in Jersey has been remarked upon by many generations of former pupils.

(6)   The Sacré Coeur Orphanage

IT was in the last months of the 19th Century that the then Rector of St Thomas', Père Louis Legrand, came to the conclusion that there needed to be a daytime crèche for the children of poor working Catholics parents, and an orphanage for the considerable number of Catholic children who had lost their parents.

His sister, Anna, was the Superior General of an educational, nursing and missionary order called *Les Soeurs de la Sainte Famille d'Amiens* and he wrote to her asking for help. She responded by sending two of her Sisters to Jersey; once again, because of French legislation against Catholic education and teaching Orders, there was a diaspora of Religious to neighbouring countries, and the original two Sisters were followed by other colleagues.

The new crèche opened at the New Year of 1901 in rented accommodation at Portland Place, Midvale Road. The Sisters also took in orphans, and by May there were 15 of them. Père Legrand started looking for a larger property to buy to locate an orphanage and a suitable house, 'Summerlands', was found at Rouge Bouillon, then on the outskirts of town. The property was purchased and in July 1901 the Sacré Coeur Orphanage was transferred there.

A new house was built adjoining to Summerlands which would become the Orphanage; the original house became the convent for the Sisters.

There were nine Sisters, 78 children and 13 babies living at the Sacré Coeur in December 1904, most of them of primary school age. The older boys would be found places as apprentices in various trades in town, while

Sister Peter with children of the Sacré Coeur. Sister Peter (Gabrielle Hamon) left the Sacré Coeur in 1972 to spend three years as a missionary Sister in the French Congo.(Photo courtesy of the Jersey Evening Post)

still living at the Orphanage, where they could also develop gardening and fruit-growing skills in the large garden belonging to the property.

For the girls, a textile factory was opened in 1905 in a neighbouring building where they could be given lessons in housekeeping and learn sewing and knitting. The factory became a larger business and employed women and girls from the town and parish, not just from the Orphanage. The Summerland Knitwear Company was founded by the Sangan family and they took over the running of the factory, although many of the employees came from the Orphanage, or the St Thomas' Parish.

A Juniorate, a college for the training of future Oblates, was founded in 1912 at Maison Sainte-Marie, a former school in near-by Roussel Street. This remained in existence until 1931 when the Juniorate was transferred to Pontmain, near Laval, where it still exists, combined with a retirement home for members of the Order.

In her book, *Deo Gratias*, Diane Moore writes: 'The Orphanage and Summerland property soon became a hub for Catholic life in St Thomas' Parish. It provided childcare, apprenticeships for both boys and girls, a market garden, a thriving knitwear business, a laundry, a printing press, a bustling student life as well as a meeting point for religious societies. There was even a *Salle des Fêtes*, a dance hall. The grounds were extensive

255

and they were developed fully, without ever sacrificing the "space, air and light" which Père Legrand had felt was essential to the welfare of children.'

After the Occupation, the Orphanage continued to play a major part in Catholic and Island life. St Mary's House provided a base for St Thomas' Sports Club and then for St Thomas' Church Club and the Salle des Fêtes was popular as a theatre and dance-room. Religious ceremonies, such as the annual Corpus Christi processions, were held in the grounds of the Orphanage attracting thousands of Catholics, as did also sports days and summer fêtes.

Quoting from *Deo Gratias* by Diane Moore: 'Many locals have confirmed that the role of the whole of the Sacré Coeur complex was crucial to the practical wellbeing of an overwhelming number of Catholics based in Jersey, especially those who were struggling financially. Whilst the churches offered religious solace, the Sacré Coeur was the "heart and warmth" of Jersey Catholic life, providing many with a dynamic spirit of Christian generosity.'

By the late 1960s, the changes in institutional childcare meant that there was less of a need for a large orphanage. The Corpus Christi processions were not taking place on such a large scale and furthermore, financial difficulties crept in that forced the Sisters to sell off parts of their property. Large areas of the grounds were sold to local businesses for development and construction. St Mary's House was sold to the States in the 1980s and became the site for the Police Station car park, the Ambulance Station and new houses.

The Orphanage itself became a nursery school, although it was still run by the Sisters. But by 1996 this was obliged to close. The property was sold.

Although it might be said that the Sacré Coeur had fulfilled its purpose and was no longer necessary, it is still sad to relate the story of the decline and fall of the Sacré Coeur Orphanage and its many 'good works' for Islanders: the care of children and vulnerable young people, the training of gardeners, the provision of work making clothes, the facilities for sports and leisure, the rooms for theatrical and musical events... let alone the loss to the townscape of its extensive grounds and fine buildings.

Space, air and light – all had gone.

So many of the social services borne by the Catholic Church in general, and by the Orphanage in particular, are now shared out between various States and public bodies, but whether they are done so well, or with such humanity and generosity is something that is impossible to pronounce upon. At a time when the States have been desperate to reduce its expenses, the Sacré Coeur must surely stand out as a memorial and testimonial to the good that can be achieved by private and religious charity.

(7) The Little Sisters of the Poor

IN October 2009 the Pope proclaimed five new Saints to a crowd estimated at perhaps 300,000. One of these, Saint Jeanne Jugan, was the foundress of the Little Sisters of the Poor, who was born in Cancale, grew up in Saint-Servan, and visited Jersey in the mid-19th Century.

On 28 October, Bishop Hollis, travelled to Jersey for a Mass of celebration at St Thomas to celebrate the canonisation.

Among the vast crowds in Rome for the Proclamation was a small group from Jersey's own community of the Little Sisters. It was led by the Mother Superior, Sister Mary Lucy, who travelled there with two couples residing at the Maison Jeanne Jugan, the chaplain, and three members of the lay organisation, the Association Jeanne Jugan. Nine other members of the association went independently.

Each one of the homes of the Little Sisters throughout the world was represented: 202 homes in 30 countries throughout five continents. One sister went from each home, their names chosen by ballot. Sister Mary Lucy's name came out of the hat to represent Jersey.

'It was an unforgettable experience,' she told the Jersey Evening Post on her return. 'The Church has set its seal on her work, and I am so proud – proclaiming Jeanne Jugan a saint was to show her as an example to others, and it has given us all an incentive to carry on what she started.'

St Jeanne Jugan was born just over the water from the Island in Cancale in 1792. She was one of six children; her father was a sailor but when she was four years old he was lost at sea and she was brought up by her widowed mother. Aged 16 she went to work as a kitchen maid in a manor near Cancale; at the age of 25 she worked as a nurse's aide, and already had a conviction that God had a special purpose for her.

Brothers Anthony and Elwin taking time off from their teaching to be photographed in front of one of the new extensions to the Beeches College, November 1973. (Photo courtesy of the JEP)

She desired to serve God and the poor – especially the weakest and the most destitute. It was in 1839 that Jeanne gave up her own bed so as to give it to a blind, semi-paralysed old lady who had suddenly found herself alone. This act committed her forever, and so the Congregation of the Little Sisters of the Poor, was born.

Some time in her life – possibly during the 1850s - it is known she visited Jersey – the only place outside France that she did visit. It was only in 1886 that five Sisters from the Order set up the first Little Sisters home in Jersey in Grosvenor Street and within days they began to take in sick people. Within a year in a house the Order had purchased a property at the top of New St John's Road called Hautville, the site that is still their home, although much expanded.

In 1970, part of the original house was demolished and Phase 1 of a development programme began. 1978, the rest of the house was demolished and Phase two of four phases got under way. This was finished in 1982; by 1985 there were sheltered flats for 20 people.

The establishment in 2001 consisted of 11 sisters and 65 members of staff, with 92 permanent residents.

Further vital renovation needed to be carried out to continue to meet health and safety standards. The estimated cost of running the Little Sisters was £1.2m, the bulk of the funding coming from pensions and the Island's civil parishes and States funding, but there was a shortfall every year. Consequently it needed the additional help of legacies, donations and other gifts.

An appeal was launched in June 2001 to cover such things as repainting the outside and new lifts.

A resident at the Jeanne Jugan Residence in 2011 was retired priest Fr Henry Donnelly, who celebrated his 100th birthday. He concelebrated a Mass with Bishop Hollis, who was paying his last official visit to the Island before retirement. Fr Donnelly celebrated Mass from his wheelchair positioned at the altar. He had been living at the Residence since 2004. He had been mentioned at dispatches for distinguished services when he was an army chaplain with the BEF in 1940 and was evacuated from the beaches at Dunkirk.

There are currently a total of 65 elderly residents for whom the Maison Jeanne Jugan is their home, looked after by a permanent staff, including seven Sisters.

(8)   French Sisters at The Limes

'THE LIMES' – or 'Maison St Marculf' was a house in St Helier that was purchased by Père Donat Michaux after his arrival in Jersey in 1882. It had been run as a juniorate for mature students and had a chapel of its own.

After his death it was sold to another Catholic order of religious Sisters, Les Filles du Coeur Immaculée de Marie (The Daughters of the Immaculate Heart of Mary), a Brittany-based Order of the Diocese of Rennes. Six Sisters arrived in Jersey in 1895 and worked as private nurses in St Helier and also took in patients at the house.

Besides their surgical work they also took in and cared for the poor. The Limes' large garden was often the setting for Corpus Christi processions.

Notable among the Superiors in Jersey was Mère Marie-Madeleine (1873-1956), Superior at The Limes for 43 years. She took her vows as a Sister of her Congregation in 1896, and in 1905 she was sent to Jersey; in 1909 she became the Superior. Under her care and guidance it became one of the most foremost nursing institutions in the Island. She celebrated her Golden Jubilee in 1946 and in 1949 was awarded by the government of the French Republic the medal of a 'Chevalier de la Santé Publique'.

In June 1956, three years after Mère Marie-Madeleine had asked on account of her advancing years, to be allowed to resign as Superior, she celebrated her Diamond Jubilee as a member of her Order. By her special request, she had been allowed to remain in the Island she had loved and served.

Of her 43 years in Jersey, the most difficult ones were the five years of the Occupation, when she appeared to do the impossible for her patients and old people.

In 1974 the Sisters were faced with the problems of not having sufficient numbers within their own Congregation to carry on the work by themselves. With regret, they approached the States, which agreed to take over the running of the house. After 79 years, the Sisters closed their house in Jersey and returned to their Mother House in Vitré.

APPENDIX B

ROLL OF THE CLERGY

'Let us now praise famous men'-
Men of little showing–
For their work continueth,
And their work continueth,
Broad and deep continueth,
Greater than their knowing.'

(R Kipling: 'A School Song')

BISHOPS OF THE DIOCESE OF PORTSMOUTH:

John Vertue	1882 - 1900†
John Cahill	1900 - 1910†
William Cotter	1910 - 1940†
John Henry King	1941 - 1965†
	(given the personal title of Archbishop in 1954)
Derek Worlock,	1965 - 1976
	(translated to Liverpool as Archbishop in 1976)
Anthony Emery	1976 - 1988†
Crispian Hollis	1988 - 2012
Philip Egan	2012 -

RECTORS, PARISH PRIESTS AND ASSISTANT PRIESTS IN JERSEY

The Pre-Oblates of the French Mission

1803 - 1807	Père Jean-François Philibert, in charge of the French Mission (Chapelle Saint Louis).
1806 - 1809	Père Charles de Grimouville, Titular Bishop of St Malo, Vicar General for Catholic Administration in the Channel Islands. He looked after the Irish workers and soldiers in the garrison,
1809 - 1836 †	Père Toussaint Le Guédois, in charge of the French Mission in 1822.
1837 - 1860	Père J Morlais , Rector of St Thomas' 1842

| 1860 - 1879 | Père Jean-François Volkeryck, Rector of St Thomas' |
| 1879 - 1880 | Père Matthieu Morin |

From 1880: The French Oblate Fathers (at St Thomas')

1880	Père Victor Fick OMI
1880 - 1885	Père Victor Bourde OMI
1885 - 1895	Père Victor Fick OMI
1895 - 1899	Père Constant Le Vacon OMI
1899 - 1911	Père Louis Legrand OMI
1911 - 1920	Père Louis Guillient OMI
1920 - 1933	Père Alain Mao OMI
1934 - 1946	Père Théodule Maré OMI
1946 - 1955	Père Pierre Jort OMI
1955 - 1961	Père Henri Verkin OMI
1961 - 1967	Père Joseph Simon OMI
1967 - 1975	Père Jean-Marie Chuffart OMI
1975 - 1976	Père Georges Laudin OMI
1976 - 1982	Père Jean-Marie Chuffart OMI
1982 - 1999	Père Vincent Igoa OMI

From 1999: Diocesan Clergy

(became the Parish in St Helier with St Mary and St Peter until 2003 and then part of the Catholic Parish of Jersey)

1999 - Canon (later Mgr) Nicholas France, Catholic Dean in Jersey

Assistant priests from the Occupation onwards:

1946 - 1960	Père Theodule Maré OMI
1947 - 1979	Père Marcel Barbrel OMI
1950 - 1952	Père Pierre Gueret OMI
1952 - 1954	Père Yves Jain OMI
1952 - 1956	Père Alexis Coatmuer OMI
1955 - 1976	Père Pierre Jort OMI
1956 - 1961	Père Louis Coty OMI
1956 - 1963	Père Yves Jain OMI
1957 - 1960	Père Ernest Capitaine OMI
1961 - 1962	Père Henri Hélouët OMI
1961 - 1972	Père Paul de Lansalut OMI
1961 - 1967	Père Jean-Marie Chuffart OMI
1961 - 1963	Père Vincent Igoa OMI
1962 - 1965	Père Gabriel Lesage OMI
1963 - 1965	Père Henri Le Douy OMI

1963 - 1967	Père Jean Bertho OMI
1967 - 1972	Père Pierre Kerzoncuf OMI
1968 - 1988	Père Charles Morel OMI
1972 - 1975	Père Georges Laudin OMI
1975 - 1976	Père Alfred Mouille OMI
1975 - 1976	Père Jean-Marie Chuffart OMI
1976 - 1977	Père Georges Laudin OMI
1977 - 1978	Père Michel Le Berre OMI
1977 - 1978	Père François Peron OMI
1978 - 1979	Père Georges Laudin OMI
1979 - 1981	Père François Peron OMI
1981 - 1982	Père Vincent Igoa OMI

Priest Directors of the Maison Saint Louis Observatory:
1933 - 1980	Père Charles Rey SJ

De La Mennais Brothers (1922-1972)

The De la Mennais Brothers, who had come to the Island in 1896, took over the Highlands building in 1922, using it as their General Juvenate and Noviciate. They left in 1972, having sold the building to the States Education Department

1942 - 1956	Père André Boutrolle SJ
1956 - 1965	Père Jean Duhr SJ
1965 - 1970	Père Jean Guervenou SJ
1970 - 1972	Père Jean Debray SJ

'THE IRISH MISSION' - PARISH OF ST MARY AND ST PETER

1821 - 1827	Fr John Carroll
1829 - 1833	Fr Matthew Ryan
1834 - 1837	Fr Timothy Riordan
1837 - 1839	Fr Edmund Murphy
1839 - 1848†	Fr John Cunningham; St Mary's Church built
1848 - 1893†	Fr (later Mgr) Jeremiah McCarthy; enlarged St Mary & St Peter's Church built
1893 - 1931†	Fr (later Canon) John Hourigan
1931 - 1940†	Canon George Clifford Bailey
1940 - 1946	Fr (later Canon) Richard Arscott
1946 - 1948	Canon Albert Lion

1948 - 1975 Fr (later Canon and Mgr)) Arthur Olney
1975 - 1999 Fr (later Canon) David Mahy
1999 - Canon (later Mgr) Nicholas France

From 2003 became the Parish in St Helier, with St Thomas' until 2007 and then part of the Catholic Parish of Jersey)

1999 - Canon (later Mgr) Nicholas France, Catholic Dean in Jersey.

Assistant priests at St Mary and St Peter's from the Occupation onwards:

1937 - 1945	Fr Donal Murphy-O'Connor
1938 - 1945	Fr Gerard Dwyer
1945 - 1947	Fr Anthony Zollo
1945 - 1948	Fr Raymond Henessy
1947	Fr Anthony Birrer
1947 - 1942	Fr John Hickey
1947 - 1948	Fr John Devine
1950 - 1953	Fr John Balfe
1950 - 1951	Fr John Groghan
1952 - 1956	Fr Denis Ryan
1953 - 1963	Fr Ronald Conway
1955 - 1962	Fr Laurence McMaster
1962 - 1967	Fr Cyril Murtagh
1963 - 1968	Fr Anthony Moore
1967 - 1970	Fr David Whitehead
1970 - 1976	Fr Francis Isherwood
1976 - 1977	Fr Damian McBride
1976	Fr Thomas Cullen
1977 - 1980	Fr Anthony Fagan
1978	Fr Vincent Quine
1979 - 1983	Fr Colin Ward
1982 - 1985	Fr Desmond Doran
1983 - 1998	Fr Ronald Lobb

The Beeches - De La Salle Brothers
1953 - 1979 Père Rene Lafraise

Mass Centre, First Tower, served from St Mary and St Peter parish
1949 - 1957 Père Christian Burdo
(This closed with the opening of Our Lady Queen of the Universe at Millbrook in 1956. In August 1955 there was a change in parish boundaries and the Sacred Heart took over responsibility for the

First Tower area.

PARISH OF ST PATRICK

Although the church was opened in 1948, it only became a parish in its own right in 1968
From 1952, served from St Mary and St Peter's:

1952 - 1956	Fr Dennis Ryan
1956 - 1963	Fr Ronald Conway
1962- 1968	Fr Anthony Moore...*who became the first parish priest*
1988 - 1972	Fr Anthony Moore
1972 - 1977	Fr Philip Quinn
1977	Mgr Sidney Mullarkey
1977 - 1980	Fr Anthony Maxwell-Ward
1980 - 1983	Fr Peter Turbitt
1983 - 1985	Fr Colin Ward
1985	Fr Desmond Doran
1985 - 1987	Fr Colin Ward
1987 - 1988	Fr Francis Guthrie
1988	Fr Frank Reynolds
1988 - 2000	Fr Colin Ward

As part of the Eastern parish:

2000 - 2006	Fr Robin Ellwood

Then assimilated within the Island Catholic parish of Jersey

PARISH OF OUR LADY OF THE ANNUNCIATION AND THE MARTYRS OF JAPAN (in St Martin)

1847	Père E Hallum settled in Faldouet and built a small school and chapel 'Notre Dame de St Martin')
1856 - 1882†	Père Joseph Guimarand started building a new church
1882 - 1884†	Père Charles Tardivon

From 1884: The French Oblate Fathers

1884	Père Victor Bourde OMI (from St Thomas')
1884 - 1888	Père Pierre-Henri Larose OMI
1888 - 1889	Père J Pierre-Marie Féat OMI
1889 - 1890	Père Jean-Baptiste Collin OMI
1890 - 1897	Père Léger Caux OMI - first priest of St Joseph's, Père Raffier in charge

1897 - 1899	Père Henri Raffier OMI

1899 - 1906	Père Jérôme Trevien OMI - opened Mass Centre at Gorey
1906 - 1911	Père Louis Gullient OMI
1911 - 1937	Père Abel Pierrat OMI
1937 - 1953	Père Eugène Méline OMI - new Mass Centre at Gorey 'Our Lady of the Assumption
1953 - 1957	Père Constant Quinton OMI
1957 - 1960	Père Henri Hélouët OMI

From 1960: The Anglo-Irish Oblate Fathers

1960 - 1963	Fr Sean Crean OMI
1963 - 1967	Fr Stanislaus Connolly OMI
1967 - 1973	Fr Donal Sorohan OMI
1973 - 1974	Fr Enda Canning OMI
1974 - 1983	Fr Thomas Magee OMI
1983 - 1989	Fr Michael Ryan OMI
1989 - 1997†	Fr Eamon Fitzgerald OMI
1997 - 1998	Fr Edward (Ted) McSherry OMI

From 1998: Diocesan Priests

1998 - 1999†	Fr Brian Cousins

From 2000: Part of the new 'Eastern Parish'

2000 - 2005	Fr Robin Ellwood

From 2005 the parish has been integrated within the all-Island Catholic Parish

	Fr Michael Marett-Crosby
	Fr Marcin Drabic
	Fr James McAuley
2014	Fr Philip Pennington Harris
2014	Fr John Lavers
2015	Fr Benjamin Theobald

Assistant priests from the time of the Occupation

1934 - 1948	Père Bernard Morin OMI
1947 - 1959	Père Albert Durand OMI
1950 - 1951	Père Louis Coty OMI
1951 - 1957	Père Ernest Capitaine OMI
1985 - 1960	Père Paul de Lansalut OMI
1960 - 1961	Père Henri Hélouët OMI
1960 - 1964	Fr Edward McSherry OMI

1961 - 1967	Fr Enda Canning OMI
1964 - 1965	Fr Christopher Dunne OMI
1965 - 1969	Fr Dermot Herlihy OMI
1969 - 1973	Fr Michael Phelan OMI
1970 - 1971	Fr Dermot Mills OMI
1973 - 1977	Fr Anthony Hanley OMI
1977 - 1978	Fr Patrick Lowry OMI
1980 - 1983	Fr Thomas Brady OMI
1983 - 1997	Fr Thomas Magee OMI

PARISH OF ST MATTHIEU

Built 1869-1872, through the efforts of Père Volkerick of The French Mission. It was served from St Thomas' by:

1869 - 1879	Père Jean-François Volkeryk
1880 - 1882	Père Matthieu Morin

1880 - 1952: The French Oblate Fathers

1882	Père Victor Bourde (from St Thomas') OMI
1885	Père E Rolland OMI
	Père Keul OMI
1886 - 1895	Père Constant Le Vacon OMI;
1895 - 1899	Père Jérôme Trevien OMI
1899 - 1919†	Père Constant Le Vacon OMI
1919 - 1920	Père Alain Mao OMI
1920 - 1933	Père Joseph Emile Pitard OMI
1933 - 1949	Père Jean-Louis Messager OMI
1949 - 1952	Père P. Le Bas OMI

From 1952: The Anglo-Irish Oblate Fathers

1952 - 1953	Fr Edward ('Teddy') Maher OMI
1953 - 1967	Fr William Hughes OMI
1967 - 1972	Fr Denis O'Connell OMI
1972 - 1975	Fr Daniel Breslin OMI
1975 - 1979	Fr Anthony Farmer OMI
1979 - 1981	Fr Edward McMahon OMI

1981 - 1989: Diocesan Priests

1981 - 1986	Fr Patrick Lyons
1986 - 1988	Fr James Keegan
1988 - 1989	Fr Andrew Lavery

1989 - 2003 The Holy Ghost Fathers
1989 - 2003   Fr Tom Friery

From: 2003 Diocesan Clergy
2003-   Fr Peter Glas
Then merged into the Catholic Western Parish,
- 2008   Fr Peter Glas

Then becoming a part of the Island parish:
2008 -   Fr Kevin Hoiles, serving three western churches

Assistant priests at St Matthieu from the Occupation:
French Oblates:
1926 - 1952   Père Yves Jain OMI
1947 - 1952   Père Paul de Lansalut OMI

Anglo-Irish Oblates:
1952 - 1960   Fr James Hannigan OMI
1953 - 1957   Fr Dennis O'Connell OMI
1954 - 1958   Fr Joseph Taafe OMI
1960 - 1971   Fr Michael O'Dowd OMI
1960 - 1961   Fr Patrick Hackett OMI
1961 - 1962   Fr James Morrison OMI
1967 - 1968   Fr Denis O'Connell OMI
1971 - 1975   Fr Anthony Farmer OMI
1977 - 1978   Fr Seamus Carroll OMI
1980 - 1981   Fr Seamus Carroll OMI

Holy Ghost Fathers
1989 - 1992†   Fr James ('Jim') Taylor CSSp

For the Portuguese Parish
1989 - 1999   Fr Doyle CSSp

PARISH OF SACRED HEART

The Chapelle de Sacré Coeur, St Aubin, was served by French Oblates from St Thomas or St Matthew from its construction in 1900.

1937 (from St Thomas') - 1946 Père Louis Choinel

From 1946 : The Anglo-Irish Oblate Fathers

1946 - 1951	Fr Francis O'Connor OMI
1951 - 1961	Fr Lawrence Hargreaves OMI
1961 - 1967	Fr Patrick Glasheen OMI
1967 - 1977	Fr James O'Reagan OMI
1977 - 1978	Fr John Dore OMI
1978 - 1984	Fr Anthony Hanley OMI
1984 - 1995	Fr Liam Griffin OMI

From 1995: The Holy Ghost Fathers

1995 - 2003	Fr James Carling

From: 2003 Diocesan Clergy

2003 - Fr Peter Glas

Then merged into the Catholic Western Parish,

- 2005 Fr Peter Glas

becoming a part of the Island parish in 2007:

(Fr Kevin Hoiles, serving the three western churches of the Island parish)

Assistant Priests at Sacred Heart:

1946 - 1952	Fr James Hannigan OMI
1946 - 1952	Fr Edward Maher OMI
1946 - 1961	Fr Patrick Lowry OMI
1946 - 1951	Fr Lawrence Hargreaves OMI
1962 - 1954	Fr Cuthbert Keegan OMI
1952 - 1963	Fr Stanislaus Connolly OMI
1954 - 1961	Fr John Creen OMI
1961 - 1977	Fr Aidan Brennan OMI
1961 - 1967	Fr Denis O'Connell OMI
1963 - 1965	Fr Francis Flynn OMI
1965 - 1968	Fr Michael Phelan OMI
1967 - 1975	Fr Francis Hynes OMI
1975 - 1977	Fr Matthew Feighery OMI
1977 - 1978	Fr Anthony Hanley OMI
1978 - 1979	Fr Dermot Mills OMI
1979 - 1980	Fr Michael Hennessy OMI
1981 - 1983	Fr Seamus Carroll OMI
1981 - 1983	Fr Michael Phelan OMI
1983 - 1984	Fr Brian Flanagan OMI
1983 - 1984	Fr Thomas O'Brien OMI

| 1984 - 1995 | Fr John Mahon OMI |
| 1995 - 2003 | Fr Ken Martin CSSp |

THE DEACONS

1993	Iain McFirbhisigh, (first Deacon to be ordained in Jersey)
1996	Tony Ward
2000	Louis Omer (suffered a stroke in 2005)
2002	Paul Hagg
2012	Brendan Flaxman
2013	David Cahill
2013	Christopher Walters

APPENDIX C

The 1994 Jersey Catholic Pastoral Review

The pastoral review was established by the Bishop in 1994 at the request of Canon Mahy.

The commission's members and their areas of responsibility were:
Canon Declan Lang - Review team chairman; Catholic organisations and
ecumenism;
Ms Vicky Cosstick - Adult formation and catechesis; collaborative ministry; pastoral councils.
Francis Davis - Community Care; immigrant communities.
Sister Bernadette Duggan RSM - Schools; catechetical needs of young people; religious life.
Canon Gerard Hetherington - The Church and the media; immigrant communities.
Miss Paula Medd - Young people in the Church; adults workingwith young people.
Dame Sheila Quinn - Health care and community care.
Father Michael Ryan - Parishes and parish administration
Miss Dilys Wadman - Schools, young people in the Church.

The text of the foreword by Bishop Hollis follows:

'The Pastoral Review to which I have the pleasure of introducing you is the result of a great deal of immensely hard work by Canon Declan Lang and his team of over the last eight months. I am very grateful to all who have undertaken this work.

The process which led to the setting up of this review began with an invitation to me from the Island Pastoral Council to consider the future shape of the Catholic Church in Jersey.

A number of factors, which had already began to be considered, led to this request being made. Not least among these factors was the prospect that the number of priests in the Island will be reduced, particularly as the Religious Congregations, who serve a number of the parishes, review deployment of their members, (Coupled with this, there was also felt the need to rationalise the considerable resources of the Island in order to maximise our effort towards mission and evangelisation.)

273

The Review team has been made up of members from outside the Island who have been able to take an objective look at everything that is going on. They have been very committed to their task and thorough in all their fact-finding and research.

They have looked at parishes, religious communities and institutions, pastoral initiatives and areas of social concern, ecumenism and the Church's work among young people. They have considered the deployment of resources in all these areas, both personal and material.

This Review represents their view of your situation. The words are not necessarily comfortable words but they represent an honest and objective view of things as they are and not as they might be.

The Review, therefore, represents an enormous challenge to you who are the Island community. It challenges you in your vision of the Church and it certainly challenges you in your willingness to be part of a Church whose watchword is to be mission, not maintenance, and whose life and work is based on interdependence, collaboration and partnership. You will be challenged in your generosity and your courage as you face the recommendations that have been made.'

The Review is therefore presented to you to be discussed, evaluated, prioritised and implemented by you. Circumstances will dictate to us some of the decisions which will have to be made; others will be mine to make and carry through; others again will be represented by choices you make as you generously and openly consider the implications of what is written in these pages.

I think, however, that things must not be left in the air; we need to impose upon ourselves the discipline of a timetable for action.

My wish, therefore, is that I receive a general response from the Island community by Christmas. This will be a response from the Pastoral Council and from all the communities and institutions whose lives and work are touched by the Review, and from any other interested parties. By Easter I would like to have a detailed response, because by September/October 1995 I want to be in a position to put the first elements of the Review into place.

We all face a difficult and demanding task and it is one and it is one which will tax our generosity and goodwill. It is, therefore, a task whichj must be combined with "prayer and fasting".

There can really be no consideration of this document which is not accompanied by prayer. We need to be in the presence of God as we are being faced with what is a God-given opportunity to transform the face and image of the Church in Jersey.

It is a turning point and I pray that we have the grace, the wisdom and the courage to grasp the challenge the Lord is giving us.

Bishop Crispian Hollis.'

The first section constituted a general preamble to the rest of the report, and its title, 'Jersey - Community and Mission ' emphasised the general thrust of the document: Jersey was about 'Mission, not Maintenance.'

Summarising this first section in its own words:

Pope John II tells us that the Church is essentially missionary. Without that sense of mission the Church will die as we will not be faithful to the invitation of Jesus.

The mission of the Church is to create communion.... Within our parishes there is a need to break down those barriers that cause division and to offer an experience of what it means to live as brothers and sisters. The pathway to communion can be both difficult and painful because it means letting go of our own personal preferences for the sake of the Gospel.

Pope John Paul II in Christifideles Laici says that there is a need 'to rediscover the Parish' as the place where for most Catholics they experience what it means to be the Church.... The Parish is not principally a structure or a building but a people, the Family of God... The Parish is founded on the truth that it is called to be a Eucharistic community which seeks to heal and form community wherever there is division.... Rediscovering the Parish is the emphasis of this report. Parishes in Jersey, as elsewhere in the diocese, need to ask themselves whether they are putting their resources at the service of Mission or Maintenance. [If the latter,] such a policy is a pathway to death.'

Section 2, headed 'Communities of Christ's Faithful People in Jersey' included these words:

'A comment that was frequently made to members of the Review Team was that people in Jersey are expecting change. Some people welcome this as a challenge for growth and mission while others are fearful of the upset it could bring. Some people want to hold on to what they have already created while others recognise that small communities can be very inward looking and destructive of community rather than creating it. Some people think time, energy and financial resources are often given to maintaining buildings rather than asking whether these buildings are the right and necessary resource for mission. One person suggested that a simple test to discover the viability of a community is to ask whether it is growing or dying.

275

... The provision of clergy both from the Diocese and Religious congregations is becoming more difficult. Jersey has been fortunate in the large number of Religious priests who have served the Island over the years. When the Religious have pastoral care of a parish they have usually lived in community - thus providing a larger number of priests than would be expected in an island of such a size. The task is to see where priests can be most effective in their ministry.'

Each section of the report was summarised in a number of recommendations. These are detailed below. The section numbers below refer to the equivalent reference numbers of the sections of the report.

2. RECOMMENDATIONS FOR PARISH STRUCTURE

The number of Parishes in Jersey be reduced to three - one in the East, one in the Centre and one in the West. The Portuguese personal parish to remain as at present.

A SUGGESTED PLAN FOR THE RATIONALISATION OF BUILDINGS

A: **The West:** The Parish in the West of the Island would have two churches (St Bernadette's and St Matthew's). Since the major population centre is around St Bernadette's the presbytery should be located in that area.

Redundant buildings could be:
Church of Ville-à-l'Evêque
Church of the Sacred Heart
Presbytery at St Matthew's
Presbytery at Sacred Heart
Hall at St Matthew's
Church of Queen of the Universe at Millbrook

B: **The Parish of the Centre Island:** The Parish in the Centre of the Island would have two church buildings (St Mary and St Peter's and St Thomas'). Because of the unique situation of both parishes covering the same geographical areas, two presbyteries could be retained as at present, and the two parishes could retain their individual identities. Alternatively, if the French OMI's were not in a position to provide a priest for St Thomas' in the future, or should either St Mary and St Peter's or St Thomas' become too expensive to maintain, there might be need for only one presbytery and one church.

C. The Church in the East: The Parish in the East of the Island would have three Churches (Our Lady, St Martin; Our Lady of the Annunciation, Gorey; and St Patrick's), which are relatively small compared to those in the centre and in the west. The Presbytery could be at St Martin's or St Patrick's.

Redundant buildings could be:
Church at St Joseph
Hall and outbuildings at St Joseph's
Presbytery at St Patrick's
Hall at St Patrick's

If this proposal for three parishes is accepted in principle, then the actual parish boundaries might be determined by a post-Review consultation process.

The rationalisation does not apply to the Portuguese parish as they would continue to use any of the Churches that would be retained.

3. RECOMMENDATIONS FOR PARISH PASTORAL COUNCILS

1. The whole process of the formation of Parish Pastoral Councils in the Island should continue, perhaps with training weekends and other modes of training.

2. All Parish Pastoral Councils should be encouraged to carry out an evaluation of their role and activities. (An outside facilitator may help this process).

3. Parish Pastoral Councils should review their method of communication with the Island Pastoral Council so that it is strengthened and clarified.

4. RECOMMENDATIONS FOR PARISH CATECHESIS

1. Sacramental preparation varies in its provision and effectiveness. This should be developed in the light of the need to provide a coherent and developmental programme of religious education and catechesis appropriate to the needs of young people.

2. The resources and programmes for young people should be properly evaluated, to ensure a matching of provision to need. Particular attention

should be given to materials for less able children.

3. Provision for faith development of 11-18 year olds must be addressed this is particularly important for those in non-Catholic schools, who are becoming increasingly distanced from the faith community.

5. RECOMMENDATIONS FOR SCHOOL CATECHESIS

1. An effective system of monitoring and evaluating the provision of catechists in the States primary schools should be established.

2. While the sessions offered in school are helpful in maintaining links and forming contacts they are not sufficient on their own. Parishes should explore ways and means of providing on-going development and catechists for the full age range. "Walk with me", currently being piloted for primary school children, parents and families, could be a starting point.

3. Contact with States secondary schools should be developed.

6. RECOMMENDATIONS FOR CATHOLIC SCHOOLS

1. All Catholic schools should be commended for their quality standards and concern for Catholic education of their pupils.

2. More publicity is needed for the Assisted Places Scheme, both to encourage applicants who would benefit, and to ensure continued support from parishes.

3. The declining number of Religious means that current Head teachers who are Religious are unlikely to be replaced so the Catholic community needs to prepare for this eventuality.

4. Effective publicity should be produced by the three schools emphasising the quality of education experienced by all who attend them.

5. All schools must ensure that there is a place in them for pupils with special educational needs and that appropriate provision is made for these needs.

7. RECOMMENDATIONS FOR YOUTH FORMATION

1. Every parish should set up a working party on youth provision, as a sub-group of the Parish Pastoral Council. The remit of this group is to explore the needs of young people in the parish, to initiate appropriate ways of meeting identified needs, to evaluate the provision and keep the needs of young people under regular review. The youth worker will be able to provide support and advice.

2. The Deanery Youth Council should review its structure and working methods, and formulate an action plan to ensure its effectiveness.

3. The Island Pastoral Council should ensure adequate representation by young people from the Deanery Youth Council and from individual parishes.

4. The Island Pastoral Council and the pastoral workers should address the issues of homelessness, alcoholism, drug abuse and racism among young people.

5. The Pastoral Centre Team should offer their 'Pastoral Needs Review' to every parish in the Deanery, together with training for leaders and volunteers where necessary.

8. RECOMMENDATIONS FOR ADULT EDUCATION / FORMATION

Adult education, according to recent Church teaching, should take place in the context of the Pastoral Plan (Christifideles Laici). There is need above all for some kind of Island vision, mission statement or a five-year pastoral plan. The vision for the Island should really now be seen as emerging from all the parishes by some process and should then be helping to set the agenda for the Catholic Community of Jersey. Parish or Church based community is central to people's understanding of the Church. Therefore Adult Education in the context of community and for community should be a priority.

1. The clearest route ahead for Adult Formation seems to be in the work of parents, family and youth. Opportunities should be provided for work with parents at the level of their own puzzlement and questions during Sacramental preparation. Sacramental preparation may also be used as

a chance for family activities, socialising and community building.

2. That consideration be given to providing courses in group leadership skills, faith sharing (rather than Bible Study), baptism preparation, courses which help people to reflect on their daily lives and culture, and courses in community building.

3. That a greater investment may be made in visiting speakers.

4. That consideration be given to putting on an Island conference on a theme appropriate to the needs of the Island.

5. That the Island Pastoral Council explore the PARISH PROJECT to see whether (with outside facilitators) it could be adapted to the needs of the Jersey Deanery.

9. RECOMMENDATIONS FOR RELIGIOUS LIFE

1. With dwindling numbers and ageing communities a rationalisation of resources, personnel and ministries is essential.

2. An openness between religious orders, the Bishop and the local community is fundamental to the harmonious handing over of property and schools in the event of religious withdrawing from the Island.

3. If Catholic schools are to retain their "Catholic" character, forward planning and the establishment of trustees needs to be instigated in the immediate future.

4. Religious in the Island have provided a powerful witness for the community over the years. There is greater need than ever for an effective witness to challenge the culture of our time. Ways of developing this need to be explored.

5. Religious would benefit from meeting together more often to pray, share concerns and to offer each other mutual support. This would be particularly helpful where the whole community is elderly and can feel isolated.

6. The local community could offer support and assistance to such communities.

10. RECCOMENDATIONS FOR SOCIAL WELFARE

1. This varies from parish to parish but where need is recognised there has been a willing and generous response. Examples of this are seen in the special Needs Sunday Liturgy at St Thomas', the Carers in Sacred Heart parish. The St Helier Conference of the SVP and its associated groups and the work of the Pastoral Centre. Efforts should be made to ensure that the social welfare work of the Church does not become over-focused on the work of key individuals. Every parish should spend time looking at ways to increase its knowledge of social need within its congregation and locality.

2. An ongoing consultation with other Christian churches and with voluntary and statutory organisations working in the field would ensure that the care offered does not duplicate that already being provided by others.

3. Raise the profile of the Church as a pressure group for Social reform.

4. Develop an Island plan for increased social care activities within which Parishes can work with their own priorities.

5. Through working with the States Overseas Aid Committee the Church could try to persuade the States to set aside 0.7% of its budget in aid allocation. Jersey's current allocation is large but in this aspect it could lead Europe.

11. RECOMMENDATIONS FOR PASTORAL CENTRE

1. The Pastoral Centre should be accountable to the Island Pastoral Council and to any Pastoral plan the Council develops.

2. The Pastoral Centre Management Committee be a sub-committee of the Island Pastoral Council.

3. The Pastoral Centre Management Committee review its structure and function to become more effective in policy making and in its management role.

4. The existing Team of the Pastoral Centre be expanded to include a priest with formation skills which complement those of present members and so increase the collaborative nature of the team. The priest should

be appointed either full time or with a major commitment to the Centre and be carefully chosen for his willingness to work in partnership with lay and religious workers.

5. As a matter of urgency efforts should be made to bring about a reconciliation between the Pastoral Centre and St Thomas' Parish, using if necessary an outside facilitator.

6. The Pastoral Centre be re-located to a place or places which more appropriately meet its changing and growing service.

a) The work concerned with social welfare should remain on St Thomas' site but on the ground floor to make it accessible to all, especially those with physical disability. The possibility of using rooms in the Presbytery or the Parish Social Club should be explored.

b) The catechetical and youth work base be re-located to the site of St Joseph's Church, Grouville.

7. The Team considers carefully how they can communicate to parishes and the Island at large the resources and skills they have to offer.

8. The Pastoral Centre continues to expand its service3 of providing training for volunteers and resource material for all groups.

12. RECOMMENDATION FOR CATHOLIC ORGANISATIONS

All organisations carry out a careful review of the way in which they fulfil their mission to the Island community.

13. RECOMMENDATIONS FOR ECUMENISM

1. The appointment in each Parish of someone who is responsible for promoting and planning ecumenical activity in collaboration with members of other Christian Churches. This person should be a member of the Parish Pastoral Council.

2. In response to the pastoral needs of the Island, the Catholic Parishes should try to work collaboratively with other Christians and be willing to share resources such as personnel and buildings.

3. Opportunities should continue to be created where Christians of different traditions can pray together and grow in appreciation of each other's spiritual heritage.

4. The question needs examining as to whether in the future the running and development of Catholic Schools could become an Ecumenical venture. A working party with representation from the Teaching Religious Congregations, the Island Pastoral Council and other interested parties could be set up.

5. On behalf of the Catholic parishes in Jersey, the Island Pastoral Council should consider the way in which "Christians Together in Jersey" can best be supported and developed.

14. RECOMMENDATION FOR MEDIA

At deanery and parish level, there to be competent individuals who take special responsibility for developing relationships with the news media, as well as providing a creative religious input to the press and to broadcasting.

APPENDIX D

'HOME GROWN'

Catholic Priests with a Jersey connection

AS the Catholic Church is essentially a Missionary Church, it is the exception rather than the rule to find priests serving in the place where they have grown up or lived before being ordained. The post-war period covered by this book includes several such exceptions, such as:

Fr Arthur Amy

Father Arthur Amy was a Jerseyman who had a late vocation as a Priest. He was ordained in his own patrimony (meaning that he relied on his own money and was not incardinated into a bishop's diocese). He was accepted by a bishop in the Sudan, where he served for a few years before he retired to Jersey, where he lived as a retored priest.

Although ordained in the years following the Second Vatican Council he maintained a devotion to the Tridentine rite; he celebrated his daily Mass at St Thomas's privately or with a few regular followers and sometimes at St Ouen's Manor. He died in his late 80s.

Fr Michael Cronin

Born in Jersey, a Priest of the Portsmouth Diocese, ordained in 1980, currently chaplain to the General Hospital in Southampton.

Père Albert Durand OMI

Born in Jersey in 1916, he studied with the Jesuits in Jersey before continuing his priestly formation in France, and taking his first vows in 1937. As the Occupation began, he trekked across France to the Oblate centre at Notre-Dame de Lumières, between Apt and Avignon, where he was ordained an Oblate priest in 1942 and assigned a parish nearby. There he was arrested by the Gestapo, who had found a British passport in his suitcase and accused him of being a British spy. He was tried and transported by cattle truck to Germany, where he was imprisoned in concentration camps, including two separate spells at Dachau. He was liberated in 1945 and after a spell in the UK, returned to Jersey - but his brutal experiences had left him a sick man.

He served as assistant priest to Père Eugène Méline at the St. Martin Catholic parish from 1945 to 1959. After retiring from his parish ministry he moved back to Lumières, where he died in 1974.

Père Joseph Kérautret, OMI

The family was French but came to the Island in 1890s. He was confirmed at St. Thomas' on 25 May 1902; he began his training for the Priesthood at St. Joseph's Junior Seminary, Roussel Street. He made his first Vows in 1912, his perpetual Vows in 1920 and was ordained that same year. He celebrated his first Mass at St. Thomas' on 31 July 1921. He received his Obedience for South Africa and died at Durban on the 28 July 1969.

Fr Ron Lobb

Trained and worked as a teacher and became head of St Saviour's School. He was a cousin of Amy and John Lobb - a talented family of Jersey musicians. The family were strongly Methodist, but he converted to Catholicism. On retirement from his teaching career he began to work at St Mary and St Peter's Presbytery, assisting in parish administration. In 1975 he was accepted by Bishop Emery as a candidate for the priesthood; he trained with the Mill Hill Fathers in North London. On ordination, he became assistant priest at St Mary and St Peter's and Catholic chaplain to the Hospital. He has been called a very devoted visitor and pastor to the sick and housebound. He died in 2002.

Fr Michael Marett-Crosby

Born in 1969, was at school at Victoria College Prep and St Michael's before he obtained a scholarship to Ampleforth College. He studied history at Oxford, and in 1990 returned to Ampleforth as a novice. He took final vows as a Benedictine monk in 1995 before returning to Oxford and obtaining a doctorate in theology and being ordained a priest in 1998. For the next four years he ran a retreat centre at Ampleforth. He returned to Jersey and started helping Canon Nicholas France in 2003, before becoming his assistant priest. He was the author of a number of books, including 'Business with Benedict'. Ill health forced his retirement in 2006.

Mgr Provost Cyril Murtagh

Born in Jersey, where his father was posted in the Army. He left Jersey as a young child, but he returned as assistant priest at St Mary and St Peter's in the 1960s. Canon of Portsmouth Cathedral, later Parish Priest in Hampshire.

Fr Gerard Reeve

He was ordained in 1956 at St Mary and St Peter's Church, Vauxhall Street; it was the first ordination to take place in Jersey for 30 years.

A very large congregation, including all the Catholic priests in the Island, were present. The ordination was performed by Bishop King; Fr Reeve had flown from Rome where he had been studying. He had formerly lived in Jersey and was a well-known member of St Helier Yacht Club.

Fr Brian Sandeman
He was a master at De La Salle College. After the death of his wife, Senator Jane Sandeman, he began studying for the priesthood. He was ordained in 1993. He served at St Patrick's and as Hospital chaplain until his retirement.

Appendix E

Catholic lay associations - spiritual and social

'The [idea] was to keep the faithful strongly related to their churches and schools. Loneliness meant weakness facing the too many occasions of drifting away from the church. Togetherness was the idea. Besides this, people in organised groups were more easily kept under control and even as a group controlled each other. So as to keep the faithful on the right path in their duties towards God and the Church, the Oblate Fathers put to use practically every kind of association, organisation, movement, confraternity, league and religious or social activities' - 'A Hundred Years of Life in Jersey, 1880-1980' by Père Vincent Igoa, OMI

IN the early years of the Oblates' presence in Jersey there were groups to foster spiritual; life and religious practice, such as the Children of Mary (with the Children of St Louis as a section for younger girls), the Third Order St Francis, the League of the Sacred Heart, the Apostleship of Prayer, the Confraternity of the Propagation of the Faith and the Eucharistic Crusade. Also, but with a special dedication in the work for the poor, were the Jersey Conference of St Vincent de Paul and the Ladies of Charity.

More secular, but with a *raison d'être* of providing healthy entertainment in a Catholic milieu, was the Cercle Catholique de St Thomas, which under different names, many difficulties and fresh starts, ending in a Men's Club with a junior branch for boys.

The KNIGHTS OF ST COLUMBA were formed in Jersey in 1929. The Order was established in the UK in 1919 as a fraternal order of practising male Catholics. It aims at uniting men for their own personal good, both spiritual and material and it seeks to give a practical meaning to the word 'fraternity'. It provides Parish Priests with a body of laymen ever ready to help in furthering any parochial activities.

In Jersey, the Order was established in 1929 by the setting up of St Mary and St Peter's Council No 216. About a year later Council 229 of St Thomas was erected, followed by Council 238 at St Martin. Among the Parochial work it undertook in its early years, before and after the war, was the organisation of the annual Corpus Christi processions.

More recently, the Jersey Council of the Knights of St Columba have organised a fund-raising event for the international charity, the Apostleship of the Sea, which supports those who live or work at sea. Catholics were 'walking on water' in May 2010 to raise money for the Apostleship of the Sea; the first year, £2,500 was raised by a small group, which included Mgr Nicholas France, walking the equivalent distance of Jersey to France by walking up and down St Catherine's Breakwater 18 times, for all seafarers around the world. It was Mgr France who came up with the idea.

The event was such a success that the charity then made it an annual event with representatives from across the UK coming to Jersey especially to take part.

THE THIRD ORDER OF ST FRANCIS was founded in Jersey in the 1880s, shortly after the arrival in the Island of the Oblates. Membership of this Lay Order waxed and waned over the years; it was revived in the 1950s by John McCartney under the spiritual guidance of Père Pierre Jort., then Rector of St Thomas'.

Other associations that combined spirituality development with social fellowship were:

THE SOCIETY OF ST VINCENT DE PAUL was founded in Paris in 1833 by Blessed Frédéric Ozanam and his companions. It is an international lay Christian voluntary organisation dedicated to tackling poverty and disadvantage by providing practical assistance to those in need - irrespective of ideology, faith, ethnicity, age or gender. It has been active in England & Wales since 1844 and seeks to help those who are suffering poverty in whatever form. Although it was founded by Catholics its members are not necessarily Catholic, nor does it limit its work to beneficiaries who are Catholic.

In Jersey, the 'Conference' (branch) of St Vincent de Paul was founded in the 19th Century, at least prior to the building of St Thomas' Church, although its early history is obscure, It was put on a proper basis in 1931 under the presidency of Mr O H Griffin.

There were, in the post-war decades, at least three Conferences in Jersey - Sacred Heart, St Patrick's and town. These are now all amalgamated into the town Conference.

From the mid-1980s to 1990s, the SVP worked from the St Thomas Community Centre in collaboration with the Catholic Pastoral Centre and later from Winchester Chambers in Val Plaisant opposite the St Thomas'. When that building was demolished for redevelopment, it moved to the Welcome Centre beside St Thomas' church in 2005.

It continues its work in providing practical help to people in need, regardless of their religious affiliation, if any, by way of assistance with food, clothing and furniture and providing a non-judgmental listening ear.

At the time of writing there are some 12 members, meeting once a month. Its main focus is to provide a food bank, second-hand furniture and, in selected and most deserving cases help with utility bills or dental costs. Clients are referred to it by the Citizen's Advice Bureau and, to some extent, by clergy.

It is planned to move the office back to the Community Centre on the other side of St Thomas' Church, as its quarters in the Welcome Centre are somewhat small and inconvenient to visit for some of those who use its services.

THE CATHOLIC WOMEN'S LEAGUE, started in Jersey in 1949. It had been established in the UK to 'unite Catholic women in a bond of common fellowship for the promotion of religious and intellectual interests and social and charitable work.' In reality, it has been a practical way of helping the Church and the Parish Priest, such as Altar work, hospital visiting, the welfare of old people, vestment and altar linen repairing, etc.

THE LEGION OF MARY, founded in Dublin in 1921, defines itself as an Association of Catholics , who, with the sanction of the Church have formed themselves in to a Legion for service in the warfare which is waged perpetually by the Church against the world and its evil powers.

A new branch was founded in Millbrook in 1957, on the first anniversary of the church Our Lady Queen of the Universe.

THE SODALITY OF THE CHILDREN OF MARY AND MARIS STELLA was an association of young women formed together under the protection and guidance of Our Lady. Young girls of school leaving age were invited to join so that they might be encouraged to advance in Christian piety. Only the unmarried were admitted to the Sodality, but could continue to be members of subsequently they married.

Besides looking after several altars and helping to clean and maintain church buildings, this Sodality taught Catechism and Sunday schools and instructed converts. Members met at Beaulieu Convent for retreats, recitation of the Office, sermon and Benediction, tea and amusement.

It was the custom for many years for the Children of Mary to arrange breakfasts of First Communicants.

The junior section, for teenagers from the age of 11, was known as the Maris Stella Club, founded by Miss M Ruellan, met regularly for prayer and games.

THE JERSEY CIRCLE OF THE CATENIAN ASSOCIATION Founded in 1954; at the time of this book's publication the Jersey Catenians have recently celebrated their 60th anniversary.

The Catenian Association is a voluntary organisation of Catholic laymen, founded in Manchester in 1908 as the Chums Benevolent Association. Its members meet at least once a month in local units called Circles, to enjoy each other's company and thereby strengthen their family life and faith through friendship. The basic unit of the Association is the Circle and members are known as Brothers. In 1910, there were five Circles with 250 Brothers; now there are around 10,000 Brothers in Circles in the UK and abroad.

The Catenians raise funds to support a wide span of charities and interests, at a local, national or International level raising in excess of £250.000 each year. Prayers at meetings and Masses are said for special intentions, or for example, deceased Brothers and for vocations; vocations are supported financially, as well.

A major function is held each year at the beginning of October when Brothers and their wives from many Circles in the UK visit Jersey for a weekend together.

Leonard Hems was the first president of the Jersey Circle in 1954. The current president (2015) is Tony Sullivan.

THE PATRICIANS - founded in Jersey in November 1957, its aim was to encourage the ordinary faithful to talk about their faith and thus help to spread it. It held its first meeting at the Sacred Heart Preparatory School, attended by some 50 people, on the theme: 'Should I keep the Faith to myself?'

CATHOLIC, SOCIAL AND SPORTING CLUBS

LE CERCLE CATHOLIQUE - This was founded as Le Cercle St Thomas in the 1870s and was based in what had been the 'old' St Thomas' Church in New Street. Following the opening of the new church in Val Plaisant, the old building in New Street was refurbished and converted into a hall with a stage and billiard room. It became the new Cercle Catholique, situated at the rear of 'The Playhouse'.

Its last incarnation was as the **ST THOMAS' MENS CLUB**. It had one of the oldest established billiards and snooker clubs in Jersey and was the training ground of many well-known billiards and snooker players of the Island and possessed four full-sized billiard tables.

This remained an active organisation well into the post-war decades.

THE CATHOLIC YOUNG MEN'S SOCIETY - The Jersey branch of the Catholic Yong Men's Society of Great Britain was formed in 1947. In the words of its president, Clarence Dupré: 'the object of the society was 'to prepare and train Catholic men to be lay Apostles so that they may help to bring back Christian Civilisation to the world'.

It was not primarily a youth club, the word 'Young' applied to the spirit, rather than the age of members. Mr Dupré said: 'The work of the Society develops the maturity of manhood in the young, and to its older members it brings the spirit of youth and adventure.'

The workings of the society might be divided up intro four headings: Spiritual (frequentation of the Sacraments and lectures); Social (socialisation in a Catholic atmosphere); Parochial (assisting parish clergy for the good of the parish); National (to further the interest of the national organisation).

It met for social events; it provided altar servers and, for example, canopy bearers and marshals for the Corpus Christi processions.

It also organised sports meetings for children of the St Mary and St Peter's parish.

FEDERATION OF CATHOLIC CLUBS - Founded in 1954, it aimed at fostering friendship between members of the different Catholic Clubs so that young Catholics could get to know each other. It grouped together, for social and sporting activities, the seven Catholic clubs of the Island at the time.

ST THOMAS SPORTS CLUB was open on weekday evenings and Sunday afternoons for such sports as table tennis, billiards and snooker.

Catholic social clubs survived until the 1980s.Writing in 1980, Père Igoa said: 'St Martin's has kept on traditional lines and is still going very strong after renewal and new premises built at St Joseph's, Grouville, in 1961; St Matthew's is now open to people of several confessions for the western part of the Island, and some people refer to this as an Ecumenical Club; St Thomas; worked hard to start a junior section - the "Boys Friendship Club"- but now attracts people of all ages even coming in families.'

BIBLIOGRAPHY AND SOURCES

Fr Gerard Dwyer: *Diocese of Portsmouth - Past and Present* (1981)

Père Vincent Igoa OMI: *A Hundred Years of Life in Jersey, 1880-1980*

Rev Francis Isherwood: *Jersey Church History* - short books published by the *Jersey Catholic Record.*

J H L'Amy: *Jersey Folk Lore* (1927)

Julie Lush: *St Mary and St Peter's Church* (1984)

Père J L Messager OMI: *The Story and Description of St Thomas' Catholic Church*

Diane Moore: *Deo Gratias - A history of the French Catholic Church in Jersey: 1790 - 2007* (2007)

John McCormack: *Channel Island Churches* (1986)

Tina Spencer-Nairn: *Matthew Francis de Gruchy - A brief history to commemorate the 200th anniversary of his death* (1997)

Wilfred Ward: *Life and Times of Cardinal Wiseman* (1897).

The *Jersey Catholic Record*

The *Jersey Evening Post*

The *Jersey Morning News*

The *Jersey Times*

Website of Der Erste Zug Living History:
www.dererstezug.com/VetHoppe.htm Interview by Malcolm Amy

INDEX

THE AUTHOR

Alasdair Crosby is a writer and journalist who specialises in Channel Island subjects.

He was for 14 years employed by the *Jersey Evening Post* newspaper, and is now the owner and editor of *RURAL - Jersey Country Life* magazine.

He was brought up in Jersey and returned in 1991 to settle in the Island, where he lives with his wife and family.